A PLUME BOOK

GETTING UNSTUCK

BOB SULLIVAN and HUGH THOMPSON are entrepr̶e̶[...]
forty years of experience between th[...]
analyzing systems and human nature. B[...]
and the bestselling author of *Gotcha* [...] *...ng
Ripped Off*. Hugh is a mathematics and c[...] ̶e̶nce professor
and speaker who teaches executives how to protect themselves from
twenty-first-century hazards.

Praise for *Getting Unstuck*

"The authors write in clear, engaging, and sometimes irreverent
prose as they dart across case studies from Amazon to Zappos. . . . A
stimulating read, offering some inventive theories and solutions."

—*Financial Times*

"Many readers will be fascinated by their descriptions of such under-
lying matters as acclimation, flow, and distortion mechanisms . . .
well written and entertaining."   —*Kirkus Reviews*

"It's got some interesting strategies that can really benefit consumers."

—Kelli Grant, CNBC

"The book's peppy tone and intriguing examples—athletes, miracle
berries, the famous marshmallow test—help illustrate the point that
people find it all too easy to get used to untenable situations. . . . Will
inspire readers to tackle major changes in some areas of their lives."

—*Publishers Weekly*

"Sullivan and Thompson have identified a phenomenon that plagues us all, robbing us of energy, delight, and successful results. Poignant stories, intriguing information, and insightful advice make this a must-read for any of us that want easier ways to keep the important fires lit. Warning: they've nailed stuff close to home for all of us!"
—David Allen, author of *Getting Things Done*

"Uncovering forces like the Greedy Algorithm that create plateaus in our lives is a great service, but Bob Sullivan and Hugh Thompson go much further. Their book is an entertaining and valuable guide that will show you how to quit the struggle and get up off the ground."
—Daniel H. Pink, author of *A Whole New Mind*

"The science behind how we can learn to excel at almost anything we care about by retraining our brains. A stimulating and *useful* handbook." —Daniel J. Levitin, author of *This Is Your Brain on Music*

"You already know what the Plateau Effect is. No matter what the endeavor, we've all experienced that feeling of diminishing returns from our efforts. Now Bob Sullivan and Hugh Thompson present the definitive guide for those who believe things can get a lot better and want to rise above their plateaus. Turn your back on the daily grind for good. Read this book now." —Ori Brafman, coauthor of *Sway*

"*Getting Unstuck* is smart, bracing, and eye-opening—with genuine pay-offs for accomplishing your dreams. It's also cheerful, funny, and greatly entertaining. Use it!"
—Amy Chua, author of *Battle Hymn of the Tiger Mother*

Getting
Unstuck

Break Free of the Plateau Effect

Bob Sullivan
AND
Hugh Thompson

Previously published as *The Plateau Effect*

A PLUME BOOK

PLUME
Published by the Penguin Group
Penguin Group (USA) LLC
375 Hudson Street
New York, New York 10014

USA | Canada | UK | Ireland | Australia | New Zealand | India | South Africa | China
penguin.com
A Penguin Random House Company

First published in the United States of America as *The Plateau Effect* by Dutton, a member of
Penguin Group (USA) LLC, 2013
First Plume Printing 2014

 REGISTERED TRADEMARK—MARCA REGISTRADA

THE LIBRARY OF CONGRESS HAS CATALOGED THE DUTTON EDITION AS FOLLOWS:
Sullivan, Bob, 1968– author.
The plateau effect : getting from stuck to success / Bob Sullivan and Herbert Hugh Thompson.
pages cm
Includes index.
ISBN 978-0-525-95280-0 (hc.)
ISBN 978-0-14-218094-5 (pbk.)
1. Self-actualization (Psychology) 2. Success—Psychological aspects. 3. Achievement
motivation. 4. Learning, Psychology of. 5. Performance. I. Thompson, Herbert H., author.
II. Title.
BF637.S4S85 2013
158.1—dc23   2012038324

Printed in the United States of America
10 9 8 7 6 5 4 3 2 1

Set in Dante MT Std with Neutraface 2 Text
Original hardcover design by Daniel Lagin

To everyone who still thinks things can get better

CONTENTS

CONTENTS

THE BEGINNING

Give us three minutes, your imagination, and your nose, and we bet we'll convince you that the Plateau Effect is the most powerful force of nature you've never heard about.

Let us take you to the Paris of the West, to a block in San Francisco where the unmistakable aroma—stench?—of garlic suddenly overpowers every other gritty smell on Columbus Avenue. About half a mile from the famous triangular Transamerica building, there's a restaurant that you can't help but notice. The unusual name, "The Stinking Rose," might persuade you to take a look inside, but that's not what really grabs your attention. No, it's that smell wafting out the front door onto the sidewalk, swirling around all the passersby.

The Stinking Rose is a sort of homage to garlic; it has every garlic dish you could possibly imagine. These range from the traditional, such as garlic spaghetti, to the exceptional, like garlic ice cream. The restaurant serves more than three thousand pounds of garlic a month, and as you walk inside, you can smell every clove of it.

But once you are seated at your table, something remarkable starts to happen. With stunning speed, the scent of garlic fades and the other smells of San Francisco return. Your wife's perfume, or the grapy wine, or the bleached tablecloth curiously reemerges, and its aroma seems to overpower the garlic.

Of course, that's not at all what's happened. Your nose has simply gotten tired of the garlic scent and stopped telling your brain that it's there. You might say you've grown numb to the garlic, but the word *numb* hardly does justice to the amazing evolutionary trait we've just described.

We've become so used to this disappearing smell phenomenon that most of us don't even think about it. It's why you might need someone else to tell you it's time to reapply deodorant or suck on a breath mint. It's why most of us grow queasy at the thought of entering a high school locker room, but the athletes don't seem to mind. With incredible speed, people become immune to even the most pungent odors.

This immunity is the body's natural defense against being constantly distracted by stimuli. If our bodies didn't adapt, our attention would be relentlessly divided by millions of smells—even our own scent—and unable to notice changes in the environment around us. The effect is called "acclimation." Without it, stopping to smell the roses would be an act of unending distraction. Acclimation is a critical element of our evolutionary design.

Naturally, acclimation is not limited to smell; it governs all of our senses. Acclimation is why people who live in big cities learn to ignore the sound of traffic outside their windows while it drives suburban guests crazy. It's why we forget that we're wearing a wedding ring, or glasses, when initially they are so irritating. Acclimation is why we "get used" to things.

Humans are hardwired to eventually ignore consistency, especially in the forms of smell, taste, touch, and hearing. At its most base level, this behavior is a survival instinct: The ability to adapt and ignore distracting information is a natural form of self-defense. It allows us to focus on changes and new things that enter the environment that might be threats. This ignoring of a persistent stimulus is generally a welcome feature of how the body works. But often, acclimation does more harm than good.

There are times when it would be very helpful to turn off this defense mechanism.

Getting Unstuck will show how athletes, scientists, relationship therapists, companies, and musicians around the world are learning to do just that—to turn off the forces that cause people to "peak out" or "get used to" things—and turn on human potential and happiness in ways you probably think impossible. *Getting Unstuck* will show you why the world is full of one-hit wonders, why all good things come to an end, why all trends eventually fall, why most people get less for more, and how you can break through again and again. Plateaus are like governors that cap your U-Haul van speed at fifty miles per hour. We will show you how to disable this secret governor and turn on your inner Maserati.

Just give us another few hours or your time.

Understanding why we reach a plateau can help us stop wasting time on things that we've stopped getting value from and focus on other things that leverage our time and energy better. The Plateau Effect tells us when to eat, what we should do in the gym, how to build a successful business, and even how to build stronger and broader relationships. Knowing how the Effect influences everything in our lives helps us get maximum value in minimum time and then move on quickly once we've reached a goal. It helps us do a good enough job quickly for things that aren't very important to free up time to concentrate on things that are. Those who master the

Effect, who can identify a plateau and break through, leave one-hit wonders in the dust.

"Just try harder. Just work harder. Just do more."

That's the advice you've heard again and again, from teachers, coaches, bosses, and parents. But what if you're already trying as hard as you can? In fact, "try harder" is often the worst advice you could possibly give. Have you ever found yourself giving more and more to a task you care about—learning to play the piano, trying to fix a broken romantic relationship—and getting less and less return for your effort? Of course you have. That's how the universe is built. Physics, biology, chemistry, even economics all dictate this truth—effort follows the law of diminishing returns. Trying harder is a failed, frustrating strategy. Trying harder to smell the garlic after your nose has acclimated to the Stinking Rose won't reawaken your olfactory nerves. It doesn't work anywhere else in your life, either.

Dieters and bodybuilders know this well. They begin a new regimen of starvation or weightlifting. For ten days or so, the results are fantastic, even inspiring. Down four pounds, or up another ten on the military press. But somewhere near that two-week mark, they hit a wall. The scale seems frozen in place. The strength gains top out. They have, cruelly, plateaued.

Plateaus are subtle at first, but once you know what to look for, you'll begin to see them everywhere. In fact, millions of Americans watch them, perhaps unknowingly, during prime time television. Fans of the hit NBC TV show *The Biggest Loser* witness cruel plateaus every season. Contestants nearly always lose an extraordinary amount of weight in week one, when their bodies are shocked by the new lifestyle. Then, what insiders call the "Week Two Plateau" hits, and the results are downright depressing. We analyzed data from all contestants during the first four seasons of the show. On average, they lost an amazing 5 percent of their body weight during week one. But even under the most scrutinized conditions, with the best possible trainers available, the Plateau Effect couldn't be beat. Week two always brings a dramatic lack of progress—and a lot more yelling by trainers. During season two, for example, contestants averaged less than 2 percent weight loss in week two. And during the inaugural season, they dropped a completely discouraging 0.6 percent, or roughly 90 percent less than in week one. Contestants who survive get as their reward the even louder screaming voice of a trainer. The screaming really doesn't help. It's just the Plateau Effect in action.

We believe the Plateau Effect is a law of nature, as real and impactful as gravity or friction. It's built directly into the genetic code of our bodies, and into the planet we inhabit, which we hope we'll prove to you in the following pages. This seemingly immovable obstacle, this frustrating success-followed-by-stuckness formula, affects us all. It foils the most modern software companies as they try to hunt for devastating bugs. It foiled ancient mystics who wrote extensively about spiritual plateaus, when prayer seemed to lose impact and passion for faith seemed to wane. To escape the plateau, they developed extreme methods to reset and restart their faith, like the Ignatian Spiritual Exercises, created by the founder of the Jesuit order in the 1500s, which must be practiced in silence for a month.

Plateaus are everywhere.

There is a comfort in merely learning about the existence of the Plateau Effect. Since you were a small child, people have told you that the solution to your problems is to try harder. We're here to tell you that every day, the universe is conspiring against people who think that *more* is the answer. It's built to stop you. At a bare minimum, we want this book to ease a burden you've probably been fighting since you were a baby, and which has become a twenty-first-century malady.

Doing more work doesn't work. You can put the BlackBerry down now and relax a little. You already look more graceful.

In fact, the very word *plateau* is comfortable—at least, far more comfortable than *problem*. We've found that's it's infinitely easier for couples, employees, and students to talk about plateaus than problems. Try this easy experiment: Ask one group of employees to talk about their problems at the company; then ask another to talk about plateaus they encounter at work. One conversation is negative, and usually descends into cattiness and name-calling. The other often leads to discussion of untapped potential and solutions. Guess which is which!

While the Plateau Effect is a fundamental part of nature, modern life has deeply exacerbated the frustrations it causes. The age of specialization and mechanization has robbed many of us of diversity in critical areas of life. Exercise is a good example. Running on a treadmill can't hold a candle to running on a golf course. Bench press exercises on a universal gym don't do nearly as much for you as lifting free weights. And that stomach-crunch rolly thing isn't worth the $9.95 shipping and handling you paid for it. Why? Because all these gadgets work to isolate individual muscle groups. That's fine if you want one very strong muscle in your life. But if you want to be healthy, you have to play outside. You have to let your body struggle with all the variety, surprise, and diversity that nature affords.

This is the madness behind the method of a small but growing number of health-conscious Americans who follow what some call the "paleo diet." John Durant, a very healthy, long-haired twenty-something living in Manhattan, is their spokesman. Sometimes called the Caveman, Durant believes that exercise requires doing what men and women did ten thousand years ago—he and his friends throw large rocks, climb trees, balance on logs, and do other outside activities that engage their minds and entire bodies at once.

"[I do] the sorts of natural movements that hunter-gatherers did just to survive in the past," he says. "It's what children do on the playground. . . . They haven't learned any fitness method. They run, they jump, they're on the monkey bars. They wrestle. They crawl on all fours, and they do these things instinctively. And it's only when we become adults that we get on to treadmills and ellipticals and do the same three or four movements over and over again."

You don't have to live in a cave to see his point. Isolationism, driven by gadgetry, treadmills, and other modern "conveniences," hastens the Plateau Effect dramatically. Now more than ever, it's essential to understand *why*.

There's an important distinction between reaching life equilibrium and being stuck in a plateau. Families need stability to thrive. People need a sense of safety; they need to know they won't be hungry and they'll have a warm bed at night. In psychologist Abraham Maslow's famous hierarchy of needs, this sense of security is one of the most basic requirements for a happy human existence. For many families, simply achieving a predictable workplace and loving home is all the challenge they need. Equilibrium like that is a primal drive, no less than the way our ancestors were driven to find food while avoiding being eaten themselves.

You might be inclined to think of creating a stable home as a plateau . . . but we wouldn't call it that. As anyone who has tried to juggle a marriage, a job, and child rearing knows, there is no such thing as status quo at home. Instead, a bunch of competing needs wrestle in constant tension: Do we go on vacation or pay for braces? Do you work late or go to the kid's soccer game? Wrestling with such tension, working toward the equilibrium required for a stable family life and the tremendous personal growth it provides, is nothing like a plateau. At best, it's a dance, a balancing act that occasionally reaches a peaceful state of equilibrium, or what engineers might call a "steady state." But then, one child takes up drumming, or another moves into high school, and the balancing act reignites again. Nope, chasing after a two-year-old and holding a baby while trying to sound professional during a conference call is nothing like a vaguely dissatisfying plateau—Hugh can testify directly to that.

Meanwhile, plenty of segments of our lives, at certain times, benefit greatly from reaching "set and forget" mode, the steady state we've already mentioned. If you have an assistant who's proven himself responsible for ten years, who always files your expense reports on time and stops you from sending inflammatory e-mails, you don't want him taking a new job, forcing you to start over with a new assistant. If you've picked an elementary school for your child, you don't want the school to close and force you to do a new round of school visits. Think of these as "background tasks," or the "commodities" of your life. You're happy with them as they are, chugging along in sustain mode. But other parts of your life, what you might consider the "entrepreneurial" part of life, deserve much more than autopilot. These are areas of life where you want to invest. They are different for everyone, and they change throughout life. Today, it might be your career. Tomorrow, it might be your marriage . . . or perhaps putting yourself in a position to help your child pick the right college. Distinguishing between the "set and forget" part of your life and the entrepreneurial part is essential for taking on the right challenges.

A real plateau means you have stopped growing. It means your mind and senses are being dulled by sameness, by a routine that sucks the life and soul out of you, by getting less and less out of life while doing more and more. Plateaus ultimately force you to make bad decisions and feel desperate. Understanding this force, and tapping into it, will let you get more from less effort and feel more in tune with the reasons you were put on this planet. It will help you be a better coach, a better parent, a better provider for your family. Frustrated men and women who are unhappy with their lot in life make poor parents; the best gift any dad or mom can give a child is to be happy, and to teach their kids to be happy. Understanding your plateaus—feeling and dealing with the places in your life where you experience vague dissatisfaction, and doing it in the most efficient, successful way—is the quickest route to the equilibrium you seek, whether you have six children, sixteen grandchildren, or you enjoy the single life.

Any business school teacher will tell you that companies either contract or expand—there's no such thing as standing still. This is true in all areas of life. Think of a shower drain clogged with hair. Running more water won't help, that's for sure. But leave it untreated, and you're soon standing in a puddle of water every morning in the shower. Plateaus are a sign—a tangible warning—that your life, your relationship, or your business is clogged. Ignore such clogs at great peril.

When humans shared the earth with predators and were under constant threat of being eaten alive, "getting used to" the familiar—and reacting only to the extreme—was a matter of life or death. Today, however, "getting used to" your job, your spouse, your exercise routine, or your local deli has become a matter of dying a very slow, boring death. The force of acclimation means even the strongest odor, or the prettiest girl, or the most amazing new rock band will soon become routine and dull for you. This is why so many things you do seem exciting at first, but within a few weeks, the thrill is gone. It's also why most exercise and diet plans fail at around the two-week mark.

The time it takes to "get used to" things can vary, but it always follows the same familiar pattern—a response curve that accelerates quickly at the beginning and slowly begins to level off. If you plotted this curve, it would look a lot like a graph you saw about a thousand times in high school math. No one ever mentioned that this simple curve is actually the key to growth in just about every human endeavor you can imagine?

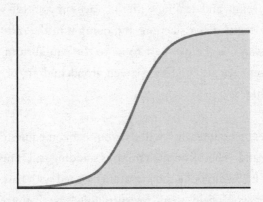

We believe that plateaus can be broken down into eight simple categories. In each case, if you identify the plateau—what kind of clogged drain are you working with?—the solution is easier to find. Remember, not all clogs respond to Drano. Some need . . . Oh, never mind. We (Hugh and Bob here!) are not plumbers. So let's kick the clog analogy—it's holding us back.

You might be thinking right now: "Wait, you're not plumbers . . . who the heck are you?"

We aren't doctors, either. We offer you this prescription as investigators who have found what we think are incredibly valuable strategies from emerging areas of scientific research. We aren't psychologists or therapists. We are entrepreneurial analysts with, between us, forty years of experience researching, writing, and analyzing systems and human nature.

Bob has been writing about the dramatic changes to life, identity, money, and culture that result from the digital age since before most

Americans had an e-mail address. He's been an investigative journalist for NBC News and MSNBC.com for almost twenty years, so you'd be hard-pressed to find a tale about technology or money that he hasn't covered. Hugh is a start-up businessman, mathematics and computer science professor, and speaker who travels the globe every year to teach executives and engineers at some of the world's biggest companies how to protect themselves from twenty-first-century hazards. A native of the Bahamas and a former Ivy League educator, Hugh brings a rare blend of Western and Island cultures to his views on life's major pitfalls and promises. After years of speaking engagements and conducting research together, we have synthesized scholarship and experiments from around the world to explain why we think today is a magical time for people to start overcoming their limits. Through the years, we've talked with executives from hundreds of firms and interviewed thousands of people. Combining our divergent backgrounds, we have found a hidden problem and some simple solutions that are just too exciting to keep to ourselves.

We turned to many experts for help explaining plateaus, their causes, and their cures. Some of those discussions led to original research conducted exclusively for this book. Later, you'll see how we enlisted the help of Carnegie Mellon University to test a theory we'd devised about the risks that divided attention pose in our increasingly cell-phone-distracted world. The results are stunning—but so is the potential solution that Carnegie Mellon's research accidentally unearthed. We don't want to spoil the surprise, but for now we'll just say the mere possibility that you'll receive a phone call while reading this passage means you will probably understand about 20 percent less of this chapter. Also in that part of the book, we'll disclose the results of a simple test of listening comprehension we devised with the Ponemon Institute. The test showed that nearly all of us (80 percent) miss important details when listening to important instructions or during a domestic squabble, but—brace for this, men—women nearly always outperform men in auditory comprehension. Don't worry, men: This simply means that you have more room for improvement, so you'll have an easier time breaking through plateaus caused by missing some of life's critical pieces of information due to poor listening skills.

A word about the way this book is organized: The first four chapters discuss the "hard science" of plateaus, with much more on topics like acclimation. They set out the three greatest forces behind the Plateau Effect we see all around us. In the middle, you'll find what we call the mechanical chapters, which talk about the nuts and bolts of how to overcome plateaus. These three chapters can be thought of as the instruction manual for the engine that can propel you off your joyless plain. Finally, the last three chapters deal with the human, emotional side of plateaus and show how people have become inspired to break through them. This final part of the book discusses the everyday behaviors that are the last step to achieving the great potential towering above the plateau that is holding you down. At the back of the book, we've added a summary of the eight steps to overcoming the Plateau Effect.

There is a story that's told by motivational speakers the world over—perhaps you've heard it—about baby elephants and circus trainers. Trainers once kept baby elephants in check by binding one of their legs with a large shackle, connecting it to a chain, and linking the chain to a peg in the ground. The baby could walk but couldn't break free from the chain, and so his life was limited to a small circle around the peg. He became settled in this circle, his boundaries defined by its circumference. Of course, baby elephants grow up into massive, hulking, powerful creatures. But circus trainers never had to increase the strength of the elephant chain. Even though the animal could easily break free as an adult, he never tried. As a baby long ago, he had learned what the circumference of his life was and never even imagined that it could change.

Many of us are elephants. We've defined our lives by the circles we move in, using years-old experiences as absolute parameters for what we can and can't do. To outsiders, we might look as foolish as a huge elephant restricted by a tiny chain. This is the cause of most plateaus. This book will help you pull in a new direction, and whatever place you are in, we hope to make your world bigger.

PART ONE
THE SCIENCE

Three Forces

1. DO THE MATH

Uncovering the Forces That Drive the Plateau Effect

Or, "An accomplished athlete is like, 'I don't want to do this because it makes me look stupid.' And then suddenly, Derek [Jeter] was killing those drills."

Most of you are probably quite familiar with the notion that people who drink alcohol develop a tolerance for it. On the first day of college, three beers might get you drunk. By October, you might need six beers to reach those same buzzy heights. And by the holidays, a six-pack might not even make you feel light-headed unless accompanied by someone like Jack Daniel's. You've built up a *tolerance* to alcohol.

The concept of tolerance spreads far across the drug world. Morphine is the best example. People in pain often receive morphine in the hospital—and after time, they need more and more of it to have the same pain-killing effect. Just as your nose stops smelling garlic, your pain receptors become saturated and start blowing off the morphine unless you administer more and more. Tales of morphine addiction that result from this tolerance are well known, but here's something you probably don't know and we hope you never encounter: Morphine tolerance, treated by higher dosages, can have far worse consequences than addiction. Take enough morphine, and it can literally kill your body's desire to breathe, something called respiratory depression. People who die of morphine overdose usually suffocate.

In far less dramatic ways, tolerance is probably suffocating you, too.

Tolerance can cut both ways, however, and doctors often use this Plateau Effect to their advantage. A patient who requires blood thinners might need to take what would be a fatal dose to achieve the required benefit. Take too much of a blood thinner, and your brain will bleed. So instead of overdosing the patient, doctors slowly ramp up the dosage over a month or two. The same dose that could kill a patient with a side effect on October 1 could be tolerated by a patient on December 1, now in an amount that provides the necessary medicinal benefit.

Tolerance—when a drug's benefit begins to slump because the receptors it targets are saturated—is only one part of the Plateau Effect in medicine, however. Toxicity is another. With drugs, as with garlic, too much of a good thing can do more harm than good. Common ibuprofen, taken as an anti-inflammatory by weekend athletes everywhere, is a good example. Ibuprofen works by blocking something called cyclooxygenase (COX) enzymes, which cause swelling and pain. The problem is, there are two types of COX enzymes. Blocking COX-2 is a good thing and helps you get back on the field quicker. But blocking COX-1 can lead to bleeding, stomach ulcers, and kidney damage. When you pop an ibuprofen, you are taking the good with the bad. Take too little, and your pain won't go away. Take too much, and you can cause permanent damage. In between is an S-shaped response curve, where the benefits are high and the risk is low. It looks like this.

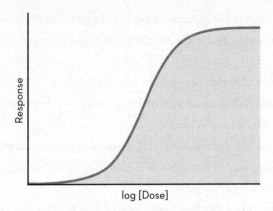

log [Dose]

Look familiar? Whether because of tolerance or toxicity, most drugs follow this basic pattern. Doctors and pharmacists are well aware of the delicate balancing act that is required to stay on the right side of a medicinal plateau. The way they handle it will begin to sound familiar as we march through the many plateau-busting techniques in this book. They often attack the problem with diversity.

The next time—hopefully far in the future—you check in for surgery, the hospital won't simply give you morphine. You'll get a complex cocktail of seven or eight different drugs, all with slightly different benefits and side effects. It's called "multimodal therapy." Giving smaller doses of multiple drugs can magnify the therapeutic effect of each while diminishing the potential for tolerance. Sometimes the multimodal approach can cause true synergism, where 1 + 1 really does equal 3. That's what Vicodin is—a preparation of acetaminophen plus hydrocodone. Over one hundred million prescriptions for Vicodin are now filled every year in the United States.

But any drug, even a multimodal cocktail of cancer-fighting chemotherapy drugs, loses its effectiveness over time. That's one reason why doctors tell patients to take what's called a "drug holiday," to give the patient's body a chance to reset, to give recep-tors a chance to desaturate, and hopefully to kick-start a drug's pos-itive effects.

What if pharmacists only believed that more is better? Drugs clearly exhibit this law of diminishing returns, or more critically, the trait that we believe is central to the Plateau Effect: Things work, until they don't. Just because you do something that works doesn't mean doing more of it will work even better. Now, we want to prove that to you mathematically.

Hugh holds a Ph.D. in mathematics, and Bob holds a college de-gree in math, which means we both spent a lot of time working through something called differential equations as teenagers. These were boring until we started looking into the Plateau Effect and real-ized that the differential equation—this most fundamental tool for solving real-world, three-dimensional problems—is simply math's way of expressing plateaus. In fact, differential equations are to the Plateau Effect what $E = MC^2$ is to relativity. Higher math, what some people call God's blueprint for the universe, is actually the language of plateaus. We'll show you how, and you won't even need a scien-tific calculator. You just need a dog.

Say you want to build a pen for your doggie in the backyard so he can frolic safely outside your house. One side of the pen is the side of your house, so you only have to build three sides (easy!). To make things even easier, you buy 50 feet of prebuilt fence, which means the sides must meet at right angles (no curves). What's the best shape to make so Fluffy has the most room to run around? Hint: We wouldn't be telling you this story if the answer were a boring square.

If you were a caveman, you might make the mistake of simply using trial and error. Your wife might argue that the sides connected to the house should be longer; you might argue the opposite. You could build fifty different configurations and measure them, after which your wife would probably divorce you for taking so long to work on the project.

Or you could solve the problem with calculus in about thirty seconds. Turns out, the right shape is a rectangle with two sides that are half the length of the others—in this case, you'd lay down one 25-foot side parallel to the house and two 12.5-feet sides, like this. (Read the notes if you want to see the evidence.)

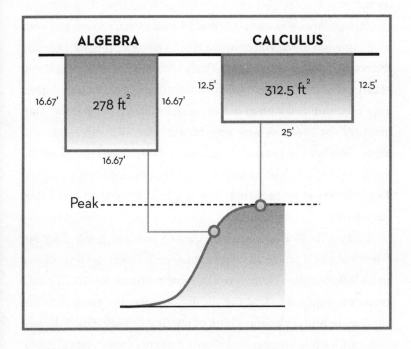

Fluffy will really benefit from the calculus. If you chose the obvious square shape, he'd have 278 square feet to romp in. But with your advanced math skills, he gets 312.5 square feet.

The real world is full of such calculus problems. There's one you probably hold in your hand nearly every day: What's the optimal shape for a soft drink can to maximize volume while minimizing surface area and thus aluminum costs? Basically, it's a can that's a little taller than it is wide. But imagine if, instead of doing the calculations, engineers inside cola companies wasted all their time idly arguing about whether cans should be taller or squatter?

Sound ridiculous? But that's how most of us live our lives. Someone gives us a piece of advice, and we try it, and it works for a while, but we keep doing it long after the suggestion has lived out its usefulness. Let's go back to the dog pen for a moment to explain what we mean.

Imagine that you started to build a square-shaped pen, and your wife came out to tell you that you should elongate the side opposite the house. She's brilliant, right? That's true, until she's wrong. If you began to follow her advice and took it too far, you'd suddenly have a very long, thin pen with even less room for Fluffy. What if the engineers for the soda can who wanted to make taller cans—let's call them "heighties"—became drunk with power and convinced the drink maker to fashion cans that resembled miniature skyscrapers? The firm would go bankrupt. The heighties were right, until they were wrong.

Solving the dog pen problem, the can problem, and millions of other real-world problems involves nuance. It involves a little of this and a little of that, but often not in equal portions. Advanced mathematics is required to find the optimal solution, but most of us live our lives in brutal algebra. Think of political debates: One side yells "tax cuts," while another yells "infrastructure investments." Obviously, the solution involves some balancing act between those things, but Republicans and Democrats have a hard time getting past $A + B = C$. One side builds a tall, thin soda can; the other builds a can shaped like a manhole cover. And we all suffer.

Many of our own personal struggles—to lose weight, to improve our relationships, to grow our businesses—suffer from this same kind of all-or-nothing, black-or-white algebraic thinking. The diet you choose works, until it doesn't. The new marketing strategy works, until it doesn't. What's fascinating is that if you really could try every possible solution for the dog pen, the cola can, and nearly every other real-world problem you could devise, and plotted those on a graph, it would look just like this:

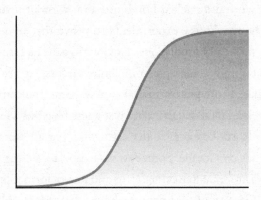

Precisely when something has reached optimal shape and size, it will begin to stop working if you keep applying the same technique. That's why it's important to reconsider the advice you've received from those diet plans, those late-night infomercial exercise machines, those business books that offer only algebra. We're here to offer you calculus: a new way to optimize all that other advice. People, companies, husbands, wives, and political parties would all do well to learn a little calculus if they want to start solving problems in the real, three-dimensional world—and, to our point, if they want to escape the plateau caused, ironically enough, by being right.

The desire to be right is among the most powerful forces in humanity. Clever teachers learned long ago how to use this power against— well, really *for*—their students. Hugh got a real kick out of toying with the highly motivated students he taught at Columbia University. They made excellent guinea pigs.

Hugh once taught a popular course in information technology at the New York City campus of the Ivy League school. In it, he covered a lot of material: why systems break, how databases become useless in the wrong hands, why it seems everyone's personal information is left lying around on the street for any creep to steal, how hackers brought down Iran's nuclear bomb program without firing a single shot. And he ran kooky experiments to prove that understanding data can be fun (and mischievous). Not long ago, he had students seed the Internet with a made-up term, "context reflux," to see how long it would take for the phrase to make its way into the common lexicon. To the students' delight, after just a few blog posts and tweets, they began to see "context reflux" crowding out all kinds of legitimate searches on Google. Someday, we expect to see the book *Context Reflux: The Media Revolution*. Fans and foes of former presidential candidate Rick Santorum know the havoc that this so-called search engine poisoning can cause. For years, web users who searched for "Santorum" found, not information about the former Pennsylvania senator, but rather a vulgar faux definition of the word *santorum* that had been created by critics. Data is easy to manipulate, and it can be fun, unless you are the victim.

Word of Hugh's pranks spread quickly, so every semester, his class filled up fast. During a recent semester, he had the usual mix of master's students, about half a dozen Ph.D. candidates, and a handful of ambitious undergrads. But what struck him was how many distractions students brought with them: laptops, iPhones, iPads, eReaders, even watches that gave real-time market updates. He felt he was in constant competition with Twitter, Facebook, and up-to-the-second stock quotes for AAPL.

It's a common teacher's lament nowadays, but fortunately, Hugh was in a position to use the students' distraction to his advantage. He wanted to prove a point about how ineffective their brain power had become, and how a small adjustment could make a huge differ-ence.

For a crop of very bright students, they never saw it coming.

"Today's class is going to be a little different," Hugh said. "No notes allowed. Please put any pens, paper, phones, or laptops away. We're going to learn about designing experiments."

Some people weren't happy; others panicked.

"Will this be on the midterm?" one said. No. "Will this be on the final?" No.

There was one student who'd had a death grip on his iPhone since the beginning of the semester who seemed particularly un-nerved. He seemed to be shaking. Hugh quickly glanced in the cor-ner to be sure the emergency defibrillator was in working order.

After deflecting two other midterm questions, the lecture began. The timing had to be perfect.

The PowerPoint slides he'd created were set to advance auto-matically and with great precision, and Hugh began to talk over them. The lecture began with a discussion about ethics in experi-ment design. A list of influential figures appeared on the screen. Don't worry if you can't recall them at first; Hugh's students certain-ly couldn't.

Harold Hotelling, Raj Chandra Bose, Herman Chernoff, Ronald Fisher.

During the next five minutes, Hugh repeatedly read through the list of names five times: first talking about their occupation, then their role, their history, their impact and legacy. The point should have been clear: Hugh was trying to burn the scholars' names into his students' brains, the same way they'd memorized multiplication tables in the fifth grade—through repetition. Of course, he knew it wouldn't work.

Next, the slides advanced to describe the most influential experiments on learning skills in history—most, naturally, having to do with memorization. The students then saw a list of some of the most prominent researchers in the field:

Hermann Ebbinghaus, Paul Pimsleur, Cecil Alec Mace, Piotr Wozniak.

The slide was only up for a few seconds, just barely enough time to read through the list. Hugh then moved on, but twenty-five seconds later the list reappeared, and again he read the names out loud.

The class went on to a discussion about how observers often affect the results of what they observe. And then, exactly two minutes after its ephemeral appearance, the second list of researchers appeared again. This happened two more times during the class—once ten minutes later, and then again an hour after that. Each time the names were read aloud quickly, and then the lecture moved on. By the time he was finished, the second list of scholars had also been shown five times—but at intervals which were precisely spaced: at twenty-five seconds, then two minutes, then ten minutes, then an hour. It's a formula that has been understood for decades—derived based on meticulous experimentation—but locked away in the annals of science.

Both lists got five minutes of airtime, but the way that time was used varied dramatically. Hugh believed he'd just given the students perhaps the most important lesson in focused learning they'd ever receive.

At the end of the class, a pop quiz was administered. After the usual moaning and groaning, the students were astonished. In fact, they were downright delighted with themselves. The results mirrored one of the best-kept secrets in cognitive psychology: Most of the students were able to recall the second list, where reviews were spread out, but hardly any remembered the first list, where reviews were done consecutively.

Every problem has its kryptonite, and for memory, that kryptonite is bad timing. With memorization, as with many things in life, doing the same thing over and over only takes you so far.

In 1879, Hermann Ebbinghaus, a professor of philosophy at the University of Berlin, set out on an exploration that would later grow into one of the most important fields of modern research. His journey would take longer than four years, and the precision and thoroughness with which it was documented are still considered to be a model in the field. Ebbinghaus's destination was one of the most nebulous regions in the world. Few had dared to investigate it, and many had thought such an investigation was impossible, even heretical. It was not an archeological dig or a trip to some besieged country. Ebbinghaus's journey was into his own mind.

His field, now referred to as psychometrics, was in its infancy. Sir Francis Galton had proposed the notion of quantifying intelligence a decade earlier, but the idea of measuring one's mind was regarded much the way that numerology is today.

Ebbinghaus wanted to better understand how memories form and how people learn new information. He had a suspicion that memory "plateaued"—that it would be increasingly less effective to spend time memorizing something by simply repeating it or using other rote techniques that you probably encountered when learning multiplication tables. Ebbinghaus used himself as a research subject. His method was simple: repeat a set of his made-up symbols several times and then, twenty-four hours later, look at the list again and see how many times he needed to re-review it to be able to repeat it by heart. What he found was that after a certain threshold, viewing the list one more time produced a shrinking benefit when that data had to be recalled or relearned later. This meant that the tenth review of the list did far less for retention than the first or second review. Similarly, the twentieth review was of so little benefit over the nineteenth review that it was hardly measurable.

Ebbinghaus developed something he called a "forgetting curve." Its shape should remind you of something. Note the first line, how quickly it falls as a person's chance to remember sinks toward zero in a dotted-line curve, like an inverted plateau. More important, note how the forgetting is overcome with each successive reminder in that familiar shape. We'll discuss this a lot more in the chapter titled "Bad Timing."

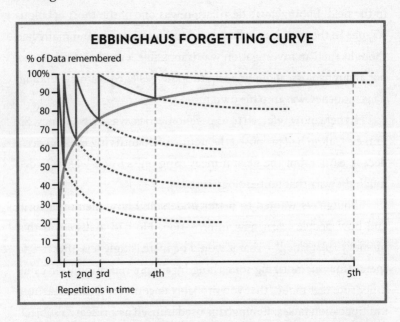

Ebbinghaus realized that people reach a plateau—a point at which additional effort produces little additional results. He started to introduce intervals of time between reviews and continually fine-tuned those intervals, eventually showing that efficiency could be raised by 500 percent through the simplest of techniques. His discovery that we reach a memory plateau, and his research into how to avoid it, led to a method of learning that has helped accelerate retention and is the basis of the world's most effective learning techniques.

Here's a taste: We've established that mere repetition won't burn facts into your brain. But well-timed repetition is pretty foolproof. How well timed? The recipe: Space reviews so that the first is done after five seconds, the next after twenty-five seconds, the third after two minutes, the next at ten minutes, then one hour, five hours, one day, five days, twenty-five days, four months, two years, and that's it, the information is locked in permanently. Don't believe it? We'll sneak in a drill shortly that will convince you.

The implications of Ebbinghaus's work and the work of others who have built upon it go far beyond memorization, or even education. World-famous elite professional athletes have rediscovered his basic premise; so have some of the world's most successful companies. Later in this book—when we discuss timing, in Chapter 4—we'll meet small tribes of people who have taken Ebbinghaus's findings to heart and use them to count, analyze, and guide literally every single step they take. Plenty of disparate groups have, without using the term, begun to solve the Plateau Effect.

Too bad the dominant family home entertainment corporation of the 1990s wasn't paying attention.

Try to put yourself back into a 1980s frame of mind for a moment. The glory days of the silver screen were fading a bit as families of four were tired of paying nearly a day's wages for theater tickets, and almost as much for cheap popcorn and soda. Meanwhile, Americans were radically changing the way they consumed entertainment, and armed with large televisions and spiffy new living room sound systems, they wanted to stay home. The times were changing, and this company rode the wave perfectly. It grew from humble beginnings in Dallas, Texas, to acquire twenty-four million customers worldwide. Its value proposition was spot-on—let people rent a movie for a few dollars, watch it on their own big screens, pop their own corn, and they'd be thrilled to save a bundle on movie tickets. Conscientious consumers did the math and discovered that after saving a year's worth of movie tickets, even at kids' discount prices, the big TV would pay for itself.

The firm that enabled this home theater transition became a household name with brand equity that rivaled McDonald's and Coca-Cola, and left old-fashioned entertainment companies in the dust. Eventually, it was acquired by arguably the world's most powerful media company, and titans like Carl Icahn and Wayne Huizenga, owner of the Miami Dolphins, fought over its spoils. The company seemed to be in nearly every living room in America.

Today, those same titans are left to pick over its near-dead carcass.

The company, perhaps you know, is Blockbuster. In October 2010, stock in this once-proud, can't-miss business fell to 4.1 cents per share after the firm declared bankruptcy.

The Goliath was slain by a slingshot fired by a "David" named Marc Randolph in tiny Scotts Valley, California. Randolph had rented the movie *Apollo 13* and, like millions of Americans, failed to return the video on time. In fact, he was very late: forty dollars late. He was outraged by the fee—even angrier than 1980s parents were about the price of popcorn. So he set on a crazy idea: What if consumers could rent movies for as long as they wanted, one or two at a time, with no fear of late fees? Would they pay ten dollars a month instead of playing Russian return roulette with Blockbuster? Test marketing showed they would, but there was an enormous hitch. The year was 1997, and the only sensible way to run such a venture would be to deliver the movies electronically, through two-way cable TV boxes or satellite dishes. But it was too early for both technologies. Clunky experiments with set-top boxes had failed miserably. There wasn't nearly enough bandwidth for satisfying on-demand experiences. Experiments delivering movies at night, while consumers were sleeping, failed, too. Like so many ideas from California, this one was before its time. Cable TV firms decided to wait until the technology caught up to the idea.

But Randolph didn't wait. Instead, he took one step backward in order to make a giant leap forward. His even crazier idea: Send movies through the mail. Put a stamp on an envelope, mail the DVD out, then have the consumer drop it in the mail and send it back. Just as the entire entertainment industry was focused on satisfying consumers' impulsive requests, and America was enthralled by e-mail, and Wall Street was making everyone with *dot-com* in the name rich, Randolph invented the Pony Express of movies.

Detractors thought he was nuts, starting his company while relying on hundred-year-old technology, right at the height of the dot-com bubble. And he was crazy to take on Blockbuster, which at its height had four thousand US locations. But he didn't care. He ran the numbers. He knew it would work.

A little more than a decade later, the same day that Blockbuster shares hit 4.1 cents, Netflix soared to $169. A month later Netflix rose to $180, and was selected to join the prestigious list of S&P 500, replacing *The New York Times*.

When Bob met Randolph in the late 1990s, the Netflix founder was on a media tour in Seattle, explaining his crazy adventure in licking stamps. Netflix warehouses were exactly what they sounded like. Armies of workers scattered around the country raced to stuff envelopes with movies as fast as they could. Consumers just getting comfortable with using websites would queue their orders. They were surprisingly patient about waiting for their flicks, and surprisingly willing to plan their Friday nights on Wednesday afternoons—after all, they *could* choose to drive to a Blockbuster and get the movies right away. But Randolph knew they would tolerate only so much delay. He raced to set up more and more regional centers so he could stand by the "soft" promise of one-day turnarounds. He also knew it had to be easy, so he swallowed the price of delivery, both ways—he did the stamp licking, not the consumer.

It worked.

By May 2000, the firm had 250,000 paying customers. At the time, the idea of getting web users to pay for anything was just about absurd: There was only porn, online dating sites, and Netflix. Three years later, Netflix had more than one million subscribers. Still, Blockbuster barely sensed the threat and ran advertisements poking fun at the quaintness of the mail-order service. It halfheartedly started its own competitive service, Blockbuster by Mail, which offered a real advantage to consumers—movies could be exchanged immediately, at the store.

But it was already too late. Netflix was cool, its website was far superior, and its reputation was growing fast. Little piles of the red Netflix envelopes formed in mailrooms at apartment complexes all across America's big cities, acting like so many Christmas presents to their recipients.

Randolph had perfect timing. A veteran of the mail-order business, he understood the infrastructure required for smooth operation. He knew the newly minted DVD format was ideal for mailing. But most of all, he knew video rental stores were arrogant and ready for a takedown (a forty-dollar late fee for a thirty-dollar product?). Blockbuster had "plateaued." Randolph refused to wait; he used available technology and made his move. By noticing its vulnerability,

mastering the timing, and being aware of changing winds and changing technologies, Randolph felled Goliath. Netflix is now the household name. Blockbuster is now the Pony Express, its thousand empty
stores now a problem of urban blight.

The story doesn't end there, though. Netflix, which invented a
category by looking backward, also leaned forward at just the right
time. Netflix didn't abandon its core consumers but began delivering movies on demand just as high-speed Internet made the experience palatable for most consumers. By 2010, Netflix's seventeen
million consumers spent more time streaming movies than watching DVDs—a boon for the company, which is licking a lot fewer
stamps these days. To encourage the trend, it offered discounted
"streaming-only" subscriptions. In 2011, it was estimated that more
than 20 percent of weeknight Internet traffic was generated by Netflix subscribers streaming movies.

The infusion of new customers attracted by streaming capabili-
ties pushed the Netflix customer base past Comcast sometime in
2011, making it the largest "pay-TV" company in America. And some
project Netflix to have forty million users by 2013, putting the service
in one out of every three US households. The firm hit several bumps
in the road as it tried to navigate the tricky change from mail-order
company to streaming giant—it tried and failed to raise prices without customers noticing when it began double-charging for its mail
and streaming services. But it always understood that its business
model, from the very beginning, was ending.

How did David and Goliath switch positions so quickly? More
important, why did Blockbuster burn out while Netflix burned
bright? Why were analysts armed with simple tools able to predict the
flameout while those titans of industry seemed powerless to stop it?
And what can Netflix's success teach you? Blockbuster failed for precisely the same reason that movie theaters lost favor and that Netflix

almost wrecked its own dominant position in the marketplace—they all plateaued when they stopped providing value to their customers and instead focused on short-term gains. We call that the *greedy algorithm*. These firms and industries got distracted and stopped listening, which meant they ignored obvious warning signs. They were victims of missing the *just noticeable difference*. And while they all had an impeccable sense of timing on the way up, that same sense betrayed them when trouble began. When these things happen, a plateau is unavoidable—as unavoidable as the impact an apple makes on the ground after falling from a tree.

Unlike gravity, however, the Plateau Effect doesn't have the last word. Blockbuster's failure wasn't inevitable.

Think you can't teach an old dog new tricks? Too set in your ways to try something totally new that would break barriers for you? If anyone would have trouble summoning the humility to shock their techniques with brand-new material, it would be an aging major league baseball superstar who'd already earned more than a quarter of a billion dollars doing things the way he'd always done. At age thirty-five, the Yankees' Derek Jeter had done everything there was to do in baseball. A surefire Hall of Famer with four World Series titles and the adulation of every available woman in New York City, Derek Jeter was the epitome of cool. But he had one nagging flaw, one Achilles' heel: bratty mathematicians who invented higher-level mathematical statistics for evaluating defensive prowess. Soon after Jeter's career began in 1995, these stat geeks began their unrelenting assault on his performance at shortstop. Jeter, they said, was at or near the bottom in all the defensive categories. One famous egghead put it this way: "He gets far more girls than his fielding talents should allow." A Wharton professor released a study concluding that Jeter was, in fact, the worst shortstop in baseball. The statisticians offered evidence to back up the words of Boston Red Sox fans everywhere: "Jeter Sucks." Red Sox Nation rejoiced: "It took world-class scientists to prove what Red Sox fans have known for years," wrote a blogger on FenwayWest.com.

If you had $250 million in earnings in the bank, would you care about taunts from statistician bloggers hurling insults using terms like "fielding runs above replacement"? Jeter not only cared about them, he used them as part of his formula to find the Fountain of Youth. How did he do it? By quite literally learning to take his first step all over again.

After years of working with the same trainer, in the same spring training complex, and winning multiple championships, Jeter listened to his critics, and he beat them at their own game. In 2008, he hired a new trainer, Jason Riley from the famed Athletes Compound for elite athletes in Tampa, Florida. Riley set about rewiring Jeter's fast-twitch muscles and focused on healing years of wear and tear in his body. Jeter's long-standing bugaboo was moving laterally to his left, limiting his ability to make perhaps the most common play in a shortstop's repertoire—gobbling up ground balls that roll up the middle of the diamond, near second base. Jeter was a step slow, Riley found, because his left hip was a bit less flexible than his right, a common condition for right-handed hitters. He had violently rotated that left hip perhaps 2.7 million times since he first grabbed a bat as a child, and at age thirty-five, he was a little slow to react when hitters slapped the ball past the pitcher to his left.

So Riley put Jeter through grueling drills to strengthen and reenergize that hip. He quite literally forced Jeter to take baby steps all over again.

"We were re-coaching his first step, over and over," Riley told Ian O'Connor, author of a book about Jeter. "I think he hated doing these drills at first, because it's almost like reeducating a little kid. An accomplished athlete is like, 'I don't want to do this because it makes me look stupid.' And then suddenly, Derek was killing those drills."

Riley sent Jeter on a simple four-step road of learning that he uses with every elite athlete he encounters—a road you can take, too. He described it to us during a lengthy exchange about Jeter's training one day. It consists of four simple steps: unconscious incompetence; conscious incompetence; conscious competence; and finally, the victory, unconscious competence.

To explain: Jeter was taking his first step incorrectly but didn't know it (Step 1: unconscious incompetence). When Riley pointed it out, Jeter knew the technique was wrong but had big trouble breaking his bad habit (Step 2: conscious incompetence). With great practice and much conscious focus, he rewired his neuromuscular communication to the point that he started to make the correct movements—but only as long as he concentrated very hard (Step 3: conscious competence). And finally, the new movements were burned into memory and could be done automatically (Step 4: unconscious competence).

"This is the goal of all movements," Riley told us. "To perform the movements effectively, efficiently, allowing for better recruitment, better synchronization, and less energy expenditure." Dancers who count one . . . two . . . three, one . . . two . . . three look silly. So do shortstops who think about their steps while chasing hard grounders up the middle. But with enough practice, the right way becomes the automatic way, and real change occurs.

Once Jeter reached unconscious competence, he smashed through his defensive plateau. When the Yankees shortstop started chasing down everything hit to his left during the 2009 season, general managers around the league wondered aloud if he had indeed discovered the Fountain of Youth. No thirty-five-year-old shortstop had ever improved his defense before. That season Jeter committed the fewest errors of his career and had his highest fielding percentage, but those results barely tell the story. He also managed to shock even the nerdiest of statisticians and shoved his way to the top of all those newfangled defensive metrics. The "Jeter Sucks" cries grew quiet. And, by the way, the New York Yankees won the World Series, providing overwhelming evidence that plateaus can be overcome with remarkable results. Know how many teams have won a World Series with a shortstop older than thirty-five since 1955? One, the Yankees, with Derek Jeter, in 2009. Know how many shortstops older than thirty-five have won a Gold Glove since 1970? One: Derek Jeter.

He's no Blockbuster. And you don't have to be, either.

2. GOING FLAT

The First Plateau Force

Or, "You're like, '... It's going to taste like a tomato.' But what if it doesn't? What if it tastes like ... a raspberry?"

I have no idea what just happened here. I'm shocked, I'm angry, I don't even know what to say."

Jennifer Lopez was pissed. She sought comfort from her fellow *American Idol* judges, producer Randy Jackson and Aerosmith front man Steven Tyler.

"I'm never upset on this show, and I'm never really mad, but this makes me mad. It's like, 'What's going on?'" Jackson added. Tyler berated the voters at home, saying, "I don't know, America, man. A mistake is one thing, but a lack of passion is unforgivable!"

Fans were angry, too. They had just watched Pia Toscano, one of the most talented and beautiful singers to ever hit the *Idol* stage, be eliminated, leaving her with a ninth-place finish. But while the judges were angry at voters, they themselves were the root of the problem. They were too nice.

The judges consistently praised nearly every performance by every contestant and did it nearly every week. If compliments were garlic, *American Idol* viewers had been sniffing cloves of it for weeks, and like it does for diners at the Stinking Rose, the scent had just faded away. Voters had become acclimated to praise, numb to compliments, and had trouble differentiating mediocre talent from the truly exceptional.

On *American Idol*, hopeful singers compete every week and face a panel of judges who comment on their performances. Then, it's up to viewers to vote for their favorite. People call, text, or click by the millions, and the contestant who gets the lowest number of votes is sent home. The role of the judges is to provide expert feedback, to point out the good, the bad, and the awful of performances with the intention of helping viewers make an informed choice.

At least that's the plan.

It worked pretty well before cantankerous judge Simon Cowell left. Cowell would berate singers he thought performed poorly and praise the ones who did well. Here are a few Cowell quotes during his *Idol* tenure: "If you would be singing like this two thousand years ago, people would have stoned you." And another: "If your lifeguard duties were as good as your singing, a lot of people would be drowning." You get the point. He was mean, downright ruthless, but he was a *differentiating signal*. You knew who he loved and who he hated.

Contrast that to the combination of Lopez, Tyler, and Jackson. Their harshest comments were equivalent to saying, "It was a little pitchy, but we love you anyway." They praised nearly every singer, making it difficult for the public to differentiate and making viewers second-guess their own negative opinions. Today.com writer Craig Berman summed up the problem the day after Toscano was eliminated:

"It would have been impossible to gauge that the panel loved Toscano more than anyone else in the competition because they gave lavish praise to everyone, and ended the show by saying everyone was great and they didn't know who people should vote for."

Simon Cowell, irascible as he was, played an essential role in the mechanics of the show: He helped amplify the talent gap between certain singers. The new judges did not. The first time Lopez, Tyler, and Jackson praised Pia Toscano, it might have meant something, but eventually it got lost in a sea of consistency.

Acclimation, as we have discussed, desensitizes us to consistency, but its impact goes far beyond reality TV and garlic-lover restaurants. It might even have led to the theft of your car.

When car alarms first started to become widely used during the 1970s, the sound was jarring. People looked, they reacted, and the alarms served their intended purpose of drawing attention to would-be thieves. But soon their effectiveness plateaued.

Had brilliant thieves figured out how to outsmart the alarms? Hardly. The problem was much simpler: all that noise. A law enforcement study of car alarm noise in New York City found that up to 99 percent of alarms were false. Thunderstorms, an unruly neighborhood cat, vibrations from a passing truck, and a close encounter with a pedestrian were all more likely triggers of an alarm than criminals. The sound was so common, and the false alarm rate was so high, that people started to ignore them. They were no longer an effective signal.

A study by Progressive Insurance found that less than 1 percent of people would call the police if they heard a car alarm. They were ruled a nuisance in the court of public opinion. The cacophony of ineffective car alarms pushed the passage of an ordinance in New York City banning the use of alarms that did not stop after three minutes—a very desirable feature for criminals. By 1997, a study of insurance claims data from more than seventy-three million cars showed that car alarms "showed no overall reduction in theft loss." That's what happens when we get flooded by false alarms and bad data; we ignore all the data.

In the battle of signal versus noise, noise has a decided advantage. It's a natural human reflex to tune out information channels that get flooded by noise. The downside is that there are a few messages in those channels that we really care about. Cars do get stolen. Some alarms are legit, but the communications channel has been burned. Car thieves actually use oversignaling to their advantage. A common yet brazen technique when stealing a car is to set off multiple car alarms in a lot at once if your goal is to only steal one particular car.

Car alarms lost their effectiveness because they stopped being unusual. When we go numb, we miss really important signals—and this can lead to some pretty major mistakes.

While the world was caught up in hanging chads and magnifying glasses in the fall of 2000, the technology community was much more interested in a glitch you might not have heard about that hit the swing county of Volusia in Florida. An electronic voting machine in a district with six hundred registered voters counted -16,022 votes for Democratic candidate Al Gore—that's *negative* sixteen thousand votes. Unless you were filming an episode of *Survivor* on a deserted island that week, you probably remember the *Bush v. Gore* drama: uncertainty, limbo, chaos. But what happened in Volusia? How could a machine so critical to one of the most important processes in the country have failed so spectacularly? (By the way, these bad results were discarded and had no impact on the final tally, as Volusia's votes were famously hand-counted later.)

It's likely that the voting machine was tested thousands of times and used hundreds of times in regional elections without the problem showing up. Yet there it was, standing in the way of selecting the next leader of the free world. If you take a look behind the curtain of the software development industry, it's easy to imagine why serious bugs like this get missed. Software is written by software developers, people who produce pages of logical instructions for a machine to interpret and act upon. In most software companies, the finished product is then put through its paces by software testers—people who poke and prod at it looking for bugs. Testers tend to do things that are similar to what they think a user would do. They press the big buttons, select the most common options, open and close files, and so on. The problem is that those common user paths aren't usually the most "bug-revealing" paths. They may catch some serious problems early on, but their ability to find bugs quickly plateaus—the system essentially becomes immune to continued standard testing techniques. But those fringe bugs that get missed—the kinds that cause a voting machine to record -16,022 votes—are usually the most critical. The normal method for bug hunting is prone to miss exactly the most critical mistakes that need to be found.

The hunt for software bugs turns out to be a handy metaphor, too. Every year, hundreds of products are recalled because of defects. Manufacturers knew about some of these defects before the product was released, but in many cases these issues were missed because testing was too methodical, *too normal*. Boris Beizer, a legend in the field of software testing, calls this the Pesticide Paradox: "Every method you use to prevent or find bugs leaves a residue of subtler bugs against which those methods are ineffectual," he says in his book *Software Testing Techniques*. Put another way, traditional inspection methods can lead to the creation of "superbugs"—scary in the world of biological infection, these should be just as scary when it comes to software that controls airplanes, or gadgets that control acceleration in a car, or devices that help pick a president.

The software testing world needed a shock to outwit the Pesticide Paradox and break through a plateau of bugs. The answer was an approach now known as fuzzing, and it can help take on nearly any plateau that comes from acclimation.

———

Fuzzing embraces the odd and unusual. It is a technique that takes a viewpoint that most engineers find difficult to accept: Most systems are too complex to fully understand, and as a result, weird things happen. Engineers are accustomed to rigid processes and live in a world of mathematical tolerances. Fuzzing accepts that the real word is more, well, fuzzy.

Hugh's first experience with fuzzing (although he didn't know it at the time) came from an urgent need for a soda while he was in school in the Bahamas. Back in the 1980s, soda machines were just making their way into local schools in the country's capital, Nassau. The Bahamas is a pretty small market for soda machine vendors, and to compound the problem, there was a unique currency situation. The coin of the realm on the island is the Bahamian dollar, which is artificially pegged one-to-one to the US dollar. Bahamian dollars and US dollars are used interchangeably, so if you go into a store and buy a candy bar, you might get some of your change back in US currency and some in Bahamian currency.

New soda machines had just been installed at Hugh's school, but there were handwritten signs on them that read "US Quarters Only." When he and his thirsty friends came across one of these machines in the school quad, none had a US quarter, so they started to experiment. One put a washer in the slot, hoping a soda would magically pop out. The washer dropped right through. They tried a US dime. Nothing. A Bahamian quarter. Nada. One of them had read something about salt water being helpful in situations like this; it just got the machine wet. For about half an hour, they put anything they could find into this stubborn machine in hopes that it would somehow produce a soda (in their defense, they hadn't even hit puberty yet). The outlook was bleak until they dropped in a Bahamian ten-cent coin.

The Bahamian ten-cent coin looks nothing like a US quarter. It is corrugated around the edges, giving it the appearance of a silver flower. To their amazement, the display instantly registered "25"—the machine mistook the ten-cent coin for a US quarter. They scrambled to find three more ten-cent pieces. The machine read "50," "75," and finally "1.00" (things are expensive in the islands). They hit "Select," and *bam*, a soda dropped down into the tray. It was one of Hugh's proudest preteen moments.

Years later, Hugh learned that the soda machine measured the diameter and weight of coins to figure out if an object dropped into the slot was a US quarter. Bahamian ten-cent pieces coincidently have almost exactly the same diameter and weight as US quarters. Without understanding the mechanics of the machine, Hugh and his friends applied essentially random inputs and hoped for something interesting to happen. This is the essence of fuzzing—applying inputs with some degree of randomness, then looking for unexpected outcomes.

The soda machine was resilient to normal use but failed in the face of an unusual scenario. This is the problem that plagues lots of systems, from the Fukushima nuclear power plant in Japan to the *Titanic*. People who evaluate these systems are typically constrained by rules of logic, while the world is rarely as rigid. To put it another way, systems becomes *numb* to testing.

That's where fuzzers come in. You can think of them as monkeys on amphetamines that just try random things in the hopes that they will break something. They have few rules, few constraints; they just do stuff. A normal sane human being would not yell at a soda machine for an hour and expect it to somehow acquiesce and give up a free soda to mollify you—an amphetamine-laden monkey might just try it. And who knows, maybe there's a sensor on the machine that is looking for a constant cacophony and then, thinking it's in some sort of delivery truck, unlocks itself. Modern systems are so complex, no one is quite sure what unusual stimuli might lead to. Hugh learned this firsthand on a flight from Las Vegas to Orlando.

Each seat in the airplane had a small touch screen built into the headrest of the chair in front, and on this particular airline, passengers could watch a variety of television channels and play a few simple games. One of these games looked remarkably similar to the classic strategy game *Tetris*, where players use their skills to manipulate oddly shaped falling blocks on a screen trying to form horizontal lines. The "options" screen for the game had a box in the center that held the number of blocks you could preview during play—zero and you're flying blind, four and you can really plan for what's coming next. To give himself the biggest advantage possible, Hugh pressed the large "+" button on the screen as many times as he could and got to the maximum value of four.

Near his armrest was a small phone console—the kind where you can call friends and family for a mere twenty-two dollars per minute. He noticed that the phone had a numeric keypad and that it also controlled the game of *Tetris*, including the level of difficulty that he had just tinkered with. He tried to enter the number ten through the phone keypad with no luck: It first changed the value in the box to "1," which then got replaced by "0"—both normal, allowable values. Frustrated, Hugh then made the assumption that there was no hope of trying to wedge a double digit value into this game. His next try was the number eight. No luck there, either; the number didn't change at all.

Hugh then tried the number five: success—the game accepted it!

The number five is an interesting test case: Software testers would call it a boundary value because it is just beyond the maximum allowed value (or boundary) of what the software was designed to accept—which in this case was four. A common programming mistake is to be "off by one" when writing the logic of software. For example, the programmer may have intended to write code that meant: "This value shall be less than five."

But what actually got coded was: "This value shall be *less than or equal to* five."

It's one keystroke difference in most programming languages.

The game was now in uncharted territory; the unanticipated value "5" was now in the box. Hugh then turned his attention back to the touch screen and hit the "+" button, which, to his complete geeky delight, increased the value to "6"! The logic that had stopped him from getting beyond the value four probably said something like: "If the value is equal to four, do not increase it." In this case, the value wasn't four but five, so hitting "+" happily increased it to six. Hugh wolfed back a bag of peanuts and then kept pressing the "+" button until he got to the value "127," where he paused for a moment of reflection.

The number 127 is very special in computer science. In fact, it's a plateau of sorts. Technically it's two to the power of seven minus one ($2^7 - 1$); in some cases, it's the largest value that a particular system can hold. To understand why this is the case, consider the problem of using your fingers to count. Let's assume that you count in the traditional way, such that if you're holding six fingers up, that represents the number six. Using this method, you run into a problem when you try to count beyond ten because you reach the maximum capacity of your fingers. A common way that kids count beyond ten is to remember that they've already gone through the cycle once, and then start again with one finger for eleven. Imagine that you had to send a photograph of your fingers to someone. It might be pretty hard to convey twelve or thirteen because the image would look like two or three. This problem occurs because at ten we've reached the capacity of our fingers, and when we add beyond ten—to a single finger representing eleven, for example—we hit something computer scientists call an "integer overflow"; we've just tried to store more information than we should. In the case of using fingers to count to eleven, once we go beyond the maximum value (ten), we "wrap around" to the smallest value we can hold (in the case of fingers this means one). The same exact problem happens in software, where we use a set of on/off switches (known as binary) to store a number. When the number exceeds the capacity of the switches, the program just resets the number to the smallest allowable value. It's like counting all the way to a hundred but only being able to see the last digit, so it appears that you're going from zero to nine and then suddenly back to zero. When this phenomenon happens in software, it can cause all sorts of problems.

Anyone remember the Y2K bug? When the calendar rolled over from the year 1999 to 2000, you might have been at some crazy party, but some computer scientists were cowering in their basements with stockpiles of food, worrying about what would happen to old computer systems (the kind that run banks and air traffic control systems) when the two-digit year 99 suddenly went to 00. Thankfully the new millennium didn't lead to the apocalypse. The same could not be said of Hugh's in-flight entertainment system.

Why is 127 a special number for some software? Like ten for fingers, it is a *boundary value*. When we add 1 to 127 (1 + 127), normal math tells us that the result should be 128. Sometimes, however, in computer math the result is *-128*, which is the smallest possible value that those on-and-off binary switches can hold—it's the equivalent of holding up one finger to represent eleven but it looking like one.

When Hugh saw 127 on the screen of this in-flight entertainment system, he considered the chance that this could cause an integer overflow for a moment as he kicked back another bag of peanuts.

Then, in the interest of science, he pressed the "+" button one more time. Suddenly, the display flashed -128 just for an instant and then, *poof* . . . screen goes black.

Poof . . . screen of the person next to him goes black.

Screens in front of him and behind him go black.

The entire plane entertainment system goes down.

After a few minutes of mumbling from some of the passengers, a fairly emotionless flight attendant reset the system and all was well. Hugh landed with a newfound respect for *Tetris* (and for the number 127).

How could this problem have been missed by the manufacturer?

It's likely that the game was tested thousands of times and used tens of thousands of times without the problem showing up. Yet there it was. As writers who also have written a fair amount of software, we find it easy to imagine why traditional software testing missed this problem. Testers tend to follow paths that are laid out in large design documents called "specifications." Those documents say things like "Given input A to the system, we expect to get result B." Testers then typically create tests that involve applying input A and then checking for B, and these tests are often codified so that they can be run automatically. Input A, for example, might be "Press the little printer button" and output B may be "Some pieces of paper should come out of the printer containing your document." There also is free-form testing, often called "exploratory testing," where testers are told to think like users and do the things that users are likely to do. Those common paths that testers explore cause them to miss uncommon but potentially damaging problems. In the case of the inflight entertainment system, the user was likely to just tap on the gigantic "+" and "-"—buttons on the screen. It turns out that a pretty horrible bug, one that could take the whole system out, sat along a very strange path.

Today, software fuzzers are used widely in the technology industry and are responsible for finding some of the most dangerous bugs in systems. They find problems that humans just aren't wired to locate. Fuzzing breaks through the numbness plateau of software testing by shocking the system and ignoring the rules. Without this "shake it up" approach, software bugs become immune to the pesticides we spray on them, and superbugs lie in wait to strike at the most inopportune times. Becoming numb to the normal, desensitized to the mundane, is a problem that goes far beyond software. The diversity of fuzzing breaks through this numbness, and its effectiveness isn't limited to software bug hunting. In fact, you can use the technique in the most complex system known to man, the human mind.

Here's an experiment. Read the following list just once:

1. Ostrich
2. Peanut Butter
3. Software
4. Octopus
5. Raincoat
6. Sandwich
7. Lemon
8. Sunset
9. Credit Card
10. Refrigerator

For most people, memorizing a list of ten items is a difficult task after only one review. Even after several reviews or repetitions, most people only remember items at the beginning and end of the list, and even those tend to fade quickly. Our memory, like our senses, tends to ignore the commonplace and look for the unusual, the extraordinary.

Without looking, can you remember what the second item was on the list? What number was "Octopus"?

The mind is not good at saving the conventional.

Hermann Ebbinghaus—who you met in Chapter 1—vastly improved his own learning skills by employing spaced repetition. This is a pretty effective approach for rote memorization, but how can we further take advantage of the fact that our minds, like our senses, tend to be more responsive to the unusual? Perhaps the best sources of information on how to escape the memory plateau are people who are able to do it consistently. To find these people, the World Memory Championships would be a good place to start.

There's a small group of zealots who see memorization as a sport, much like track and field, football, or competitive chess. Athletes get together in events and compete for the title of world's best. Amazing things happen in these games. In 2006, competitor Andi Bell memorized the order of a randomly shuffled deck of fifty-two cards in the fastest time. Most of us would find it difficult to remember the order of a deck of cards; we might review it dozens of times and still only remember the first few cards in the deck. Ebbinghaus's spacing technique is of little value here because speed is critical. To memorize all fifty-two cards, an optimistic average for most people would be several hours through repetition.

Bell did it in thirty-one seconds.

Thirty-one seconds! That's less than a half-second glimpse at each card. When asked how he did it in an interview with the BBC, Bell modestly said, "I think I have the same mental equipment as everybody else, so it's something anybody can do." He may be right.

He uses a memorization technique known as the method of loci, which has its origins in ancient Greece (the word *loci* comes from the Greek word for "location"). The technique relies on using a familiar location, such as your house, and then mentally pegging the words, numbers, or items you want to memorize to locations that you're already familiar with.

The invention of the method is attributed to Simonides of Ceos, a Greek poet who was attending a dinner in honor of a prominent member of the community. At some fortuitous moment during the dinner, Simonides stepped outside—just in time to avoid the roof of the banquet hall collapsing and killing everyone inside. Simonides was asked by Greek authorities to help identify each of the guests who had perished. He was able to visualize the table in his mind, and then, by moving clockwise around it, he was able to remember each guest. His mental journey around the table let him tie people to physical locations along the way. This insight—that we can tie objects to familiar physical locations to remember them more easily—is the foundation of many modern memory techniques.

By taking a physical location that you know well, such as a room in your house, your office, or the street you live on, you can create what Simonides referred to as a *memory palace*: a set of reference points for storing future information. For example, in your bathroom, you're likely to have a toilet, a sink, a showerhead, a floor mat, and a door. Using Simonides's method of loci, you first would mentally "walk through" this room and choose some sort of order, such as moving clockwise or counterclockwise. For example, when Hugh looks around his bathroom clockwise, he sees a toilet, a sink (with a plastic cup of toothbrushes), a showerhead, a floor mat, and then the bathroom door. If he puts numbers to the order, the list would look like this:

1. Toilet

2. Sink

3. Showerhead

4. Floor Mat

5. Door

These things are familiar to him. He doesn't have to memorize them. He sees them every day and can just shut his eyes and visualize the layout of the bathroom. He's created a memory palace.

Now, imagine that you have a list of new things that you need to remember, such as the list we saw earlier. To memorize them, you need to create a mental image of them somehow interacting with items in your memory palace. The trick is to make the relationship between the two items as crazy, outlandish, or unspeakable as possible. Once you've set up a memory palace in your head, the necessary skill shifts from *memory* to *creativity*. Like our senses of smell and taste, memory is predisposed to notice the unexpected and unusual. It's the reason that people vividly retain traumatic memories and why you remember the person wearing the funny hat or glasses at a party. Our body is wired to react to oddity. By taking the items in your memory palace and finding creative and unusual ways of tying them to the things you want to remember, you shock your memory into retention.

Take another look at the first five items on our original list that needed to be memorized:

1. Ostrich

2. Peanut Butter

3. Software

4. Octopus

5. Raincoat

Now take a couple of minutes and try to associate the objects in your memory palace with the items on the list. When you're thinking of these mental pictures, try to be as detailed and wild as possible. For Hugh, using his bathroom as a memory palace, here are the associations he makes:

1. Toilet and Ostrich—There's a very hungover ostrich, his eyes rolling back in his head, and he's leaning over the toilet. He's grabbing the bowl with wings outstretched.

2. Sink and Peanut Butter—There's a big glob of peanut butter clogging the sink; water's building up, and it's starting to overflow and spill onto the tile floor.

3. Showerhead and Software—He turns on the shower, expecting Niagara Falls, but instead tiny 1's and 0's flow out. They don't just drop into the tub with a clatter like a bunch of change would; instead, they float to the ground like mini clouds.

4. Floor Mat and Octopus—There's a small octopus with a towel around its waist stepping onto the floor mat. Each tentacle is dripping water, which is being soaked up by the long fibers of the mat.

5. Door and Raincoat—There's a very heavy raincoat hanging on a small hook on the back of the bathroom door. The coat is bright yellow, and the weight of it is starting to bend the hook. It'll probably break any second.

Each of the associations has something unusual, something striking. As Hugh thought of the ostrich, he also wondered what unusual antics the bird had been up to that night to leave him in that state. For the peanut butter, Hugh knew that it was chunky and not creamy. He imagined that the octopus had a very embarrassed look because somehow he knew that someone was writing a book with him in it. Details help to make the image more vivid and absurd. If you haven't thought of a few of your own, then try it now.

The amazing thing about this technique is that it works, and it works well. With practice you can train your mind to create these absurd associations and images very quickly. The technique is virtually limitless. If you spend time setting up some memory palaces in your head with a hundred unique points to store information, you can read a list of a hundred words just once and then recall them with or near 100 percent accuracy after a very minimal amount of practice. Sound impossible? Try it with ten, then twenty, and you'll be hooked. The heavy lifting is setting up your memory palaces—figuring out the rooms, coffee shops, or parks that you can see vividly in your mind and then numbering the items as you move around your memory place. Once they are set up, memorizing a list is the easy part.

Even though rote memorization plateaus, as Ebbinghaus correctly pointed out, we can break through by shocking our mind into remembering through the unusual. But as you experiment with this technique, be grateful you don't live in the sixteenth century. Back then, the method of loci could get you into some serious hot water. Some religious groups at the time were highly suspicious of the need to think in unusual and provocative ways to make images stick.

"The animation of the images which is the key of memory is impious because it calls up absurd thoughts, insolent, prodigious and the like which stimulate carnal affections," said religious leader William Perkins in those times. Using memory palaces can make you a rebel!

Andi Bell, the man who can remember the order of a shuffled deck of cards in barely more than thirty seconds, is a master of creative association. For him, the process of memorizing a deck starts way before he sees the first card. He first sets up a memory palace—

a familiar building, room, or city (like the bathroom we used to remember the list earlier). Next, he's associated one item with every
card in the deck. For the Queen of Clubs, he might picture a caveman
wielding a spiked club, and for the Three of Diamonds, he may
choose a diamond engagement ring that has three stones. When Bell
sees cards whiz by, he instantly pegs the item associated with the card
to a numbered location in his memory palace. To recall the cards and
the order, he simply takes a journey through his memory place, sees
things like cavewomen and engagement rings, and knows which
order the cards are in. In another event in the World Memory Championships, Bell was able to memorize the order of more than twenty
randomly shuffled decks of card—a thousand cards!—in under ten
minutes. When asked questions like "What is the twenty-third card
in the seventeenth deck?" Bell was flawless. He also memorized a
hundred-digit sequence of 1s and 0s.

Bell's skills come from battling the mind's numbness with creativity. Our minds and our bodies are wired to respond to diversity.
The unusual is the antidote to plateaus caused by going numb. If you
don't believe us, we invite you to grab a bottle of water and do some
stretches as we visit a website that might just convince you. This may
hurt a bit.

It's five A.M. on a Thursday. While most of the world sleeps, a growing
number of fitness junkies wander over to a website. On this particular Thursday, here's what it says:

For time:

Run 400 meters

95 pound Thruster, 21 reps

21 Pull-ups

Run 300 meters

95 pound Thruster, 15 reps

15 Pull-ups

Run 200 meters

95 pound Thruster, 9 reps

9 Pull-ups

Welcome to the world of CrossFit, an exercise regimen that is . . . different. Each day brings a new and diverse set of exercises called the Workout of the Day (or WOD, in CrossFit speak). These routines are designed to push the body to its limit. Every day, thousands of people all over the world gather in fitness studios or gyms, or stay at home and start running, jumping, lifting, pulling, twisting, or whatever else the website demands. Readers are encouraged to post their WOD completion times in the comments section of the site. One Thursday, a man from Korea writes: "7:42 fun!" Another person adds: "AWESOME WO!! 21:52 as rx'ed! 20th day with CF; The workout took me a while, but it was my first time doing a weight WO as rx'ed, so I'm pretty psyched! Woke up @ 5am for this.. Cant wait for tomorrow!!"

Among its most committed followers, CrossFit is a religion, and its churches are the thousands of workout studios around the world known as "affiliates." Inside, you'll find the WOD on a wall or whiteboard. One CrossFit enthusiast we spoke to described it this way: "I can't wait to get up in the morning and see what's waiting. Yesterday, I hung on a bar and had to pull my knees up to my elbows ten times. Every part of me hurt." Another CrossFitter proudly says, "CrossFit doesn't let you cheat any of your muscles—everything gets covered. It's the most intense few minutes you feel like you've ever spent."

CrossFit is to muscles what fuzzing is to software—it forces you out of your comfort zone. "Our specialty is not specializing. Combat, survival, many sports, and life reward this kind of fitness and, on average, punish the specialist," reads its website.

Sometimes the exercise routines are simple but deceptively exhausting. On Tuesday of that same week, the instructions were simply: "Deadlift 1-1-1-1-1-1-1 reps." That means lift maximum weight once, then rest, then repeat six more times. Quick, tough, but efficient.

CrossFit's success is rooted in its diversity. Exercise routines often plateau because muscles become acclimated to the same routine. Strength gains quickly top out when people work the same muscles and repeat the same exercises. To escape strength plateaus, you need diversity—twisting and turning, pushing and pulling, strengthening the little muscles so you can build the big ones.

CrossFit is part of a group of other exercise regimes such as the popular P90X exercise program that *confuse* muscles. But CrossFit also uses diversity in a different way—to fight the mental fatigue that comes from repetitions. There's an element of surprise to CrossFit. You never know what the website will instruct you to do the next day. It is this surprise, this *diversity*, that moves people past the plateau of acclimation. If you don't have diversity, eventually you become numb, and what worked yesterday will be less effective tomorrow. We've seen this in action with your brain, your muscles, and your sense of smell. Now, let's see how acclimation and plateaus affect your taste buds.

Deep within the meatpacking district of Chicago, you'll find elevated trains, lots of old warehouses, and a deceptively highbrow restaurant called Moto. The exterior of the eatery is a study in contrasts: opulent food amid rows of rundown warehouses.

It's a fitting spot for a restaurant that has turned deceiving the mind into a scientific discipline. If you stay for the twenty-course dinner, you'll quickly notice that nothing is what it seems. For starters, your printed menu is actually your first course. Once you place your order, you bite into the end of what Moto owner and chef Homaro Cantu calls "printable food." At Moto, he says, you should expect the unexpected. Even that admonition can't prepare you for what comes next.

On Hugh's first trip to Moto, the evening tasting menu began with Caesar salad—except that there was no lettuce; his salad was in the form of soup. It was a deliciously mind-blowing experience—you can't help but slurp your salad. The adventure continued: a printed picture of cotton candy that tasted just like the real thing. Pancakes fried on a griddle—except the griddle was ice-cold and the sizzle when the batter hit the surface was liquid ice cream freezing instead of frying.

The basement kitchen, where Caesar salad soup and other gastronomical oddities are hatched, looks like a lab you might find at a pharmaceutical company. Canisters of liquid nitrogen and helium, along with centrifuges and lasers, line the walls. The science-experiment-turned-restaurant was born from the scientific curiosity of Chef Cantu.

"We had been creating all of these dishes out of a kitchen that was more like a mechanics shop than a kitchen, and the next logical step for us was to install a state-of-the-art laboratory," he said during a talk at the famous TED conference, held annually in California.

Cantu's laboratory takes foods, flavors, and textures and transforms them in unexpected ways. You might say it is the antidote to palate plateaus, shocking the senses and challenging a lifetime of sensory experience. At a discussion of Cantu and pastry chef Ben Roche's methods at the TEDx conference, Roche put it like this: "When you see a tomato, you're like, 'Oh, I know what that's going to taste like, it's going to taste like a tomato.' But what if it doesn't? What if it tastes like . . . a raspberry?"

Or what if your plate of cheesy nachos tasted like . . . dessert? In the basement of Moto, Ben taught Hugh the alchemy of taste bud disruption. The dish began with candied corn chips. Mint syrup poured over diced kiwi acted as the green salsa on top. Need sour cream for your nachos? Try some lime cheesecake thrown into the blender and dolloped on top. Next up, the cheese, which was actually a frozen glob of mango sorbet shoved into a food processor that spat shreds into a tub of liquid nitrogen, creating a perfect cheese-looking topping. And finally, a sprinkle of chocolate shavings that had the look and texture of ground beef. And there you have it, dessert nachos. "You don't actually know it's a dessert until you begin eating it, until you experience the flavors and you're like, oh my God, what's going on here?" Ben Roche said.

Roche and Cantu's obsession with taste deception runs deep. "It's pretty cool because the dish actually begins to behave like the real thing," Roche told Hugh during an interview. "The cheese begins to melt, so when you're looking at this thing in the dining room, you have the sensation that it's actually a plate of nachos."

This flavor morphing makes for an interesting dining experience, but can the technique be used for more than just a culinary curiosity? What problems could be solved if you could manipulate the way food tastes and shock the palate? Could you help people eat healthier by making them enjoy bad-tasting but good-for-you foods? Could you revitalize the taste buds of someone undergoing chemotherapy? Could you reduce world hunger by making local edible plants more palatable? Solving these problems is harder than conjuring up dessert nachos. You could say it would take a miracle.

In the early eighteenth century on an expedition to West Africa, a French cartographer named Chevalier des Marchais observed a curious practice of one of the native tribes. Before their meals, they chewed a small red berry from one of the indigenous shrubs. The tribesmen would then proceed to eat their meals, some containing extremely bitter foods. This berry was no simple aperitif; it contained a substance now called miraculin, which, for an hour or so after you eat it, transforms the taste of other foods. These "miracle berries," as they're called, reengineer your taste experience, making sour foods taste sweet. Sucking on a lemon goes from mouth-puckering torture to an experience akin to eating the sweetest tangerine. Limes taste like succulent oranges. What was old and sour is now oh so sweet.

This little berry has been responsible for a phenomenon known as "flavor tripping," where people gather at highbrow parties and taste old foods again for the very first time. It's the type of event you might find in the Hamptons or Beverly Hills, with trays of lemons, club soda, and other foods being carried by well-dressed servers, waiting to surprise your taste buds. Guests begin their evening by sucking on the miracle fruit and then eat their way through the night.

The trick to miracle berries is the odd behavior of miraculin. For about an hour after the berry juice coats your tongue, the miraculin protein binds to the sweet receptors there. When something acidic touches those receptors, the miraculin protein changes shape, igniting the sweet receptors, and the effect is that even the most bitter and acidic foods taste sweet.

Miracle berries have a history that reads like a John Grisham novel. Back in the 1970s, entrepreneur Robert Harvey founded a company called Miralin that was poised to disrupt the sugar and sweetener industries. His vision was to combat diabetes and break the country out of rising obesity rates caused by the overconsumption of processed sugar. Using miraculin, Harvey's company created the experience of eating sugar-laden snacks in food that was actually good for you. In one of his early attempts to find out how impactful the miracle berry could be, Harvey conducted a series of experiments where children were given two sets of Popsicles: one made with traditional sugar and the other laced with miraculin and no other sweeteners (and weighing in at just over zero calories). The miraculin Popsicles won out every time.

Miralin's backers bet big on the idea, but they were looking at more than helping diabetics; they sought to attack the sugar and sweetener establishment. Their roster of investors included Reynolds Metals, Barclays, and Prudential, and expectations were sky-high. The company expected miraculin to be approved in the Generally Recognized as Safe (GRAS) category by the FDA—a classification commonly bestowed on foods that occur naturally and have been eaten widely for a long period. This classification would allow miraculin to be included in foods and act as a sugar substitute. In 1974, a day before the company was set to launch its first product with miraculin, devastating news arrived. In a dramatic reversal, the FDA classified miraculin as a food additive, meaning that it would have to undergo years of testing. Miralin folded, and the miraculous little berry was relegated to low production levels and "flavor tripping" in the Hamptons . . . until 2005 when Chef Homaro Cantu was asked to help an elderly woman who was suffering from cancer.

Chemotherapy, in addition to attacking cancerous cells, can have much broader effects on the human body. One common side effect is altering taste buds in the tongue, causing patients to have greatly diminished senses of taste and smell. In some cases, patients have reported a heavy metallic taste to food. After a call from a friend who was trying to help an elderly cancer patient who hadn't eaten in six months and was reduced to feeding tubes, Cantu and Roche worked on the problem of revitalized taste buds numbed by chemotherapy. They ate their way through a series of offensive-tasting foods, looking for an ingredient that would help make them more palatable. Of everything they tried, miracle berries ended up having the greatest effect. "The interesting thing about the miracle berry in chemo patients is that it actually straightens out their taste buds, whereas for you and I, it blocks our bitter and sour receptors," said Cantu in an interview with CNN. He got a voice mail from his friend saying that it had actually worked. The patient had started to eat her way back to a healthier lifestyle.

The concept of using miracle fruit to help cancer patients also intrigued Dr. Mike Cusnir, an oncologist at Mount Sinai Medical Center in Florida. One of Cusnir's patients who worked at a botanical garden brought in some miracle berries, talking about how they had helped make certain foods palatable again. Intrigued, Cusnir began clinical trials to see how the fruit affected patients. In a preliminary trial of a small group of cancer patients, 30 percent showed taste improvement. "In our preliminary analysis, the response to the MF fruit appears encouraging," he writes in his research report. His work is inspiring others to continue the investigation.

Homaro Cantu thinks that miraculin's benefits could go much further: "How can we take this idea of tricking your taste buds and leapfrog it into something we can do today that could be a disruptive food technology?" he asked an audience at TED. Cantu previously had challenged his staff to make dessert nachos, to create a burger from the food a cow eats (to, as he put it, take the actual cow out of the equation), and to make edible paper that tastes like pictures of the food printed on it. Their next challenge: tackling world hunger. Cantu's idea is seductive: Can you use miracle berries to make local vegetation in developing nations—plants such as hay, shrubs, and the like that are edible but unpalatable—taste like something you'd want to eat? The results remain to be seen, but after you've downed a few lemons under the influence of miracle berries (as Bob and Hugh have), you may start to think that he's on to something.

Cantu realized that he could manipulate taste buds and harness the power of diversity to break the plateau-inducing force of acclimation. Fuzzing, the unusual, the shocking, and the unexpected all beat back plateaus that make food bland, make software fail, make memories fade, and make exercise ineffective. So we're going to practice what we preach and pivot abruptly right now. Please try to be patient with us. After all, patience is the only way you can be effectively greedy.

3. THE GREEDY ALGORITHM

The Second Plateau Force

Or, "As part of the hook, the teacher discusses with students how long division helps us develop grit because it takes time, patience, and a refusal to stop."

It's one of the most memorable movie scenes ever, but somehow, most people remember it incorrectly: Gordon Gekko's "Greed is good" speech from the movie *Wall Street*. What Michael Douglas's character said is a gross, morally corrupt slogan, right? Actually it was a bit more nuanced.

> *Greed, for lack of a better word, is good. Greed is right. Greed works. Greed clarifies, cuts through, and captures the essence of the evolutionary spirit. Greed, in all of its forms; greed for life, for money, for love, knowledge, has marked the upward surge of mankind . . .*

The lost nuance is important. Research during the past century has shown that long-term greed *is* good—but short-term greed, the kind that maximizes for the here and now, seems to work for a while but almost always leads to a plateau.

So greed is good. . . . and it's bad. How do we tell the difference?

We'll give Gordon Gekko, and you, the better word he lacked. It depends on your *gratification horizon*.

A short gratification horizon (think of a two-year-old who wants everything right now) leads you to make the right choice for today even though it puts tomorrow in jeopardy. It puts on blinders that block out the future, forcing you to look only at the next step, not the final step. These choices almost always end up boxing you in and put you in a worse position for the future. Long-term greed, on the other hand, the kind that pushes you to suppress your immediate wants and desires and instead looks at the long-term outcome, is one of the most direct pathways to success.

In mathematics, there's a name for this short-term greed, the process of always choosing the option that gives you instant gratification. It's called the "greedy algorithm," and following it almost always leads to a plateau.

To understand how the greedy algorithm works, imagine that you're standing at a street corner in Manhattan. You need to quickly get to a building that is twenty blocks north, and money is no object. Let's imagine we have three travelers: a native New Yorker, a tourist, and someone who lives and dies by the greedy algorithm—we'll call him "the greedy guy." For simplicity, let's say it takes one minute to walk the length of one block.

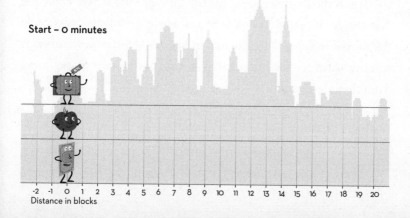

Start – 0 minutes

-2 -1 0 1 2 3 4 5 6 7 8 9 10 11 12 13 14 15 16 17 18 19 20
Distance in blocks

One option to make your way north is to walk two blocks south, get to a subway station, and then wait another three minutes for a north-bound train to arrive. The train travels at about four blocks per minute.

Another option is to spend two minutes hailing a cab that travels at two blocks per minute in traffic.

A third option is to just start walking north.

Our native New Yorker knows that trains are the fastest way to navigate the city; they get past traffic jams, accidents, and cab drivers who try to take you on unsolicited tours. He's willing to make *retrograde progress*, to lose ground now with the expectation of future benefit. The New Yorker decides to walk two blocks in the wrong direction (making him now twenty-two blocks away from his destination), and then waits the requisite additional three minutes for the train.

The tourist on the other hand, sees an ocean of yellow cabs in front of her, spends two minutes struggling to flag one down, and finally jumps into the back seat.

Meanwhile, the greedy guy thinks his fellow travelers are insane. Neither is making immediate progress toward the destination. He sees an opportunity to make instant progress by starting to walk north.

If you took snapshots of our travelers along their journey, you'd see that in the short term, the greedy guy appears to have made the best choice. Two minutes into the journey he's made progress while the tourist is just getting situated in her cab and the New Yorker is waiting patiently for his subway—a full twenty-two blocks away from their destination.

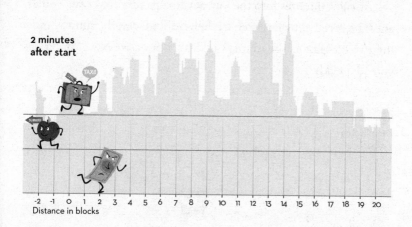

After five minutes, the landscape starts to change. The tourist is now speeding past the greedy guy in a taxicab, both making progress while our New Yorker patiently boards his train.

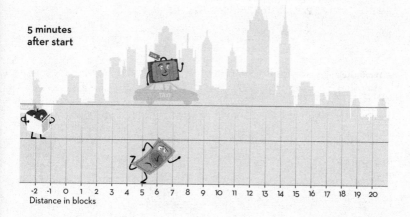

At eight minutes into the journey, the picture looks very different. The greedy guy has been left behind, and with the subway moving twice as fast as the tourist's taxicab, our native New Yorker has gained quickly.

At eleven minutes, the subway-savvy New Yorker has just arrived at his destination, waiting eagerly on his travel companions.

Notice that the New Yorker was able to suppress his short-term greed and focus on long-term greed. Our greedy algorithm guy, however, would not compromise. He saw an opportunity to make progress and took it, no questions asked. While this approach seemed effective early on, greedy guy's effectiveness plateaued—whereas our New Yorker's strategy ultimately triumphed.

We all have a little greedy guy in us. Anyone who has ever had to make a choice between waiting for the bus and walking knows what we mean. We want to save for a home, but then we buy the new iPhone. Or the iPad. Or the new iPad. Speaking of which, is it time to get in line yet for the newest one? Where was I?

Oh, yes. We react to recent events, situations, circumstances without looking at the big picture. When this happens, we often fail; we plateau.

The greedy algorithm hardly ever leads to the best long-term outcome. We are conditioned to think that short-term greed leads to good solutions. Consider the problem of making change. In the United States, there are pennies, nickels, dimes, and quarters in common circulation (for the moment, let's leave out the fifty-cent coin—we haven't see one of those in years!). When the greedy guy makes change, he always picks the largest denomination coin until the total adds up to what he needs. For example, if the greedy guy needs to give you thirty cents, he'll first pick a quarter and then a nickel, making a total of thirty cents. It's the same way you or I tackle the problem when we buy a caramel macchiato at Starbucks for $3.30 (OK, by the time this book comes out, $4.30) and search through our pockets for change. If we follow the greedy approach, we'll probably make the most efficient choice.

But the greedy algorithm is only efficient and helpful in using the fewest coins if all the coin denominations are available. Imagine that your Starbucks barista is impatiently waiting on your thirty cents but you only have pennies, dimes, and quarters—no nickels.

Let's look at what the greedy guy would do. When he chooses his first coin, he always picks the largest denomination that is less than the total: in this case, a quarter. In mathematics, we call this the *locally optimal choice*. That's twenty-five cents, but now he's got five more cents to turn over. Since he doesn't have any nickels, the greedy guy next chooses a penny to add up to twenty-six cents, then another penny to add up to twenty-seven cents, and so on until he reaches thirty cents. That's six coins and one agitated barista.

How would our native New Yorker, the person who's willing to wait for the subway instead of starting to walk ahead and make instant progress, handle this nickel-less change situation? Hand over three dimes, of course. That's half the coins (and half the hassle). The native New Yorker knows that by looking at the big picture he can get to a better solution. In mathematician speak, he looks for the *globally optimal solution*.

In life, we often don't have any nickels. The difference between people who look for the globally optimal solution and people who look for the locally optimal solution is often the difference between success and failure. The greedy guy stretches himself to the limit every month to live in an extravagant house he can't afford, but the native toughs it out in a small apartment to save money for the big house he'll get someday.

It's very rare that the greedy guy ends up ahead in the end. The challenge is that the greedy guy always looks smarter at the beginning. Imagine if you were that Starbucks barista and saw the first coin slapped on the table. The greedy guy is way ahead with twenty-five cents, and the native, by comparison, only has ten cents on the table. Because of the quick wins, the instant progress, it's tough to suppress the urge to be greedy. The greedy guy indulges today, but the native New Yorker is better off tomorrow.

What makes some people suppress their need for the quick win, for instant gratification, to focus on the globally optimal solution? Are some people naturally greedier than others (purely in the algorithmic sense)? How do these two groups fare over the long term? There is some evidence that we are wired for either indulgence or delayed gratification from an early age. It turns out there's a test for this. It takes about fifteen minutes and three marshmallows. Oh, yes, and you have to be four years old.

At first glance, the Bing Nursery School in Palo Alto, California, looks like many others across the United States. There are tables and chairs, crayons and play dough, children and teachers, silly songs and craft projects. But take a closer look and you'll see long mirrors— actually one-way glass—lining the classrooms where the youngest kids play. On the other side you'll often find psychologists—lots and lots of them. Bing sits on the campus of Stanford University.

The first thing you'll notice as you walk inside Bing's main court-yard is a bulletin board with a sign that reads "Bing Nursery School, Child Development Research, Current Research Studies." Below it is a long list of research projects, each entry detailing a current study being conducted with the children at Bing.

Standing inside Bing's courtyard you are surrounded by a series of doors. Some of those doors lead to expansive playrooms with slid-ing outer walls that, when open, allow kids to wander outside and inside freely. The whole school feels very open, unencumbered. Dur-ing a visit there in summer 2012, Hugh watched a group of children play as he toured Bing with Jennifer Winters, Bing's director. "Does she love [Bing]?" asked Winters as a mom walked out with her four-year-old daughter. "Loves it . . . unbelievable!" the mom replied.

Winters walked Hugh through the courtyard, through one of those doors, and into a space called a "game room." This room was tiny, painted all white except for the one-way glass. Inside there was a table and two tiny chairs, and in the corner, a video camera was mounted on a tripod. The space on the other side of the glass, where researchers sit, was small and cramped, with filing cabinets on the floor and stools set up to observe the game room. But this tiny space has had an outsized influence on learning around the world. Some of the most influential research on behavior has come from psychologists sitting on the other side of that one-way glass. In 1968, that's where you would have found Dr. Walter Mischel, most likely snacking on a marshmallow, unlocking the secrets of greed. Mischel, now a professor at Columbia, is perhaps the world's leading expert on delayed gratification—one's ability to resist indulging in something now in favor of something better later. Back in 1968, Mischel found himself on the other side of one of those long glass walls at Bing, using a radical but deliciously simple technique to understand impulse control in four-year-olds.

We begin life as slaves to impulse; our actions are a direct result of how we feel. To put it another way, babies are naturally very greedy (no offense to any precocious babies reading this book). They cry when they're hungry; they squirm when they need to be burped; they fuss when then need to be changed. There's no negotiating with a one-year-old. You can't say, "Hey, I know you're uncomfortable, but could you hold out another half an hour while Mom takes a nap?" Babies want what they want, and they want it now. As we grow, we learn to suppress our immediate desires. If we didn't, we'd never do something unpleasant or boring; we'd constantly switch to the more pleasurable task. In life, we learn, sometimes you just have to wait. Mischel wanted to understand the ability to delay, to hold back our natural desires and work toward some grander goal.

The experiment was simple. Mischel would put a marshmallow (or an Oreo or pretzel stick if the child preferred) on a desk in front of a four-year-old with these instructions: You can either ring this bell and eat the marshmallow now—or, if you can wait till I get back, I'll give you two. Then he receded into the next room and watched the children as they tried to hold out. Some sang a song. Others hid under the desk. A few tried to cover their eyes. Some stared directly at the marshmallow, willing the time to pass. Some succumbed to temptation quickly and ate it before Mischel returned about fifteen minutes later. The experiment showed huge variability: Some of the kids ate the marshmallow almost as soon as they saw it, but others were able to wait. About 30 percent were able to hold out and got their just desserts.

Mischel found the kids who were able to hold out particularly interesting. Why were they able to wait? It wasn't that some really liked marshmallows and some didn't: Before the experiment began, Mischel and his colleagues pretested their subjects and knew they had picked the right treat. The desire was there; some kids were just better able to manage their desires. Mischel's now famous "Stanford Marshmallow Experiment" and similar studies on delayed gratification have found that people who have a larger gratification horizon— the so-called high delayers—still have the same impulses as others; they have just developed better techniques to distract themselves and avoid temptation. On balance, kids with a short gratification horizon, the "low delayers," tend to focus on the marshmallow. They stare into its fluffy goodness and eventually succumb.

To better understand the differences between high delayers and low delayers, Mischel tried a few variations on the experiment. In one of them, both the single and double marshmallows were in clear view. Mischel and his colleagues thought that if the child could see the two marshmallows, a real tangible outcome, they'd be more apt to hold out.

The results were disastrous.

Even though they could focus on their end goal, the fact that all that puffy goodness was in clear view made it too hard to resist eating one of the marshmallows now instead of holding out for two later. Mischel then tried another experiment. This time, he showed kids a life-sized picture of the marshmallows instead of the marshmallows themselves. He would keep the pictures in view while they sat in the room, trying to resist ringing the bell. They were able to delay longer—actually much longer. The average delay went from six minutes to eighteen minutes. There was a big difference between seeing a picture of a marshmallow and seeing the marshmallow itself.

When the kids talked about the picture of the marshmallow, they did it dismissively. Some kids would say, "It's just a picture." There was a clear distinction in their heads between the flat image and something sugary, fluffy, and three-dimensional. The physical marshmallow evoked an emotional response; it prompted what psychologists call "hot ideation." The real marshmallow was visceral, attainable, ready to be devoured. The picture of the marshmallow, on the other hand, prompted a more cerebral response, so-called cold ideation. It's the difference between thinking about how delicious that pastrami sandwich will be when you sink your teeth into it and imagining what region of the world the meat came from.

In another experiment, Mischel again put the marshmallows back in the room, but this time he asked the children to think of it as if it were a picture. "Imagine a big frame around it," he instructed the children. The results were startling. The average delay time jumped from six minutes, when kids were given no instructions, to eighteen minutes, when they were told to think of it as a picture. Eighteen minutes! That's the same self-discipline threshold as when only the pictures were shown. This result tells us it's not our desires that need to be put in check—instead, it's the way we represent them mentally.

When children were directed to focus on the "cool" properties of their reward—thinking of their marshmallows as a picture or as a puffy white cloud—they were able to resist. If they were asked to focus on the cool qualities of something else that they wanted but that was unavailable—like thinking of pretzels as logs when they were trying to hold out for more marshmallows—they were not able to distract themselves effectively. Their ability to resist plateaued. On average, they rang the bell within five minutes.

Here's the takeaway: It is valuable to "cool" the things you're trying to resist, to abstract them, to think about them cerebrally instead of emotionally. The greedy guy looks at cheesecake and thinks how that first bite will melt in his mouth. The person with willpower to resist might think about the cheesecake as a list of ingredients, or the abstraction could be as simple as Mischel's, thinking of it as a picture of a cheesecake—something unattainable.

Mischel also found that if children were instructed to think of the "hot" properties of their treat—like the sweet, chewy taste of a marshmallow—temptation became extremely difficult. In one variation, he showed kids a picture of a marshmallow but asked them to think about how delicious and chewy it would be to eat it, which led to very short delays. This type of hot ideation, fantasizing about the properties that invoke emotional thoughts, is what leads us into temptation, derails our long-term goals, and causes personal plateaus.

It's natural to think about objects of desire in a "hot" and emotional way. We think about the creamy goodness of a cheesecake when we see it listed on a restaurant menu. The art of detoothing these objects, of defocusing the delicious marshmallow sitting in front of you and getting through the next fifteen minutes, is a critical life skill.

Succumbing to impulse is akin to picking the locally optimal solution. It's greedy. It's hedonism in its most basic form. It can be hard to resist picking the option that is going to give you the greatest benefit right now instead of the option that gives you the greatest long-term reward. The ability to look beyond that instant progress, to wait two minutes for a subway, to ignore the quarter when you're trying to put together thirty cents, to make *retrograde progress*, is a distinct skill. You need to be able to ignore shiny new objects and focus on a task to ever complete anything of substance.

That skill has never been more in need. In a world where the Internet offers an unlimited supply of shiny new objects, where one can indulge any new thought or desire in unchecked depth, the ability to stay on task is critical. We must often suppress our immediate greed to achieve longer-term goals.

Part of the problem is how we discount the value of future rewards. Extensive research has been done on the phenomenon of *discounting* over the past half century. Psychologists now believe that discounting follows a hyperbolic curve. That means we discount rewards in the near future heavily but our rate of discounting falls in the distant future. For example, when given the choice of five dollars today or six tomorrow, most people would take the five dollars, heavily discounting the value of the extra dollar relative to time. But if you asked them whether they'd rather take five dollars a year from now or six a year and a day from now, most people would choose the six dollars a year and a day from now. Both the five-dollar and six-dollar amounts are so heavily discounted a year into the future that they are roughly equivalent, so why not wait the extra day? This leads to a strange contradiction. A year from now you would likely make a different choice—you'd probably choose to take the five dollars and not wait another day.

It turns out that discounting has a biological basis. Several experiments during the past twenty years have shown increased activity in specific areas of the brain that evaluate immediate versus delayed rewards, which leads to the possibility that a person is predisposed to a certain pattern of discounting.

This weighing of immediate rewards versus delayed rewards varies substantially from person to person. Walter Mischel saw huge variance in his marshmallow experiments. While there are clearly differences in how people respond to the choice of waiting for a big reward or instead going for the immediate reward, does it matter in the long term? Are high delayers, people who have a longer gratification horizon, ultimately better off?

Back in 1968, when Mischel's subjects ate their first marshmallows, he had three young children of his own. They grew up with some of the other kids who were also at Bing and went through the marshmallow experiment. As he watched them grow, he became curious about the long-term life implications for low and high delayers, which prompted a tantalizing question: Did the ability to hold out on eating a marshmallow correlate to success later in life? In a now famous article from 1989 Mischel wrote: "Because intentions to practice self-control frequently dissolve in the face of immediate temptations, it is also necessary to go beyond the study of initial decisions to delay gratification and to examine how young children become able to sustain delay of gratification as they actually try to wait for the outcomes they want."

Mischel conducted a longitudinal study of participants in the marshmallow experiment, following them for nearly forty years. The results were shocking: Those four-year-olds who delayed gratification, who were able to suppress their impulse to follow the greedy algorithm, turned into adults who were more successful, better on aptitude tests, and better able to cope with stressful situations. In one study, Mischel and his colleagues found that each additional ten seconds of delay back in 1968 was worth one extra point on the SAT twelve years after the marshmallow experiment! Hold out an extra five minutes? That's an extra thirty points on the make-or-break college entrance exam. High delayers exhibited other differences, too. Friends and their parents used words like "well adjusted," "good student," and "conscientious" to describe them.

What about the low delayers, the ones who went for the marshmallow immediately? They plateaued. They consistently underperformed compared to their impulse-controlling brethren.

Mischel's work indicates that a large gratification horizon might be the single biggest indicator of long-term success, an even better predictor than IQ. MRI tests conducted in 2011 show that there were actual biological differences in people who performed at the extreme ends of Mischel's test forty years earlier. Mischel's work, and the now more than four decades of research that followed, shows that there is a dimension of humanity that is highly correlated with long-term success that has largely been ignored.

There were still several open questions: How could one test for this ability later in life? And more important, can people be taught strategies—much like Mischel's instruction to think of a marshmallow as a picture of a marshmallow—to break through the plateaus that come from following the greedy algorithm? Dr. Angela Duckworth may have the answer. If you don't find her in her office at the University of Pennsylvania, she's probably just north of New York, trying to unlock the mysteries of perseverance at one of the grittiest places on earth.

It's affectionately called Beast Barracks, some say because it's the scariest thing they've ever encountered. It has to be scary and brutal; after all, the men and women who make it through will go on to lead soldiers in some of the most stressful situations on earth. These first six weeks of cadet basic training at the West Point military academy in New York are designed to help build soldiers, but also to push cadets to their limits. Its purpose is to see who has the toughness to stick it out for the next four years and the eight years they'd be required to serve in the military after that.

Not many people even make it to Beast Barracks—the average acceptance rate at West Point is around 13 percent. If you think it's just the academics that are tough, you'll quickly be corrected. The days at Beast Barracks begin at 5 A.M. and continue through an intense program of physical, combat, and leadership training till 10 P.M. No cell phones are allowed, no outside food, either. It's a tough transition for incoming freshmen, and all you have is your personal grit and determination to get you through.

The military does extensive testing of candidates to try to figure out who will make it through Beast Barracks for those highly coveted freshman class spots. You have to make daily sacrifices, choose to persevere despite setbacks, and suppress your short-term wants (and pain) for the long-term goals. At some point during this first summer, about 6 percent drop out, likely lying flat on the grass during a push-up drill. It's difficult to know who they'll be. Will it be the son of a military officer who enrolled for all the wrong reasons? Will it be a woman from the Midwest who took a year off after high school to figure out what she really wanted to do with her life? Nobody knows, with the possible exception of Angela Duckworth. Duckworth is an assistant professor of psychology at the University of Pennsylvania, and an expert on the quality of stick-to-itiveness, the ability to persevere, to suppress short-term wants for long-term goals. She calls this quality *grit*. And she can measure it.

By any standard, Angela Duckworth epitomizes success. She graduated with a degree from Harvard, finished a master's degree at Oxford in neuroscience, and got her Ph.D. in psychology from the University of Pennsylvania, where she's now an assistant professor. She founded one company, has been a chief operating officer, and worked as a management consultant. She has a confidence about her, a presence, and speaks with the polish of a businesswoman who can close a multimillion-dollar deal in the boardroom and the patience of a teacher showing a child how to solve a math problem in the classroom.

You might say she's a two-marshmallow kind of person.

But somewhere in between graduating from Harvard in 1992 and starting her Ph.D. in psychology a decade later, she hit a plateau in her efforts to help people. As a senior in Harvard, she founded Summerbridge Cambridge, a year-round, tuition-free academic program in Massachusetts that serves middle and high school students. She left two years later to study neuroscience at Oxford. She then worked as a management consultant at McKinsey for a few months and was the COO of a nonprofit for a while. She followed her interests wherever they took her. In one case they led her to Lowell, Massachusetts, where she taught high school for two years.

"I didn't feel like I had that abiding commitment that would take me through the future," Duckworth told us in an interview. It was perhaps this unfocused pursuit that prompted her to ask: Can you measure stick-to-itiveness, good old-fashioned grit? And would grittier people, akin to Mischel's high delayers, do better in life?

After several years of correlating gritty qualities with the ability to persevere, she's developed a test for grit that has just twelve questions. Here is an example of a question she asks:

I often set a goal but later choose to pursue a different one.

Very much like me

Mostly like me

Somewhat like me

Not much like me

Not like me at all

Here's another:

I have achieved a goal that took years of work.

Very much like me
Mostly like me
Somewhat like me
Not much like me
Not like me at all

Using questions such as these, she calculates a "grit score." This score, combined with other attributes of a person, such as IQ, is strongly correlated to achievement. Grit is particularly important in areas where one is tempted to trade some long-term but difficult goal—like graduating from West Point military academy—for an easier alternative—like going to a liberal arts school that doesn't make you do pull-ups. By expanding your gratification horizon, you can push through times where the incremental benefit is small.

"If you're myopic and only look at the next moment in time and you base your decisions on 'what am I going to get out of this in the next nanosecond' versus 'what do I have to put into this in the next nanosecond,' then when you hit a plateau, your natural conclusion is to quit and move to the next thing," Duckworth told us. "If you're able to think about things in much bigger chunks, you can make good long-term choices and investments of your effort and time."

In July 2004, about twelve hundred cadets entering their six-week stint in Beast Barracks took Duckworth's grittiness test alongside an extensive battery of personality, aptitude, and other tests. Candidates were also assessed using something called the Whole Candidate Score—a measure created by the military that factors in school rank, SAT score, Leadership Potential Score (which reflects participation in extracurricular activities), and physical aptitude. About 5.8 percent of the candidates dropped out during the summer. The grittiest ones—cadets who scored more than one standard deviation higher on the grit scale—stayed in. In fact, grittier candidates were 60 percent more likely to make it through the summer. In contrast, the Whole Candidate Score—the method the military uses to predict performance—did not predict retention with any statistical significance.

Looking at a monumental task in its entirety can be daunting. Duckworth believes that gritty people naturally break down a large task into a series of milestones and that allows them to push through.

"My research team breaks down a task into little steps so that we can get that little dopamine hit of checking off a box. 'Write the first section of the methodology section.' Check. 'Organize files.' Check," Duckworth told us. Perhaps it is the ability to graft incremental progress onto a task where incremental progress is difficult to measure that is the true skill of gritty people. If you see yourself as taking little steps forward, the perceived benefit stays high, even though the end goal may still be far off in the future. "It's really a strategy to keep the perceived benefits high without saying, 'Well, the only box to check off here is to complete the entire manuscript.' There probably is a little bit of gamesmanship that goes on within yourself."

Duckworth has since repeatedly applied her grit test in lots of different situations. In one case, Duckworth tested about two-thirds of the participants in the Scripps National Spelling Bee, where students from seven to fifteen years old competed to be the nation's best speller. Again, the grittiest prevailed. Students with a gritty score were 41 percent more likely to advance to the next round.

Grit, it turns out, is a key component of success, but is it a fixed quality? Are our brains hardwired for grit at birth? Can one learn to push through and get the second marshmallow? Could the strategies and mental skills exhibited by high delayers and gritty soldiers be taught? Could they somehow be made available to children (and adults) and perhaps reshape their destiny? In 1996, in a book chapter titled "From Good Intentions to Willpower," Mischel openly wondered if there was a direct connection between marshmallow-eating delays, SAT scores, and life success, and if the techniques of delay could be taught to children.

"Such strategies within their own control may make their efforts less aversive, enhance their self-esteem, and allow them a freer hand in building their own futures. But this is a personal hope, not a finding," he wrote.

A decade later, in a school in the south Bronx, that hope turned into reality.

The KIPP schools in New York City serve one of the most economically disadvantaged groups of students in the five boroughs. While most schools focus on GPA, KIPP takes a slightly different approach. At KIPP, administrators believe character, not grades, defines students and determines their achievement later in life. KIPP even has its own scale to measure it, the CPA—Character Point Average. KIPP looks at twenty-four indicators of character measured across seven domains: zest, self-control, hope/optimism, curiosity, gratitude, social intelligence, and, yes, grit. You might find Angela Duckworth or some of her psychology students roaming the halls at KIPP. You may also run into a child wearing a "Don't eat the marshmallow" shirt.

At KIPP, teachers are exploring techniques to makes students grittier. They weave lessons on morality into courses on math and English. The core philosophy is that character counts—maybe more than anything else. KIPP aims to create *dual-purpose experiences*: learning experiences in which the teacher offers both an instructional objective and a connection to character strengths. Here is an example of how KIPP integrates lessons on grit into a concept in mathematics:

Aim: To evaluate two different algorithms for long division and determine which works best for you.

Character Connection: As part of the hook, the teacher discusses with students how long division helps us develop grit because it takes time, patience, and a refusal to stop.

The idea is that if we can teach perseverance, most other things will fall into place. There's a specific type of perseverance, though, that has proven most effective. Psychologist K. Anders Ericsson calls this "deliberate practice." Ericsson believes that in any area of human endeavor we need ten years of focused attention to achieve true proficiency, after which we plateau. What's interesting is the gap between proficient and extraordinary. The way to escape this plateau is deliberate practice. The idea of deliberate practice is that you problematize whatever you're doing. A world-class violin player is going to be proficient at playing the violin, but just playing new pieces is not likely to make her any better. The violinist has reached a plateau—a place where she is good enough to continue to achieve success but where simply continuing to practice is unlikely to improve her skill level. In their book *Human Performance*, psychologists Paul Fitts and Michael Posner call this stage of skill mastery the autonomous phase. The only thing that is going to get someone who is proficient off their plateau is to isolate some small component that needs improvement and concentrate there. This deliberate practice approach relies on "augmented feedback" from expert coaches. It's how a good golfer turns great—a hundred more rounds of golf likely won't improve his skill level, but sessions with a pro that focus on a nit in his swing will. It's how a skilled pianist turns into a master. Or, if you recall Jason Riley's strategies with Derek Jeter and other athletes, it's how unconscious incompetence turns into unconscious competence—or how an old dog becomes one of the best shortstops in baseball.

The idea of deliberate practice is how you overcome the equilibrium of "good enough" skill that naturally ensues. Deliberate practice is uncomfortable; it has to be to have any material effect. If you want to improve your typing, for example, you're likely very comfortable with keys in the middle of the keyboard and what you really need to do is home in on the action of your pinky fingers, reaching for the numbers, and other feats that require you to move out of your comfort zone.

If you browse through papers on human performance, you'll see words such as *derivative* and *thresholds*, which make them look like scholarly articles you might see in fields such as physics or mathematics. It begs the question: Is there some universal law that ties these plateaus together?

Johannes Eichstaedt, a researcher at the University of Pennsylvania (and a collaborator of Angela Duckworth), believes that what we know of achievement, plateaus, and breakthroughs is actually governed by laws of mathematics, much like the greedy algorithm.

"Our current thinking is actually quite mathematical," Eichstaedt said. He believes that human achievement is the function of a set of variables that psychologists can then get their heads around. Such a model might help explain the results of researchers like Mischel, Ericsson, and Duckworth on how we reach accomplishments.

"We think about achievement, skill, and talent sort of like distance traveled, velocity, and acceleration," he says. In his model, achievement can be thought of as the sum of all your accomplishments. This is a value that never decreases and is constantly building over time. Skill is velocity, the rate at which achievement is attained.

Someone who is a highly skilled golfer, for example, will accumulate achievement (such as tournament wins) at a much faster rate than an amateur. The golf pro is traveling down the freeway of achievement at ninety miles an hour in a Maserati while the amateur pedals along on a bicycle. Eichstaedt sees talent as acceleration, the rate at which skill increases. Think of it as achievement potential. To continue on the car metaphor, a Maserati has a much higher capacity for speed than a bicycle—even if Lance Armstrong is pedaling it.

In Eichstaedt's model, when you multiply talent by units of time using focused effort to develop that talent, you get an increase in skill.

"That's where people are a little different in terms of their talent, and then it's a function of time on task that actualizes talent into skill," he says. That's where grit comes in. Gritty people put in the effort to move from talent to skill and then from skill to achievement. This model may also help explain why people with high IQs (akin to talent in Eichstaedt's model) can become skilled with little effort but also how people with average IQs, through the hard work of focused effort, can get to the same skill level. The model underscores why it is so important to teach grittiness to children (and adults). According to Eichstaedt, Ericsson, Duckworth, and others, this combination of potential and tenacious pursuit of one's goal is the hallmark of consistently high achievers. What is interesting about this model is that it has a heavy dependence on "time on task"—meaning that if a person is able to marshal all their skills of concentration and focus, they can control the most dominant factor in their own success: time spent working on a task.

"The kicker is that if you look at the data from Angela's [Duckworth] research on grit, we explain more of the variance in achievement with grit—time on task—than we can with IQ," Eichstaedt says. That means that grit gives you a better handle on peoples' personal achievement—like their GPAs—than knowing their intelligence. A plateau then can come from a few different places: We can either stop putting in the effort—the time on task—to turn skill into accomplishment, or we can exhaust our talent. "At some point we run out of that potential to be actualized into skill through focused effort and we plateau."

It's at this point that people settle into an equilibrium that is comfortable.

Most people are happy to be a mediocre-plus keyboard player or typist. According to Eichstaedt, at some point many people prefer to focus on turning the skill that they've acquired into accomplishment instead of focusing on turning their talent into additional skill. For the occasional pianist, that might mean learning to play a few intricate pieces.

"Further skill development beyond the exhaustion of their talent potential tends to be not as rewarding," Eichstaedt says.

In the beginning, when you pick something new up, it's actually quite rewarding because you can see your talent potential being actualized into skill. You pick up the elementary aspects pretty quickly and fluently. Then the rate of skill acquisition diminishes. The results follow the plateau curves you saw in the introduction of this book. To get past that plateau you need to problematize your practice, focusing on the difficult to attain skills, like stretching your pinky finger over to hit the plus sign on a keyboard instead of typing the letters A S D F over and over again. Zeroing in on those problematic elements, according to Eichstaedt, requires "giving yourself the benefit of the doubt in a situation with incomplete information."

"You aren't getting direct feedback that you're becoming a better typist when you start doing stretch drills with your pinky, but you believe that this effort will benefit you in the future," he says.

Psychologists call this positive future-mindedness. Others might call it faith. It's the belief that you can attain some future outcome without direct evidence.

Several studies in domains of expert skill—such as chess, mastery of a musical instrument, and sports—have shown that only after extended practice does one reach mastery. It takes a lot of faith and grit to dedicate ten years of one's attention to a pursuit. It is perhaps this faith that allows a child at Bing to hold out for fifteen minutes for the second marshmallow. Or perhaps it is what allows the native New Yorker to walk several blocks in the opposite direction to catch the subway. Maybe it's why a cadet at West Point does one more push-up, or a pro golfer watches slow-motion footage of his swing.

"I think the biggest barriers to doing great things are not cataclysmic events that require heroic action. It's more important to focus on incremental effort and results than the heroic acts that typically get the lion's share of the attention," Duckworth told us.

In 2012 the KIPP foundation opened its 109th school in the United States. More than thirty-two thousand students have passed through their doors. "Grit is basically a combination of persistence and resilience," explains Dave Levin, cofounder of KIPP, in a video on KIPP's website. Levin believes that grit—along with other character qualities such as self-control, zest, and gratitude—helps shape a child's future. He puts it this way: "If these strengths are highly predictive of life outcomes, why not make our schools focus on them?" KIPP is very open about students' scores and report cards, which trend well above the national average. If Mischel, Duckworth, Eichstaedt, and a slew of other achievement psychologists are right, it's the measures that don't mean much to the rest of the world, their learned grit and Character Point Average, that will turn them into the next Johann Sebastian Bachs, Derek Jeters, and Garry Kasparovs. But if they're going to get there, they'll need more than time on task. They'll need to have an incredible sense of timing, too.

4. BAD TIMING

The Third Plateau Force

Or, "You can forget about forgetting."

You are about to be a part of an experiment that requires the utmost precision.

To fully engage, do not pause while reading this chapter. If you need to get a sandwich, go to the bathroom, or make a call, please do it now.

Back? Great.

Sorry to be so strict, but Piotr Wozniak would absolutely insist on it.

Please review the following symbols—say them aloud to yourself once—and then move on.

EBH ➔ DRE ➔ SQT

You'll see them a few more times in this chapter, and we'll need you to do another review soon. Wait . . . not yet . . . another moment. . . . OK, now:

EBH ➡ DRE ➡ SQT

We'll come back to them in twenty-five seconds (about two hundred words from now), but first it's time to introduce Wozniak, a man who knows how to stick to a schedule.

Wozniak holds a Ph.D. in cognitive psychology, but his real passion is pushing the limits of the human mind. Inspired by the introspective memory research of Hermann Ebbinghaus (you do remember him, don't you?), Wozniak has lived the past twenty years of his life as an experiment in optimization. Everything he reads, every conversation he has, every moment he spends exercising, in fact every facet of his life is conducted like a symphony, each activity summoned at precisely the right moment to harmonize into a masterpiece.

Wozniak was particularly intrigued by the *spacing effect*, the phenomenon Ebbinghaus defined that showed that waiting between reviews of information drastically improves memory retention. Wozniak wanted to see if he could live his entire life following this principle. To do so, he takes every piece of data about himself he can find and feeds it into an algorithm for optimal understanding or performance.

Wozniak knows that the human mind can absorb an incredible amount of information, but timing matters. Once again, consider these symbols (that's right, time for another review—don't just gloss over them, read each symbol, perhaps aloud).

EBH ➡ DRE ➡ SQT

They are similar to the character strings Ebbinghaus used to measure his own memory 130 years ago. They are random—they don't follow a recognizable pattern—yet we can be trained to remember them if we only correctly time, and space, our reviews. The amount of time to wait has been determined with some certainty since Ebbinghaus's first experiments, and while cognitive psychologists know this principle of *spaced repetition* well, it is one of the most underutilized insights into how our own mind works, and into the learning process. Spaced repetition is the antidote to learning plateaus. Know that tired old elementary education debate about rote memorization, good or bad? Both sides are wrong. The best way to learn, it turns out, isn't brute-force memorizing, but it isn't abandoning old-fashioned rote techniques, either—it's *occasional memorization*, following this spaced repetition pattern. We'll remind you of that in a little while.

Wozniak hadn't heard of spacing effect in 1982, when he was a young student of molecular biology at Adam Mickiewicz University of Poznan in his native Poland. Like all molecular biology students— heck, like all students—he realized that he wasted immense amounts of time memorizing a small encyclopedia of facts to pass tests, only to forget 90 percent of what he'd learned within a few weeks. Unlike most students, Wozniak wasn't satisfied with good grades. He wanted to learn, and he wanted to remember everything.

"I was collecting all knowledge in piles of notebooks. Quickly I realized that it all cannot be kept in memory with traditional methods. There was more and more material to learn. Rehearsing this all verged on impossibility. I needed more tricks and intuition to cope with it," he told an interviewer in 1997.

Adding to his frustration was his insatiable desire to learn English. From the little English he spoke back in the early 1980s, and the little Western media he could get his hands on, he had come to understand that the Soviet-controlled Polish government was lying to him. He desperately wanted to know the truth about the world, which, to him, meant being able to read and understand English. These dual motivations combined with his intuitive understanding of his own mind and his amazing observation skills to lead Wozniak down the same path Ebbinghaus had found more than a hundred years earlier.

We must stop now for a moment and continue our experiment. The average English-speaking adult reads 200 to 250 words per minute. That means that by the end of this sentence it'll be about four hundred words since you last reviewed those odd three-letter symbols, so it's been about two minutes. OK, again:

EBH ➔ DRE ➔ SQT

Now, back to Wozniak.

Like Ebbinghaus, Wozniak realized that the key was not simply repeating information over and over; it was repeating the information at precisely the right time. Wozniak's insight proved far more powerful, however, because his timing was much better. Ebbinghaus's plan for memorizing random symbols was a mere curiosity. But the advent of the computer age made Wozniak's discovery practical for nearly every person on Earth. The system he developed for countering memory plateaus offers this bold promise: "You can forget about forgetting."

Modern computers provide a rough approximation for how the human brain works. PCs have both short- and long-term storage— Random-Access Memory (RAM) and a hard drive. Facts in RAM can be recalled and observed quickly. Facts on hard drives must be loaded, which can take a long time. For both humans and computers, having facts at "top of mind" is far more useful. There's no way to compare and analyze alternatives, such as potential colleges or job offers or airplane departure times, without being able to hold the relevant facts in mind all at once. What good is knowing your boss's wife's name if you can't recall it at that moment you bump into her in a Starbucks? Having it pop back into your brain five minutes later, or with the aid of Facebook, does you no good. You, like your computer, work better with items in RAM.

Of course, hard drives will always be bigger than RAM, and our brains must constantly discriminate between top-of-mind facts and long-term, might-need-to-know-this-someday facts. Sadly, evolution has given us brains with a built-in system that no longer suits our needs. Our brains are built to keep only certain things in our version of RAM: that fire might burn you, for example, and that a trauma you experienced when you were young is to be avoided at all costs for the rest of your life. Anything that doesn't pose a clear and present mortal danger is tagged for the hard drive. The periodic table of elements doesn't seem so pressing compared to menacing, hungry bears, so after it seems like it's passed its useful time in your brain's RAM (a microbiology test, perhaps), it's given a place in the dusty basements of your brain. It's "forgotten."

Everyone forgets things at different paces, on different schedules. Different kinds of facts follow different timing. But all forgetting occurs the same way, following the same pattern, along intervals that if plotted on a chart would look just like the back end of a bell curve—the familiar plateau. As an example, three days after a test, you might have a 50 percent chance of remembering something. After seven days, a 20 percent chance. After two weeks, a 5 percent chance, and so on.

For centuries, the "fix" for this problem was simply more beatings—beatings on the knuckles, beatings on the brain. Try harder, the teacher would say. Use those flash cards over and over. And yet, no one reading this passage today will have trouble recalling the pain surrounding an attempt to memorize something as a student . . . while at the same time being unable to recall the very thing that was studied. In other words, the only fact that was beaten into your brain was the way the beatings felt. (Go ahead, try to recite that Shakespeare sonnet.)

The solution isn't repeating more often, Wozniak found. Successive repetitions quickly plateau, and quickly do no good at all. The trick is, ironically, repeating a lot less often. In fact, the magic formula lies in one simple but profound observation: You must repeat the fact to yourself at that very moment when it is about to be forgotten, right as the librarian in your head is about to hop on the elevator to the basement of your brain and deposit the knowledge there. You stop her, tell her to bring the book back to the front desk, and your recall is preserved, this time for a bit longer. Then, right as your recall chances fall to 10 percent or so again, execute another reminder. Just as the fact is about to sink into the sea of your mind, nudge it up above the waterline, and it will float for a little bit longer. Do this enough times, and you will "never forget," Wozniak claims. The fact will become forever buoyant for you.

This is great news for overwhelmed students of everything. It's not the time you put into studying; it's the timing.

A helpful reminder above a piano teacher's classroom says, "Music is the silence between the notes." Wozniak's insight might be phrased in this similar way: "Learning happens in between the times you are trying to learn."

Look at the chart on the next page, which shows the progressive impacts on well-timed remembrances and the normal forgetfulness response curve.

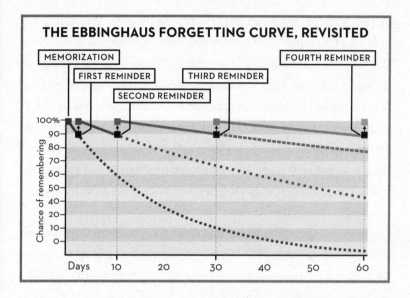

THE EBBINGHAUS FORGETTING CURVE, REVISITED

MEMORIZATION

FIRST REMINDER

SECOND REMINDER

THIRD REMINDER

FOURTH REMINDER

Chance of remembering

100%
90
80
70
60
50
40
30
20
10
0

Days   10   20   30   40   50   60

Note the "forgetting curve," and how it is climbing higher and higher toward the surface with each reminder.

The human brain is designed to limit the amount of information you can recall on short notice at any time. It's a biological plateau. But the brain can be tricked, hacked, reprogrammed, to unlock an immense amount of learning potential. It's all a matter of timing.

Well, it's not quite *that* simple. Calculating and scheduling the correct timing for repetitions of thousands of vocabulary words and biology terms—imagine a world of a million flash cards popping up like so many random billboards in front of you—would be beyond the capacity of even the smartest genius.

Computers, on the other hand, love that kind of work. Wozniak can easily do what Ebbinghaus could never dream of. To paraphrase *Wired* magazine's Gary Wolf, who has long chronicled Wozniak's adventures in timing, Wozniak has learned how to let a computer program him.

Back in the 1980s, using these timing insights, Wozniak got a hold of a black-market PC and wrote software that could flash him English words and phrases at just the right times, monitor his progress, and adjust its algorithms accordingly. Within months, he mastered English. He shared the program with colleagues, who immediately recognized its value. He quickly turned it into a commercial software product called SuperMemo (short for Super Memory), and within a couple of years, he was demonstrating the software at the world's largest technology trade show at the time, COMDEX, in Las Vegas.

Users of SuperMemo, in a survey, claimed they were able to learn and retain about 250 items per minute, and master an entire new language vocabulary in months, all the while feeling like they were accomplishing something that might seem unthinkable—they were training themselves to be geniuses. Cognitive psychologists raved that the software might finally materialize Ebbinghaus's dream of freeing schoolchildren from memorization drills that have repeatedly demonstrated their ineffectiveness and replacing them with a far more efficient and less stressful learning strategy.

Meanwhile, Wozniak started having bigger dreams. He realized the software—and the spacing effect—had implications far beyond memorization. What if there were optimal times to read and digest new journal articles . . . to eat . . . to swim . . . to make love?

Since the late 1980s, while selling SuperMemo all over the world, Wozniak has become essentially a hermit, living his life moment by moment according to the algorithms he's created. Software tells him when to run, what passages to read and read again, when to eat, when to relax . . . when to do nearly everything. If you'd like to contact him, Wozniak says don't bother trying. You aren't part of the program. Here's an admonition from his website:

I use only e-mail communication, where I can apply incremental mail processing. Freedom from meetings and deadlines makes it easier to use tasklists, proportional schedule, and adjust the timing of mental effort to the body clock.

Please do not see my refusal to attend important business meetings even in my hometown of Poznan as unkind or a sign of not attaching sufficient importance to an issue in question.

For exactly the same reasons as above, I do not have a mobile phone; not even for private purposes. Nor do I use Internet telephony. If I do not provide contact information, it is not of ill will. It is solely the question of time management.

You probably like taking phone calls and having random encounters with friends. We're not here to recommend otherwise. But in a world where time seems scarcer and scarcer all the time—time is, after all, the universe's most significant nonreplenishing resource—a hard look at wasted efforts in your life will unleash your potential and liberate you to do the things you love.

In a moment, we'll meet a whole society of people who are doing just that without becoming hermits, or slaves to a computer algorithm. But first, your experiment has hit its next phase. Nearly 1,500 words and ten minutes have passed since you last saw these letters. Insightful research done since Ebbinghaus's first experiments tells us that we should space reviews so that the first is done after five seconds, the next after twenty-five seconds, the third after two minutes, the next at ten minutes, then one hour, five hours, one day, five days, twenty-five days, four months, two years, and that's it, the information is locked in permanently. It's time for your fourth installment.

EBH ➜ DRE ➜ SQT

You're now nearly halfway to never forgetting them, for better or worse.

Wozniak, Ebbinghaus, and the users of SuperMemo all know that timing matters. They are not living some life of lunacy. They are drawing on an accepted principal—spacing—that has been well known to researchers for more than a hundred years and, more recently, is well accepted by cognitive psychologists. The lesson from Wozniak and SuperMemo is that we're not beholden to plateaus created by poor timing or poor use of time. In fact, their powerful, counterintuitive insight is this: There is great power in doing nothing at just the right time. The in-between time is just as important as every other time.

It's easy to imagine all sorts of possibilities if you master this "spacing effect." Sure makes elementary school math easier. Foreign language vocabulary, too. And the names of coworkers, or sales targets.

But what if having a good sense of timing, and the way our bodies work with the rhythms of life, really does go far beyond this memory trick, as Wozniak is trying to prove? Life and nature are full of cycles—the moon's twenty-eight-day trip around the earth, the four seasons and their consistency. Physics offers the perfect image for the flattening force of bad timing, of being out of phase with life. Perhaps you remember it from high school science class? If two powerful waves meet each other at the wrong time, they cancel each other out, creating essentially a flat line. It's called "destructive interference." Picture these two waves as ocean waves, if you like, but this is also true of sound waves, light waves, radio waves, etc. If they meet in the right phase, they amplify each other. If they meet at the wrong time—about half the time—they diminish each other. And if they meet at precisely the wrong time, they make each other invisible. Anyone who's ever lost a lover and uttered the words "It was just bad timing" knows the sad results of being out of sync with nature.

But what if there were a way to match our entire lives with the cycles that seem to naturally occur all around us? What if we could learn the best time for everything? Imagine the implications of a world where each one of us knows the best time for our brains to remember things, for our stomachs to digest food, for our blood to carry the oxygen from deep breathing.

It so happens that there is a quiet, small tribe of timing seekers, disciples who are working hard to systematically unlock the secrets that clocks—and time—have kept from humans for centuries. These disciples of the clock are something halfway between scientists and experiment subjects, between hacker hobbyists who would have been ham radio operators fifty years ago and philosopher-artists willing to spend hours sitting under a tree waiting for the right five-minute stretch of afternoon light for painting.

Their basic notion is simple: Google knows more about us than we do. It's time to flip that equation.

In a gritty part of Brooklyn that is slowly making the transition from warehouses to Starbucks, only a few blocks from the famous Greenpoint Pencil Factory that used to provide most of the jobs in the area and the most important tools for schoolchildren, we found this inspired group of true believers at their regular meeting. In a glorified attic above a yoga studio, in a loft that serves as a makeshift low-budget film studio by day, this group of ferocious self-examiners hurried to set up projectors and chairs on a sweltering summer evening.

A couple of presenters rehearsed nervously in the corner. Paper cups for wine and fruit were placed on a counter covered with newspapers posing as tablecloths. It was hotter than hell, nearly 100 degrees outside on this June afternoon, but in this loft—really, a barely converted attic—an old thermostat showed closer to 110 degrees. We were dripping with sweat by the time we climbed the stairs. A couple of old fans pushed the hot air around. But none of the men in the room—the gender ratio was probably twenty to one—seemed bothered. On closer examination, most of them were annoyingly muscular and fit. Eventually, nearly a hundred people crowded the attic, making it even hotter.

Right on time, organizer Steve Dean flicked on the projector and started the proceedings. Dean—a 35-going-on-25 computer programmer with perfect, thick hair, a booming voice, and a commanding presence—had no problems quieting the room. Ninety minutes of five-minute presentations followed. One programmer/presenter showed how he had logged the pace of every mile he had run for months and mapped them to air temperature, precise time of day, liquid intake, and dozens of other factors. He had determined that he runs his best at ten fifteen in the morning. Another programmer found a way to tweet his feelings into a database several times each hour, aiming to see if he could flatten out his down times and extend his happy times. Then, a couple spoke about a database they'd built that charted the state of their relationship—in some cases, minute by minute—with the theory that they had found the fastest road to marital bliss. With each talk came engaged questions, and offers of free software downloads to experiment with the tools being discussed. If it seems like this group rather obsessively wants to count everything, that's because they do. In fact, you might call counting their religion.

They are the early disciples of the "Quantified Self" movement.

Dean had the biggest news of the day. He had just returned from San Francisco, where he had attended the first-ever Quantified Self national conference.

"Things are really ready to take off," he announced. "We really are ready to change the world."

QS'rs, as they call one another, are everywhere. While they might be meeting in warehouse attics or backyards, hundreds of local

Quantified Self groups have formed in nearly every major city in the United States, Canada, and Western Europe. Their origin is generally traced to *Wired* reporter Gary Wolf, one of the few journalists to conduct extensive interviews with Wozniak in the past two decades. Wolf began running very public self-examination experiments more than a decade ago. But now, any QS'r can tell you what the movement is about.

Counting calories isn't the least bit controversial. Nor is counting the number of hours you sleep, or even the time you spend exercising or practicing piano. But for centuries, counting is all we've done. Quantifying the data is another thing entirely. What if there was a way to link your lunch meal to your ability to retain lessons learned in piano classes? Or if the best time for husband and wife to have difficult conversations turned out to be seven thirty A.M.?

We know this kind of timing can have a major impact on the outcome of challenging discussions—and early morning seems to be optimal, before a day's worth of decisions makes the parties involved weary. In a landmark study on something dubbed "decision fatigue," two researchers found that prisoners applying to the parole board in Israel vastly improved their chances at success if they managed to schedule their hearings early in the morning. In fact, morning candidates were paroled 70 percent of the time, while end-of-day applicants succeeded only 10 percent of the time. Postponing or procrastinating on that hard conversation throughout the day is probably really hurting your chances. The next time you want to ask your husband or wife for a guys' or girls' weekend, try asking during breakfast instead of dinner.

Google has built its entire company with the premise that these kinds of details matter and that their power can be harnessed. The firm takes billions of pieces of data—when you surf the web, what places you visit, who you e-mail and what you say—and runs them through massive algorithms in an attempt to put just the right adver-tisement in front of you at just the right time. QS'rs ask: Why should Google have all the fun? Their slogan might be: "Skip 'know thyself.' Google thyself."

QS'rs believe we all should think like Google, about ourselves.

While all this might sound cumbersome, life as a QS'r is getting easier with each passing quarter, with each new gadget or expansion of Internet bandwidth. Sensors are getting smaller and smaller, and more wired. It's trivial to create devices that log heart rate minute by minute, then upload the information wirelessly to a web server. Cross-referencing such information with other inputs—like mood or hunger—can begin to unlock amazing mysteries about our bodies and minds. More important, we can use that information to optimize our lives, the way Google optimizes our ads.

Sure, QS can sound odd. It definitely sounds obsessive-compulsive—("Wait, I forgot to turn on the pedometer when I was climbing the staircase to the bedroom!")—and we wouldn't be sur-prised if many of the people we met in Greenpoint that night would readily be diagnosed as such. Nearly all of them were fitness nuts, with all the good and bad that come with that.

Crazy or not, in fact, the concept works. Roger Craig is a dedi-cated New York QS'r and a regular attendee of those Greenpoint meetings. A computer programmer, he had always dreamed of being a contestant on the game show *Jeopardy!* So, encouraged by his club, he set about building a database of every question ever asked on the show. He created quizzes for himself and scored the results to deter-mine his weakest subject areas. Then he redoubled efforts to learn about those areas, using the spacing effect to ease his efforts to re-member foreign facts. He fought his way through trial rounds and onto the show. But that was just the beginning.

In September 2010, Craig not only won but also, by clearing

$77,000, set the record for one-day winnings on *Jeopardy!*, breaking legendary contestant Ken Jennings's record. Then he was invited to the 2011 Tournament of Champions, and his name is now the answer to a not-so-trivial question.

Answer: "Roger Craig, the November 2011 *Jeopardy!* Tournament of Champions winner."

Question: "Who made the Quantified Self movement's first leap into the mainstream world?"

The attraction of QS for programmers and fitness nuts is obvious. But what about the sick and infirm? There was another group of curious onlookers at the QS meeting we attended: entrepreneurs. As sensors get smaller, and the ability of databases to crunch numbers gets larger, medical device makers are taking a hard look at the medical magic that might come from "Googling thyself." What if a diabetic was outfitted with a moment-by-moment blood-sugar meter that was also able to predict peaks and troughs? It could beep at two thirty P.M. and say, "Have a banana now . . . or else." One wildly optimistic entrepreneur (aren't they all wildly optimistic?) predicted that quantified self-analysis could one day make traditional medicine irrelevant. Others are trying to hack their own genetic code, examining their DNA to find predictive characteristics that might help them understand why they learn better at night than during the day, or why certain foods make them queasy.

Most critically, many Quantified Self followers believe in the pooling of resources—the sharing of data from group to group across continents and around the world. What if there's a magic formula for the number of times a twenty-five-year-old male in marketing has to ask his boss for a raise before he gets it? QS volunteers will figure that out. Or what if a hundred thousand thirty-two-year-old women shared data on their efforts to become pregnant? The patterns that emerged would go oh so far beyond old wives' tales or message boards.

Unity Stoakes, founder of a health care information company named OrganizedWisdom, is at the forefront of this incredible concept. We spoke to him on that hot night in Greenpoint. He's crafting a solution to one of science's oldest problems. Testing software is easy. Testing medicine is hard, dangerous, and time-consuming. The cycle of trial and retrial is painstakingly slow.

In 2009, it took an average of eighteen months for the Food and Drug Administration to approve new medical treatments such as new prescription drugs. But even before drugs get to that final stage, it's not unusual for pharmaceutical companies to take a decade or more testing and retesting their drugs, biotech devices, or exercise programs. Imagine if a million adults signed up to be part of a standing panel, ready to kick the tires at a moment's notice and generate massive amounts of feedback data. There are immense safety hurdles to this kind of informal drug test, and it would be impractical in some cases involving more dangerous drugs. But in others, crowd sourcing would be a researcher's dream. Imagine if a hundred thousand adults who complained of sleep deprivation volunteered humidity measurements in their bedrooms for thirty days . . . and discovered that 67 percent slept better when the rating was between 50 and 55 percent? The number of tests you could run thanks to such an army of ready volunteers would be nearly infinite. Stoakes hopes to take the technology world's open-source software model—where an army of volunteers works collectively to write and test new programs, with all their work out in the open—and apply this strategy scientifically, to some of life's biggest health problems.

It's only a matter of *timing* before the Quantified Self movement succeeds. It's already making inroads into pop culture by helping regular people study one of the most basic functions of life: sleep. There's an emerging industry that's been dubbed "slumbertech" by *Boston Globe* columnist Scott Kirsner in which gadgets worn on the wrist or the head help adult sleepers log the time and the quality of rest they get every night. It's not science fiction: Zeo Mobile users wear a headband outfitted with an EEG sensor that can assess deep REM sleep and transmit the data to a smartphone for analysis. In a few weeks, Zeo's software can help users understand why they feel so tired every day, even if they are spending eight hours every night in bed. In typical plateau fashion, the time isn't what's important— the timing is. Five hours of REM sleep trump nine restless hours every time. Similar gadgets are smart enough to wake users just as they exit REM sleep, which can make for much easier mornings.

But the key is this: A night in a hospital sleep study lab can cost thousands of dollars. Now, for about a hundred dollars, anyone can track and painstakingly log sleep patterns at home. Googling thyself has become a consumer product, or at least electronics giant Best Buy thinks so. It carries Zeo products in its stores, and its Best Buy Capital arm is an investor in Zeo's parent company. All over a seemingly simple matter of timing how much you sleep.

Quantified Self habits and gadgets have already gone mainstream.

Whether you're a budding comedian, a struggling musician, or just a husband who wants to improve his marriage, you can benefit from developing a better sense of timing. Breaking through the blocks in your life could very well be as simple as getting in sync with some basic rhythms around you and within you. So we'll give you an easy place to start.

Breathing.

An average adult completes twelve to twenty breath cycles every minute. If you talk to most Yogis, or yoga instructors, that's at least two times too much. Try this experiment now; it'll only take a minute, we promise.

Breathe in. Count one Mississippi, two Mississippi . . . three . . . four . . . five . . .

Breathe out. Count one Mississippi, two Mississippi . . . three . . . four . . . five . . .

Breathe in. Count one Mississippi, two Mississippi . . . three . . . four . . . five . . .

Breathe out. Count one Mississippi, two Mississippi . . . three . . . four . . . five . . .

Repeat this set three times—six full cycles of slowly breathing in and out.

You won't have to look far to find claims that you've just lowered your heart rate and, more important, your blood pressure. Some scientists claim you've just optimized the way your body produces energy and spreads oxygen around to your muscles. You've almost certainly relaxed your limbs, and you are probably thinking a little more clearly. If you're a person of faith, you probably feel closer to your Maker, too.

And if you are a normal adult who is surrounded by gadgets that beep and ring and could demand your attention at any time, keeping you in a state of slightly heightened anxiety, your breathing rate is probably right back up to the eighteen times per minute or so that it was before we started this experiment. (Tell the truth . . . did you look at your e-mail while breathing?)

While the precise benefits of slower breathing are the subject of much debate, the fact that it's a good thing is nearly universally accepted. Just about every exercise program, yoga program, meditation program, spiritual journey, prayer program, and even vocal instruction begins with this simple but powerful instruction: Breathe slower and deeper. Focus on your breath. Feel your abdomen rise and fall. Pause.

When you breathe more slowly, you will quickly feel more in tune with your body and with nature. The exercise is so simple that even a one-minute pause in an otherwise dreadful day has shown measurable health benefits. Faster breathing is the most obvious symptom of that most common twenty-first-century malady, anxiety, and it is the first, almost instinctive advice that any friend offers to an anxious person:

"Just breathe."

There are few health practices that inspire such universal agreement. And yet when was the last time your doctor wrote you a prescription to breathe more slowly?

Richard Davidson, director of the Laboratory for Affective Neuroscience at the University of Wisconsin, spent years studying Buddhist monks in Tibet, with the Dalai Lama's blessing. Tests repeatedly showed increased gamma wave activity in their brains during meditation—indicating superior attention and awareness. It might not shock you that monks are mindful. But science is beginning to suggest that we can meditate our way to stronger brains, kind of like lifting weights to increase muscle mass. A researcher at Massachusetts General Hospital found that adult Americans who meditated forty minutes per day managed to quite literally increase the thickness of their cerebral cortex. In 2003, *Time* magazine called meditation the "Smart Person's Bubble Bath," but it's a lot more than that. Davidson's work with brain imaging has shown that meditation shifts brain work in the prefrontal cortex from the right hemisphere—famous for its aggressive fight-or-flight responses—to the left, where responses are more measured and, often, more positive.

But research maintains that better breathing can heal the body, too, merely by bringing it into sync with other bodily functions.

Breathing is unique among bodily functions in that it is automatic—that is, you don't have to try to breathe—but can be consciously directed, too. It's this conscious breathing that lines up body functions in a way that may offer amazing health benefits, if early research is confirmed over time.

In 2006, an Italian doctor named Luciano Bernardi published a paper in the British medical journal *BMJ* that the popular press has taken to calling "Why the Ave Maria is good for your heart," causing quite a stir. There is rhythmic magic, he found, in saying the Christian rosary (with its many Ave Maria, or Hail Mary, prayers) or in repeating the traditional yoga mantra "om-mani-padme-om." Both exercises slowed breathing to the critical six breaths per minute. In other words, it takes a Catholic devotee about six seconds to say a Hail Mary, and a yoga practitioner about the same time to repeat a mantra—a dramatic link of East and West spiritual practices that show our forefathers had more wisdom than we know. Bernardi also found that praying or repeating a mantra enhanced heart rate variability and arterial baroreflex sensitivity, which allows the body to adjust properly to changes in blood pressure. In other words, patients with hypertension who prayed actually had their prayers answered with lower blood pressure.

There's more—much more. Dr. David Anderson, who studies aging at the National Institutes of Health, has even conducted research showing that slow breathing increases adults' ability to break down salt. Adults who suffer from cold hands and cold feet often suffer from poor circulation; slower breathing can improve this condition by improving the blood's ability to carry oxygen. Other research shows dramatic improvement among asthma sufferers from slower breathing.

There's still plenty to learn about why better breathing means better health. One theory, espoused by advocates of the Coherent

Breathing method, holds that breathing is the brain's doorway to all the body's other autonomic functions. Bringing it into rhythm or coherence with the heart rate and other basic body functions improves everything from cardiopulmonary efficiency to emotional response, making life much easier for the heart in more ways than one. Again, it's not the amount of breathing that matters; it's the timing.

But you don't need a doctor to tell you that a stuffy nose (blocked air intake)—can quickly make life miserable and exercise almost impossible. It stands to reason that better breathing—and better timing when you breathe—is among the quickest, easiest paths to a better day. With a simple adjustment—waiting another three seconds each time you inhale, for most of us—you can change your life. Sometimes, timing really is everything.

Of course, breathing in time is just the start of all the ways that good and bad timing might have a major impact on your life and, to our point, might be the direct cause of an unexpected plateau. Mastering the spacing effect means you'll never forget things; mastering your breathing can help you live longer and healthier. Now let's look at how a better sense of timing can help in numerous unexpected places—such as ordering lunch at your local deli, or finding lost treasure on a Caribbean beach.

There's a deli near Bob's home that has the amazing ability to craft ham, salami, and provolone sandwiches on savory made-that-morning rolls for $3.95. They're not skimpy, either, stuffed deep with meat and cheese that would put most chain delis to shame. Bob can hardly walk, or drive, past the place without stopping to get one.

Sometimes, starting on Monday morning, he'll get one every day of the week. Ah, his favorite sandwich.

But by the time Thursday rolls around, something changes. Suddenly, he simply can't stand the idea of stopping at the deli. When that switch flips, the mere thought of that tangy salami makes him lose his appetite. Even the smell of the deli becomes repulsive.

What happened? He's overdone it. He's smothered the object of his affection. He has become *saturated*. You're familiar with the phrase "You always hurt the ones you love." Well, that's a little too gentle. We'd like to put it another way: We often kill what we love, or kill exactly what we love about the things we love.

When you think of the word *saturation*, no doubt the phrase *market saturation* comes to mind—as in, Coca-Cola has saturated the US soft drink market. There are no virgin Coke drinkers left. The company can't grow by simply making more Coke. It has to make new soft drinks, or acquire new complementary product lines (pretzels!), or find remote, Coke-less corners of the planet (Angola!). Market saturation, of course, is a very traditional form of a plateau, and it's obvious that some radical new thinking must be applied to bust out of that plateau.

But that's only one form of saturation. People can become saturated, too. As we've seen, your food tastes can be saturated. Your relationships can be saturated. Sex can be saturated. Your career can be saturated. The simple cause of these kinds of saturations is excessive repetition. But the consequences can be even more dire than market saturation. When you've overdone your favorite sandwich or the same sexual experiences, you don't merely find yourself with a flat quarter. You can end up hating what you do, who you date, even who you are. You end up killing what you love, when a simple plateau-vaulting trick or two could bring you to new heights.

The good news is that if you learn to sense this potentially deadly feeling early enough, it can be your best friend. When you get that slightly queasy feeling on the first day of too many days in a row at your favorite deli, you can back up, turn around, and find something else to eat. Long before slightly queasy turns to hatred, you can add a splash of change to your routine and find hope in your marriage or your workplace.

That queasy feeling is the canary in the coal mine of plateaus. Learn to recognize it, and you're halfway to solving one kind of plateau problem in your life. When you "kill" your favorite sandwich . . . or your favorite song . . . or your favorite sex position . . . how long does it take to bring it back to life? You probably don't need Quantified Self software to tell you that a week or two of salads will have you craving that salami again. Improve your timing, improve your life.

It's important to distinguish between some tasty terms here. *Saturation* means killing what you love because of overfamiliarity— too many ham sandwiches this week. It usually can be fixed within a few days. *Acclimation* of taste buds, like the acclimation to smell we discussed at the beginning of the book, is a much more subtle, and more pernicious, problem. American palates have become acclimated to high-fructose corn syrup and salt in nearly everything we eat. Slowly but surely, our taste buds have become desensitized to sugar and salt, meaning it takes more and more of these things to register with our tongues. Hence, the need for triple-decker Oreo cookies. Instead of a dramatic cycle of love and hate that eventually pushes people away from hyperfamiliar foods, or pop music, or even friends, acclimation doesn't push things away. It slowly erodes our ability to sense, increasing our need—perhaps even our addiction— for something.

"Cleansing" taste buds from acclimation is a much deeper problem to solve than "reviving" a preference killed by saturation. Dieticians recommend thirty-day experiments with cutting out fatty or salty foods like potato chips in an attempt to "reset" the palate. Here's one great variety tip from behavioral science that might help you reset your palate with just a little planning. Eaters often choose the same thing at lunch, or for a snack, day after day. But those who plan the week's lunches on Sunday night are far more likely to mix it up. It's called "diversification bias," and here's a simple example. A yogurt eater who might buy one container of peach yogurt every day in the cafeteria would never buy five containers of peach yogurt at the supermarket on Sunday night; instead, the urge to pick variety when choosing for the future is just too great, while there is no such diversity urge when choosing in the moment, day after day. As you might suspect, the effect of diversification bias goes far beyond yogurt. Music listening, exercise, friendships, almost anything can benefit from the power of planning ahead and increased variety.

Recognizing the difference between saturation and acclimation will dramatically improve your ability to effectively treat these plateaus. If you are a writer who has hit writer's block, are you tired of writing because you've been writing every day this week for twelve hours, and you just need a weekend away? Or have you been writing about the same subject matter for 147 weeks in a row, and a more substantial change is needed? Couples' therapists will tell you that many marriages end unnecessarily when a simple break would do the trick and rekindle the magic, and we're sure we don't have to remind you how unsatisfying love/hate, passionate/violent breakup love affairs turn out to be. Our point here is this: People in the middle of these kinds of situations are often the last to properly distinguish between saturation and acclimation. Each problem has a very different sense of timing.

Here's one determining factor that can really help. Earlier, we promised that we'd take you to a Caribbean beach. Let's go there now. Imagine you live in a bungalow along a long white sandy shoreline. It's peaceful and quiet at night, but every morning the beach is crowded with sun worshippers. How can you afford to live in such a luxurious place? You've become very proficient at wielding your

Viper Hybrid All Purpose Metal Detector. You are a professional beachcomber. When the sun falls and everyone leaves the beach, you go to work. A couple of hours later, waving your magic tool above the sand and into the shallow waters of the pristine beach, you find buried treasure that pays the rent on your beautiful bungalow and much more.

Successful beachcombers have a tool that's much more important than their model of metal detector. It's their ability to know when to quit. Or, put more accurately, they know when to pause.

As you might imagine, beachcombing is easiest right after dusk, when the maximum amount of misplaced jewelry lies nearest the surface of the beach. But after an hour or two of hunting, when the "low-hanging fruit" has been grabbed, the work gets progressively harder and less fruitful. The time gaps between "hits" start to grow. As the beach becomes more and more picked over, the treasure gets slimmer and slimmer. It's never empty, mind you—the tourists drink a lot, and they are pretty reckless. But our successful beachcomber eventually reaches a point of diminishing returns where it's just not worth searching any more. Search efforts have plateaued, and it's time to head to dinner and count the winnings.

But by all means . . . it is not time to quit.

Tomorrow is another day. The sun will rise, new tourists will sunbathe, and they will leave a new set of earrings, watches, and coins buried like treasure in the sand.

To the beachcomber, the beach is a *replenishing* resource. More critically, it replenishes on a regular basis. First, it's important to understand that the slim pickings that hit an hour after dark are no cause for despair; they are simply cause for a pause. Second, by understanding the rhythm—the timing—of the replenishment, the beachcomber can become much more efficient. It's easy to imagine our beachcomber building a database that might include dozens of characteristics—how the amount of sunshine during the day impacts the "fishing" haul at night, or what days of the year turn out to yield the most treasure. Eventually, by employing a better sense of timing, he can find the same amount of treasure in half the time, leaving more time for joining the tourists and relaxing on the beach.

Saturation and temporary depletion of a replenishing resource might not seem related at first glance, but they are. Your ability to enjoy a sandwich from your favorite deli can be used up rather quickly, but it also can be restored quickly. We both can say from experience that a taste for salami is a replenishing resource.

If you run a small coffee shop, offering a rare Ethiopian Harrar flavor might move the needle on sales for a week or two . . . but then, it is no longer rare, and sales return to normal. Fortunately, coffee lovers' tastes replenish, so it would be smart to offer the flavor for a limited time . . . then to stop . . . then to offer it again in a few months. This pattern has worked for decades with McDonald's McRib, which means it can work for any kind of food. The trick is uncovering the timing. How often can you sell rare coffee and tell people it's rare? The beach might refill with treasure every day, but a clear-cut forest can take twenty years to recover. Taste for the McRib seems to cycle every year or so. Understanding the time cycle of your replenishing resources will keep you on the right side of the plateau curve.

But before you turn the page, look below and read them one more time.

EBH ➜ DRE ➜ SQT

Now, read them once more when you finish this book, another time a month from now, then four months from now, and then one more time in a year or two. Then, you will never forget them. And you won't be able to say you didn't learn anything reading *Getting Unstuck*.

Of course, we don't want to stop there. We've described the problem now: why, despite what you've been told, hard work isn't always rewarded, and how nature can make you numb, greedy, flat—stuck on a plateau. But Mother Nature doesn't want you to be stuck. The very elements that seem to hold you back can also set you free, can be used as tools for breakthroughs. We'll begin with the most practical of these tools, the engines that drive breakthroughs. You just need to go with the flow.

PART TWO
THE ENGINE

Building Your Approach

5. FLOW MECHANISMS

Step Functions, Choke Points, and Mystery Ingredients

Or, Why your chicken noodle soup never tastes like the one mom used to make

It's the stuff that SAT question writers dream of: If two people can paint a house in six hours, how long will it take if three people work on it? If you want to get into college, the answer is four hours. If you want to paint a house, things get a little more complicated.

How many paintbrushes do you have? How many ladders? What's the quality of the third painter? Can the three work together; can they communicate? There are a lot more issues to consider than manpower, and a lot more measurements to take before coming up with an answer. The problem has to do with the flow of the process and obstacles along the way that can trip you up and, if you're not careful, lead to a plateau.

Farmers know this all too well. If you double the seed, double the fertilizer, and double the water, you're unlikely to get double the yield. Other factors must be considered: Is the area too small to have crops planted closer together? Will the land be depleted of a key mineral? Can the plant that processes the crop handle an increase in capacity?

We call those stumbling blocks, the things that go wrong when you increase capacity, *flow issues*.

Think about what happens when you turn on your shower at home. Water flows through a series of pipes and then magically sprays through a bunch of tiny holes in your showerhead. Now, think about what can go wrong with that process. Maybe you need to replace part of the infrastructure—and spend some serious cash doing it (a *step function*). Maybe those big pipes underneath your house lead to a very small pipe that's limiting the flow (a *choke point*). Maybe part of the pipe is old and about to bust (we call that *erosion*). Or maybe, just maybe, your spouse was right and you need a professional who has a knack for fixing things just like this (the *mystery ingredient*).

During these next two chapters, we are going to discuss what we call the mechanical causes of plateaus.

Step Functions

Hugh had been thinking about it for days—the way steam came out when he pulled the bun apart; the roasted pork inside, cooked to succulent perfection. It was at one of his favorite San Francisco restaurants, his first stop on a weeklong trip to the city. You couldn't be in a rush with this place; things took time. There were two cooks, both from South Korea, who spoke "I passed my driver's test" level English, and they were stretched to capacity. Plus, the place was way too small.

You accept these inconveniencies because your reward is the most perfect blend of fat, pork, sugar, and dough that is known to exist in the western world. When the taxi pulled up, Hugh was already prepared to wait out a fifteen-person line, but instead, tragedy: His go-to roast pork bun place was now a big Laundromat. How could a restaurant where you had to wait half an hour in line to get a five-dollar piece of bread with pork in it go under? Hugh wandered inside, and amid a set of spinning dryers he got the tragic tale from the Laundromat manager. The restaurant had expanded and signed a two-year lease for a space next door. They knocked down the walls in between and hired another cook. The American dream realized. At peak dinnertimes, they had enough customers to fill the place, but at other times it was relatively empty. The huge increase in rent was too much for a five-dollar roast pork bun to shoulder, and eventually they needed to close. The restaurant clearly had the customers—the line for the old restaurant was around the block at dinnertime—but the owners fell victim to one of the most vexing flow issues in any business: the *step function*.

A function, as it's defined in the field of mathematics, has input and output, action and consequences. Step on the gas a little more (input), and you go a little faster (output). Sometimes, though, this input-to-output relationship isn't so smooth. If your car is at a standstill in snow, you might have to floor it before the car starts moving (and then it's really moving!). This concept of a sudden "step" from stopped to moving after you hit a threshold is one of the most important flow issues because it can often be mistaken for a plateau. You might just need a little more gas for the wheels to get traction.

We call these things that happen in chunks "step functions." You want to add just a little more of something, but that thing is only available in bundles. The result is a jump in cost, effort, or benefit. Bakers know this rule well; it hits them right between the eyes every time a recipe for cookies calls for a pinch of baking powder, and they need to buy a whole box. Grocery stores, naturally, don't tend to sell by the pinch. That painful purchase can have a happy ending, however. If you decide to bake two batches of cookies, your cost per pinch actually goes down because you still only need one box. (Leftover batches of cookies can be mailed to Bob and Hugh, courtesy of our publisher.)

Airline loyalty programs are usually step functions—after you fly some number of miles, you hit a threshold and then, *boom*, you move to a new status and get an extra bag of peanuts when you fly (given airline cutbacks, you may only get one extra peanut, not a whole pack). Step functions are not inherently good or bad; they are just the way some processes work. But if you don't recognize and plan for them, they throw off the theory that incremental effort yields incremental reward.

While buying some extra baking powder to make us cookies is unlikely to break the bank, sometimes the cost of an additional input can be staggering and unexpected. In some cases, you may not even realize you're about to hit a threshold. To see this on a big scale (and to take the vacation you've always dreamed of), you need to visit the island of Nassau, just off the coast of Florida.

At the beginning of every year in Hugh's home, the island nation of the Bahamas, homeowners and insurance companies make huge gambles on the weather—specifically, hurricanes. In a perfect world—the world where you'd only get insurance when you knew for sure that something bad was about to happen—you would hear that a hurricane was traveling and had a chance of hitting the country, and you would promptly run to an insurance company to protect your home. If the hurricane hit, you'd be covered. If it veered off into the Atlantic, you'd drop your insurance policy and repeat the process when you got word of the next hurricane.

In the real world, though, Bahamian insurance companies won't let you buy insurance when there is an active threat of the hurricane actually striking; it's a losing proposition for insurance companies and makes the business unviable. You have to gamble: either buy hurricane insurance before you can know if there's a real danger, or go without it and risk losing everything.

Things get even more interesting for hurricane insurance companies. They make those same bets, just on a much bigger scale. It's a process called *reinsurance*; one insurance company takes out insurance policies with bigger companies just in case a hurricane goes on a rampage through the islands. Hurricane season in the Atlantic runs from the beginning of June through the end of November every year. Every December, on the heels of one hurricane season and well before the next, Bahamian insurance companies make multimillion-dollar bets on the number of hurricanes that will hit the next year. Placing those bets is a combination of intuition, input from experts (who are also guessing), and pure luck. They bring to Nassau a set of "weather handicappers," crystal-ball-wielding meteorologists who guess on weather patterns six months in the future (think sports handicapper–meets–Al Roker—who, coincidentally, is from the Bahamas . . . but we digress). After discussions of El Niño, La Niña, and the migration patterns of pelicans, the companies call their brokers and place their bets.

Each hurricane that you have reinsurance for is known as a "cover," and each cover is a huge step function. Here's how it works. If you knew for sure that three hurricanes would hit the Bahamas during the course of the year, you'd buy three covers, which would guarantee, for a fixed cost, that you would only be on the hook for some hefty deductible—the reinsurers would take the rest of the hit. If you bet accurately, you'd make big profits. If you were too cavalier and got only two covers, you'd need to come hat in hand to the reinsurers for an emergency third cover after the second hurricane hit—sometimes at triple the original price. If, on the other hand, you were too paranoid and bought too many covers, you'd be committing to a huge fixed cost (a big step function), which would eat heavily into profits. It's high-stakes gambling.

To put things in perspective, the first tropical depression (the category right below "hurricane") of the season begins with the letter *A*, and naming continues alphabetically after that, excluding the letters *Q*, *U*, and *Z* (which are apparently too hard for meteorologists to come up with hurricane names for). The average number of named systems in the Atlantic in a year is 11.3—that's the letter *K* in the alphabet. This means that if Hurricane Ophelia is floating around and it's only September, it's time to go cover shopping—and take a big step up in cost.

Insurance companies aren't the only ones that make bets with step functions. You do it every month with your cell phone provider. Think you'll only use nine hundred minutes? Go with the one-thousand-minutes-a-month plan. You're covered, but if you go over, you'll be talking to your best friend at twenty cents a minute. On the other hand, if you go with the two-thousand-minute plan, you're leaving money on the table because you've got excess capacity you aren't using.

Most people (and businesses) are loaded with excess capacity. Think about your car. Maybe you use it to get to and from work—but what about the rest of the time? It just sits there, excess capacity created by taking the step from not owning a car to owning a car. What if you could rent your car out while it would otherwise be sitting at home or in your company's parking lot? Your bedroom might follow the same trend; you use it at night, but what about the other sixteen hours of the day—empty, excess capacity. Filling the excess capacity you commit to with a step can be a plateau-busting game changer. Just ask Seth Rubin, owner of Rise & Shine Biscuit Kitchen and Cafe in Denver, Colorado.

Like so many Americans, Seth Rubin was a victim of the recession of 2009. He was laid off as a project manager for a construction company as home building plummeted in Denver. An avid cyclist, he had always dreamed of opening up a coffee and biscuit shop, but the huge upfront investment and the risk was too much for him to pull the trigger.

"I always had the idea of biscuits and coffee in the back of my mind, but it was never a step I was willing to take because a restaurant is quite possibly one of the riskiest operations out there to start," he told us.

To put it in context, in 2009 the economy was imploding. Jobless rates had hit their highest level in two decades, and credit sources for small businesses had all but evaporated. Seth was thinking about what to do next, and on one of his long rides he had a crazy idea as he passed Basil Doc's Pizza, a small local chain owned by Mike Miller.

Mike and Seth had met a decade earlier at a cycling event in Denver. Back then Mike had one Basil Doc's location. Now he had four. Seth walked in with a plan to open up a biscuit shop in the morning and then hand things over to Basil Doc's for dinner. "I figured I'd bounce the idea off of Mike, hoping that he'd talk me out of it," Seth said.

But Mike didn't talk him out of it. In fact, he offered to keep Seth's share of the rent low while he was feeling his way through it. His fortuitous bike ride to Basil Doc's was in September 2009. Four months later, Seth served his first biscuit as Rise & Shine Biscuit Kitchen and Cafe—recession (and plateaus) be damned.

To get going, the work was mostly cosmetic at the front of the store. The two restaurants shared equal billing on the signs out front, and Seth changed the colors inside to make it seem friendlier for customers to dine in.

"Just about everything I needed in the kitchen was there. A lot of what happened early on was making use of what was there and purchasing what I needed and not what I wanted," Seth said. He bought a used cappuccino machine and some equipment on Craigslist, then repurposed everything he could from Basil Doc's. "At the get-go, we were cooking eggs on a griddle pan on a stockpot range, which is functional but not ideal. But it was also a seventy-dollar investment versus a six-hundred-dollar investment." All in, Seth went from an idea to selling his first egg and biscuits combo for just under five thousand dollars, pennies on the dollar for a new restaurant.

While Seth's biscuit business was peaking in the morning, Mike's pizza restaurant waited out the slow period of the day. And when Seth's business would have naturally waned in the afternoon, Mike was being pummeled by dinner pizza orders. The two realized their businesses had *complementary peaks*: They were busy at opposite times. Even more interesting, their needs were similar. Both needed an oven; they both needed a similar layout to display and then deliver their goods. They both wanted stability for their businesses, but the step function of being the sole renter of an oven-equipped store, only to have it sit idle for half the day, was a serious drawback.

It was a partnership baked in heaven.

Rise & Shine opens at seven A.M. and closes at one P.M. After that the kitchen is cleaned, supplies stored, and then the Basil Doc's team gets prepped to open at four, with pizzas coming out of the oven by four thirty. "We clean up everything that we were doing, and we switch out coffee condiments for pizza condiments. We turn the pizza ovens on and walk out the door." Were customers confused? Sometimes. "We have a couple of people now and then coming in and looking for slices of pizza at lunchtime, but we've managed to talk most of them into a biscuit instead."

Fourteen months after Seth took the leap of faith on the first store, he opened up a second location, taking the morning shift at one of Basil Doc's other properties.

Mike and Seth were able to monetize their downtime by creating a symbiotic relationship, smoothing costs and cutting the biggest step in the restaurant business—rent—in half. It was more than a marriage of convenience. They started to get crossover customers—a stop on the way to work for biscuits and on the way home for pizza. They turned a liability, a mutual drag on their respective businesses, into a game-changing, plateau-busting, dough-powered dynamo: "We still have people coming in saying, 'Oh, we had pizza here last night and found out you guys were doing what you're doing in the morning, so we decided to come back.' Mike gets the same kind of thing."

Basil Doc's only has two locations left for Seth to move in on, but one of those doesn't have much space in the front to serve the biscuit-consuming crowd so he had to pass. It may work out for the best.

"Mike does have someone who's moving in now doing jams and jellies. We're looking into them supplying the jelly for our biscuits, you know, and keep it all in the family," Seth said.

This idea of complementary peaks, maximizing the utility of a resource and smoothing out step functions, transcends dough. It has caused one of the biggest revolutions in information technology: the cloud.

Computers—the kind that power the websites of companies such as Amazon, Google, and Yahoo—are expensive. The cost of power to run them, buildings to house them, air conditioning to cool them, and people to maintain them is even more expensive. Even worse, these expenses come in big chunks. Getting one of these systems up and running requires a serious outlay of cash, all before your business makes its first dollar. This start-up cost made the barrier to entry for entrepreneurs overwhelming. The expensive step function of buying your own technology infrastructure might have dissuaded the next Facebook or Twitter founders from changing the world. But what if several companies could band together and share the cost of buying all the expensive equipment? They could cut costs dramatically with little downside. But there are logistics problems. How would these budding entrepreneurs find one another? How could they be assured that they were keeping up their part of the bargain and not stepping on one another's toes? What if they were competitors? How would that work?

There was a huge opportunity for someone to make a really big investment, create a bunch of capacity, and then rent out space on their computers to Internet entrepreneurs or even established businesses wanting to expand.

Enter the cloud.

It all started with the creation of virtual machines (VMs)—computers that can run within other computers. Virtual machines let a single server hold multiple "virtual" servers, allowing companies to push the capacity of a computer's hardware to its limit. Virtual machines solved a serious problem in big businesses: excess computing capacity. Before VMs, adding another computer server meant buying another expensive piece of hardware. Some of these servers operated at a fraction of their potential. It was like driving a Greyhound bus around twenty-four hours a day carrying only one passenger. Now you could fill every seat on the bus, saving a ton of money that otherwise would have gone to buy new hardware.

The cloud concept went a step further: If you ran out of your own capacity, you could seamlessly "spill over" into someone else's idle capacity. You could "rent" that time from them, but only when you needed it. It'd be like the now defunct San Francisco roast pork bun restaurant just renting the new space at dinnertime and only paying for the time and extra space they needed. This concept of being able to spill over into somebody else's space saves companies a fortune, and also creates a huge business opportunity for holders of the space.

Companies like Amazon bet big on this idea, creating massive data centers and renting out virtual machines to anybody who wanted them. You could rent them by the minute. Because everything was happening behind the scenes, it was seamless to customers. More load meant more time rented on more servers, but it also meant more revenue to cover the cost.

It's midnight, and you only have a few customers online? You're paying pennies. It's the Friday after Thanksgiving, and you're selling thousands of digital picture frames per minute online? You're paying a premium, but you're making money hand over fist. Need more space, bandwidth, or servers? Just pay as you go. Cloud service providers smoothed the step function.

The concept of seeking incremental solutions until you can justify the step up in resources is the key. Can't afford to hire a new person in your business? Bridge with a contractor till you can. Can't justify paying for the two-thousand-minutes-a-month plan? Get a family plan and share resources. Identifying step functions, smoothing the ones that you can—and planning for ones that you can't—can help your business (and your life) flow like Niagara. That is, until you hit a choke point.

Choke Points

A choke point is the part of the system that breaks first and slows everything else down. Failing to identify a choke point can bring a gushing flow to an unexpected trickle. When you hit a choke point, the whole system can slow or even stop. It's the equivalent of tripping a circuit breaker by plugging in one too many strands of Christmas tree lights.

A common cause of plateaus is not recognizing when and where choke points will occur. For example, insecure managers often hit a plateau because they make themselves a choke point; they micromanage, reviewing every tiny decision and putting other people on hold while they deliberate. Their part of the business is held back by their need to ponder, consider, and digest. You know who they are: walking "blocking issues."

Choke points can occur in the strangest of places. In 2009 alone, it is estimated that more than 143 million personal information records (credit card numbers, social security numbers, etc.) were stolen in the United States. That's a big problem for consumers, but think about the challenges from the criminal's point of view.

The supply of stolen credit card numbers has gone way up, and competition among bad guys has forced the price of a single stolen credit card number down to about one dollar (that's complete with that CVV2 security number and billing zip code). More "reputable" stolen credit card dealers will even offer twenty-four-hour customer support for buyers: If any of the stolen credit card numbers don't work, they will replace them within hours (seriously). Consider how familiar the customer service policies of one such, ahem, merchant are (please excuse the less-than-stellar English).

Try before you buy (quoting from their online advertisement): "If u want test please buy one and then if the cvv is good u can buy more from me."

Bulk discounts—why buy one stolen credit card number when you can get thirty? C'mon, treat yourself: "If u buy over 30, I will sell for u good price."

No "credit" policy (seems a bit unfair, considering): "Cvv will be sent to you after receiving payment. Orders will be sent via e-mail or when you want."

And finally, a commitment to quality and customer service: "I have a replacement policy for bad Cvv. Warranty 24 hours. All my cvv are inspected before sale . . . not good mean change!"

The people who buy these card numbers are usually members of an organized crime group. Now comes the tricky part: How do you turn a stolen credit card number into cash without getting caught? It's at this point we run into the real choke point for credit card fraud: housewives in Middle America.

The process works like this: Bad guys publish job opportunity ads online, and some even go as far as posting flyers on lampposts. They make promises like "Earn $100,000 in your spare time from home." Sounds pretty appealing. People respond and become "employees."

Within a week, trucks begin delivering a steady stream of big-screen TVs, gaming systems, laptops, and other high-end electronics, all ordered from online retailers using stolen credit card numbers. The person's job is simple: pack the items in a box and send them to a warehouse outside of the country.

The scheme is called "repackaging" and often the housewives ("mules" in criminal speak) don't know they're doing anything wrong until the FBI breaks down their front door a few months later. The whole process of monetizing a stolen credit card number is limited by mule recruitment—how fast criminals can get these unknowing accomplices to sign up. It's the choke point.

Much of the effort in the stolen credit card supply chain is now focused on recruitment. It's big business. Cybercriminals are turning to online dating sites, job posting boards, hobbyist chat forums—anywhere and everywhere they can cultivate a relationship.

This kind of creativity is key to dissolving choke points . . . or, where appropriate, to creating them. To understand this dynamic, we'd like to invite you to visit the strange world of CAPTCHAs (Completely Automated Public Turing test to tell Computers and Humans Apart).

You may not know them by name, but if you use the Internet, you've certainly seen them. CAPTCHAs are the annoying squiggly words you need to type into a box online before you can buy a ticket to a baseball game or sign up for a new e-mail account. It's a test: Is the person filling this thing out a human or a computer?

The modern CAPTCHA was the brainchild of Luis von Ahn, a computer scientist at Carnegie Mellon University. CAPTCHAs have been integrated into almost every major website—including Google, Yahoo, and Ticketmaster. You may be wondering what purpose these incredibly annoying, sometimes indecipherable words really serve. They might be frustrating to read for a human, but good CAPTCHAs are darn near confounding for computers to figure out automatically.

Before CAPTCHAs, cybercriminals would write automated tools to try a thousand different passwords for your online account in seconds. After CAPTCHAs, the process got derailed. The tool would get to the part where it had to guess what the squiggly word was and then give up.

CAPTCHA was a game-changer for websites that were being inundated with spam or password guessers. But again, if we may, let's think about it from the cybercrook's perspective. The CAPTCHA became the ultimate choke point.

Organized cybercrime groups had invested significant time and energy in writing tools to advertise their wares and break into accounts; they weren't about to see all that effort wasted and revenue lost, especially to a series of letters that looked like they were written by an intoxicated roller coaster rider. It is here where we see what a motivated group can do to work around choke points creatively.

The first attempts to circumnavigate CAPTCHAs were technological. Bad guys wrote a series of special-purpose optical character recognition (OCR) software tools specifically designed to help computers read CAPTCHA characters. The tools succeeded in some cases, which led CAPTCHA writers to make the letters even more unreadable.

The next approach to bring down CAPTCHAs was to pay people in low-income countries to solve these things by hand. For a hundredth of a cent, you could get someone to figure out if those three letters on the screen spelled "Cat" or "Car" or "Let" or whatever. It worked, but this pay-per-solve approach actually started to get pretty expensive. Imagine trying to guess someone's password. You might have to try a hundred thousand different combinations to get to the right one, that's ten dollars . . . you'd be better off buying ten stolen credit card numbers!

And then, finally, a breakthrough. Crooks leveraged the most powerful force on the Internet. It's the force that pushed web browsers to start showing images. The juggernaut that made the VHS format win out over Betamax. The hundred-billion-dollar industry that has spawned some of the most disruptive advancements in technology and video production. Pornography.

Cybercrime gangs set up porn sites online. The service was free. You didn't need to sign up, no membership required. All you needed to do to see the next image or video was fill out a few CAPTCHAs. It was a brilliantly sordid scheme. The CAPTCHAs were taken from the websites that their tools were actively trying to attack. Whenever one of their tools hit a CAPTCHA choke point, *bam*, they would take a picture of the squiggly word and cue it up to appear on the screen of the next porn site visitor. Some of these porn sites even used quality control procedures—they'd take the same CAPTCHA and present it to five different porn hunters and only trust that the typed word was correct if all five people gave the same answer. It is estimated that, at the peak of the porn-CAPTCHA frenzy, several thousand CAPTCHAs were being solved by unsuspecting (and somewhat rushed) porn site users a minute. It was a choke point remover that had staying power: No matter how complicated you made the CAPTCHA, there would always be a motivated human who was willing to solve it for free.

In this battle of good versus evil, of choke point insertion and removal, CAPTCHAs continue to evolve and push the bounds of human computation. In an ironic twist, the man responsible for creating one of the biggest choke points in cybercrime, Luis von Ahn, has refocused (perhaps out of guilt?) on removing choke points in a completely different area: the digitization of old books.

If you haven't figured it out, Luis von Ahn likes to solve puzzles. After CAPTCHAs started appearing everywhere, he realized that people were doing all of this wasted work figuring out these little puzzles. Could he put their efforts to better use? More than two hundred million CAPTCHAs are filled out every day; that's more than 150,000 hours of labor per day wasted on those squiggles. Were there problems that humans could solve that could be broken up into little chunks but then pieced together to solve a bigger purpose? It was out of this desire that the reCAPTCHA project was born.

Before we get to reCAPTCHA, a bit of background on the challenges of computers reading the written or typed word. During the past several decades, computer systems have become pretty efficient at being able to recognize typed text from pristine documents. But what about old documents and books, the kind that are riddled with coffee stains, stray marks, bad typesetting? In those cases, the software starts to get less reliable and the digital content starts to look like gibberish. Ultimately, a human that must intercede, eyeball the page, and make the call, and here's where von Ahn and reCAPTCHA come in.

Instead of completely fabricated puzzles, reCAPTCHA presents users with two squiggly words to type in: one that the website knows the right answer to and the other that's a picture of a word from an old book. Users don't know which word is the bogus one and which one is correct, so you are incentivized to give your best guess on both. reCAPTCHA then gathers and cross-checks your interpretation of the word that was scanned in from the old book, and if enough people agree, voilà, you've just helped preserve history by turning an old masterpiece into a digital document that will live on forever.

reCAPTCHA also goes a step further. Instead of just looking at a contorted word, the software gives you the option to listen to some slightly garbled audio and then type the words you hear. This makes the CAPTCHA concept workable for the visually impaired, but through the lens of reCAPTCHA, it also created an opportunity to turn old recordings into transcribed documents.

reCAPTCHA was disruptive. It removed the choke point in digitizing less-than-pristine documents and recordings. reCAPTCHA now serves up more than thirty million puzzles a day and has digitized millions of old books and documents. It quickly captured the attention of Google—a key player in the book digitization game—and in 2009 the Internet juggernaut acquired reCAPTCHA.

Choke point removal is transformative. The key is to find out where the choke point is and creatively route your way around it (hopefully without having to get into the porn business).

Erosion

Once a year, on the small island of South Bimini in the Bahamas, hundreds of people gather for a hunt. Bahamians from neighboring islands have made the pilgrimage by sloop, sailboat, and weathered, sputtering Boston whaler. It's become a tradition, a rite of passage for some. A group of volunteers have worked through the night to prepare, and every year they've been forced to up their game. Welcome to the annual Out Island Easter Egg Hunt.

Things kick off around noon, and until then, children under the age of ten are held back by their parents like horses behind a race gate. When they're let go, the kids spend hours turning over rocks, peering into trees, and combing through grass looking for painted hardboiled eggs.

Hugh remembers being attacked by a duck as a child after stumbling across a nest full of unpainted eggs. Hey, every hunt has its risks.

Wizened ten-year-olds—veterans of the hunt on their final run— know that it's important to be focused early on. Most of the eggs are found in the first few minutes: a pink egg that contrasts with the grass, an egg lazily thrown on the side of a rock, or one protruding out from under the leaf of a seagrape tree. The egg-per-minute ratio then trails off as fewer and fewer eggs are left to discover.

They may not know it by name, but on this island kids get a harsh exposure to *erosion plateaus*.

Usually, more than half of the eggs in someone's basket are found in the first few minutes. No matter how hard the kids hunt, the same effort yields fewer eggs as time passes. The problem is that even though effort remains constant—kids hunt just as hard in the second ten minutes as they do in the first—their reward for that effort decreases. When we consume a resource that is fixed (or that replenishes slower than the rate we consume it), erosion must occur.

Erosion plateaus tend to happen smoothly. There is no sudden drop in effectiveness or flow that often comes with a step function or choke point; effectiveness just gradually falls.

So it was with the egg hunt. The wise hunter would get out way in front of the pack, where the pickings were bountiful, grab while the hunting is easy, and then coast through the end. But even that strategy eventually fails.

In the mid-1980s, there was a breakthrough; it was an innovation that would reshape the hunt and bring joy and fulfillment to even the slowest of preadolescent egg seekers. Hugh was about ten years old, near the end of a lengthy but fairly unremarkable tenure. Here's what changed: Instead of using a pre-seeded field of eggs—static and ready to be depleted—the organizers moved to a staged pattern where the hunt would take place in two different areas, at different times, on opposite end of the island (it was a pretty small island). After fifteen minutes of hunting on the south end of the island, an area in the north would open up, and driven by the allure of an untouched field of eggs, kids would rush in. Then a group of adults would restock the old area, setting up for the cycle to repeat. The hunt went on for an hour instead of fifteen minutes—and could have gone on forever.

The plateau-smashing solution, the acid that melts erosion plateaus away, is to find a *counterbalance*: something that restores what you deplete, gives what you take and takes what you give. On South Bimini, parents hid eggs and the children discovered them. A perfect counterbalance. Counterbalances are different from the complementary peaks that allowed Rise & Shine Biscuit Kitchen and Cafe to thrive in the same location as Basil Doc's Pizza. Instead of sharing resources, a counterbalance replenishes a resource that gets eroded.

To see the power of counterbalances in action, we invite you to fly to Seattle, Washington, drive five hours due east, and ask anybody you see on a tractor for Kevin Mader. They'll know where to find him.

The Palouse region in southeast Washington is home to Washington State University and lentils, lots and lots of lentils. In fact, 90 percent of the lentils grown in the United States come from this area. If you drive down Washington State Route 27 in the Palouse, you'll see endless fields of green and brown, lentils and wheat stretching over the horizon. What you'll also see is the name "Mader."

There's the Mader farm, an empire of combines and storehouses. There's Mader Road. There are trucks marked "Palouse Brands" heading in every direction carrying Mader lentils and wheat. And if you stick around long enough, you may get a personal greeting from Steve and Kevin Mader, fourth- and fifth-generation farmers who cultivate more than twenty thousand acres (an area bigger than Manhattan) of wheat and lentils in the region.

Farmers like the Maders have perhaps the purest grasp of counterbalances. Each crop gives something to the land and also takes something away. Lentils, for example, enrich the soil with nitrogen. They also encourage a specific type of pest. That's why you can't plant crop after crop of lentils in the same field; each season will be tougher to grow, and you'll hit a plateau, despite doing the same thing that was successful in the last crop.

One solution is to leave the ground fallow; let nature rejuvenate the soil and then come back a year later with a new round of seed. Leaving the ground fallow to rejuvenate has both biblical and scientific roots. The Hebrew concept of Jubilee speaks to a year of rest for the land at the end of seven cycles. A crop can deplete resources, and Mother Nature must step in as the counterbalance to make it whole again.

Beyond periods of rest, modern farmers use other types of counterbalances to keep the land in equilibrium. The nitrogen that the lentils leave behind is the perfect food for a counterbalancing crop: wheat. Wheat consumes the nitrogen, removing what is essentially a waste product for lentils. The two work together in harmony, each giving what the other needs and reaping what the other discards. In addition to making the land productive, the crop diversity helps to stop the buildup of pests and keeps the soil rejuvenated.

Wheat feeds off the nitrogen and flourishes. Lentils leave it behind; wheat picks it up. You can't get much more counterbalanced than that.

Mystery Ingredients

Why does your chicken noodle soup never taste like the one Mom used to make? Why does this diet plan work for everyone except me? It might be due to a factor we call "the mystery ingredient." Failure to identify a mystery ingredient is another common cause of plateau. It's why your raspberry pie never tastes quite as good as the one Grandma used to bake. It's why you can't re-create the magic in a movie sequel (*The Dark Knight* excluded, of course). It's why businesses are often hit with surprising efficiency losses after moving production offshore.

The defining characteristic of a mystery ingredient is that even the chef doesn't know what it is. The mystery ingredient could be changing market conditions, interpersonal issues between coworkers, or just a team member with a can-do attitude. It's the elusive catalyst that makes things work.

Outsourcing is a good example. In the early days of outsourcing, India looked irresistible. There was a large talent pool of technologists, workers were fluent in English, and the labor rate was a fraction of that in the United States. On paper, success seemed inevitable. In the gap between cost savings charts and actual implementation, though, something happened: India's economy boomed. The average salary for IT workers went up by double digits annually between 2000 and 2009. Technology centers like Electronics City in Bangalore saw new office buildings go up every week. People would resign at one company in the morning and be able to get a job paying 10 percent more that afternoon at a company across the street. The boom led to unexpected changes; employee turnover went through the roof. That meant employers constantly had to retrain workers on policies, procedures, and tools. Companies that weathered the storm recognized the mystery ingredient: people who moved from the home office to India and managed employees on the ground there. On-site managers were able to adapt to changing conditions and align the goals of the company with actions in a fluid situation.

Data is often the enemy of the mystery ingredient. Mystery ingredients don't tend to show up on spreadsheets or checklists. Over-analyzing a situation can lead you to make decisions that destroy the very essence of a company or a relationship. To put it another way, the deification of data has eroded our belief in mystery. Maybe you don't believe in some mysterious force at your company, a mysterious relationship between coworkers that provides something special, but that doesn't make you immune to any consequences if you remove it. You don't have to believe in gravity to fall off a bridge. Maybe your spreadsheet doesn't show that one member of a team is the glue that keeps everyone going, but fire that person and you'll face the consequences.

Mystery ingredients go by different names. In business, they might be called "institutional knowledge"—the know-how to get things done that somehow just can't get put down on paper. No one can say with certainty how many employees you would have to lose to deplete institutional knowledge. But you sure know when it's gone.

Today's mystery ingredients might be tomorrow's facts. In 1847, a Hungarian doctor named Ignaz Semmelweis noticed that women who delivered their babies at a hospital with the help of doctors suffered a significantly higher mortality rate than women who delivered their babies at home with midwives. Back then, people believed that disease was something that happened spontaneously—an accepted "fact" that didn't explain the mortality discrepancy Semmelweis observed. He began to suspect that doctors were somehow causing the infections that eventually led to the death of these women and that the disease was somehow contagious. He forced doctors to wash their hands with chlorinated lime water before treating pregnant women. The results were dramatic. Mortality rates for women giving birth at the hospital dropped from 18 percent to 2.2 percent. His belief in the mystery ingredient, something now accepted as *germ theory*, literally saved lives.

Mystery ingredients often can be hard to find but seem obvious in retrospect—much the same way that the handling of disease outbreaks hundreds of years ago seems insane under the lens of germ theory. Often, it's just important to recognize that a mystery ingredient might exist, that what you see isn't the whole story.

One amazing example of a mystery ingredient is the placebo. The well-known phenomenon of the placebo effect can actually help manipulate the Plateau Effect. How so? It has been well documented that placebo treatments can result in improvement in actual disease state. Exactly what happens here is still a subject of much debate, but it is obvious there is a complex interaction between the mind and body that can result in real physiological changes. There is evidence that placebos can even have effects in treating cancer, and placebos are routinely used in cancer clinical trials. A placebo presented as a stimulant will significantly increase heart rate and blood pressure, while a placebo presented as a depressant will have the opposite effect. There is even the phenomenon of *nocebo* effects, adverse events associated with administration of a placebo—yes, you can cause side effects by giving a someone a sugar pill!

Doctors can use the potency of the placebo effect to manipulate the Plateau Effect of a drug. For instance, doctors could better educate patients on the effects of drugs so that the information not only allows the patient to be well informed but also serves as classical psychological conditioning, magnifying the placebo effect. It has been shown that providing a placebo to patients whose doctors treated them with "warmth, attention, and confidence" increased their response to placebo from 44 percent to 62 percent. Since the placebo effect tends to wane over time, you can introduce new treatments in sequential fashion to ensure the placebo effect is fresh. The placebo effect teaches us that even if we don't fully understand how a mystery ingredient works, it can still have a big impact. Quite literally, the most important element of a recipe, a cure, or a successful venture could be all in your head. And if so, you'd be wise to accept that there's more to this story than what you can see.

Perhaps there's a little mystery ingredient in every situation. Maybe it's sprinkled on the top of Rise & Shine Biscuit Kitchen and Cafe or swirled into the squiggly words generated by reCAPTCHA. It's the "it" factor that we ignore at our peril. But if we accept its existence, embrace the fact that there can be more to our plateaus than the data tells us, that there may be some greater force at work that we can't fully understand, we are moving toward what on paper looks like an impossible breakthrough.

6. DISTORTION MECHANISMS

Navigating Bad Data and Other Tricks of the Plateau

Or, Why Everyone Wants to Believe in Magic

You're at Newark airport. It's eleven thirty A.M.

On a glowing yellow status board the word "DELAYED" seems permanently seared next to your ten A.M. flight to Washington D.C.—mechanical difficulties. You glance one line down. The eleven A.M. flight on the same airline to the same city shows "DEPARTED." The noon flight just switched to "BOARDING."

You're angry, stranded, and left wondering: Why are they picking on me and my flight? Why not just give the ten A.M. passengers the plane that's ready and make the next group wait a bit? That might fit the rules of common sense, but when was the last time an airline—or any global industry—obeyed common sense?

Watching others depart while you are stuck in an airport lounge is a frustratingly common occurrence for the frequent traveler. But it happens for a very good reason. OK, a very obvious reason: because airlines, government agencies, and even consumers often measure and count the wrong things. We're going to call this malady "bad metrics," the first distortion technique you'll find in the circus of bad data that most of us live in every day.

Welcome to Bob and Hugh's Hall of Mirrors! It's fun on a Saturday night with a bottle of pop and your date, but the Hall of Mirrors is a nightmare to anyone trying to feel their way through a relationship, a business model, or any kind of training. You wouldn't start a diet based on a big belly you saw in a distorted mirror, would you? Most of us do something exactly that silly every day. What's worse than having no data at all? Having bad data.

As we continue with the book's mechanical section, which shows you how to build a platform for regularly breaking through the Plateau Effect, this chapter sets out the ways that our perceptive abilities let us down. The Enlightenment brought us the scientific method because smart people realized that they couldn't trust their own eyes—if they wanted truth, they had to develop a method for boiling out impurities and bias. Still, most of us ignore this wisdom and live in a hall of mirrors, a place of half-truths that lead us to various states of getting stuck. What follows are the most pernicious causes for these false truths—counting the wrong things, risk miscalculation, opportunity cost, magical thinking, measurables and unmeasurables, data idolatry, overweighing Grandma, bad norms, accidental reinforcement, and a few other tricks—and what you can do about them.

Now, back to the airport.

Counting the Wrong Things

Why is the airline picking on your ten A.M. flight? Simple. Airlines are benchmarked on their percentage of on-time arrivals and departures. So on paper, it's better to delay one flight by five hours than to delay five flights by one hour while catching up on the original delay. An 83 percent on-time rating is better than a 0 percent rating, right? That's bad metrics in action. (Other factors contribute to the way airlines handle this situation, too.)

The goal of airline scorecards was to provide some accountability and transparency to fliers, but the metrics don't quite align with traveler satisfaction. There's common sense, and then there's metrics. Falling slave to bad metrics can and does lead to disaster. The media was not kind to JetBlue when it kept some passengers in a plane on the tarmac for more than ten hours in 2007. No one cared how many other JetBlue flights were on time that day.

Bad metrics are often the cause of a false plateau—and that can be worse than a true plateau. False plateaus can convince you to stop doing something that's actually working. You want to get healthy, so you exercise and change your diet. But what if you measure "health" only by weight loss? You know what happens next. You lose seven pounds. Then weeks go by and the scale gets stuck on 195. You become disheartened. Even a spot on *The Biggest Loser* wouldn't help. You start reaching for the Twinkies and skipping the gym.

But even while the scale isn't budging, your health may still be improving. Often, the way you measure improvement is too narrow. Maybe you're building muscle. Maybe you're starting to chip away at your cholesterol. Maybe you're a little stronger than you used to be. But if all you care about is the bathroom scale, you are bound to fail, even if you are succeeding. You will stop exercising, gain the weight, re-start exercising, re-lose the weight, hit the same point, stop again, and so on. You've plateaued via the going-in-circles trap. All because you have defined success too narrowly.

Often, the most important question is this: How do you effectively measure progress toward those goals? Long-distance runners don't set out to run a sub-four-minute mile. That would be too much to handle all at once. Instead, they set out to run a fifty-eight-second quarter mile, followed by two sixty-one-second quarters, and then hope to finish with a fifty-nine-second last lap sprint.

The "splits" we use to mark progress at the quarter pole, halfway point, and so on might be even more important than the goals themselves. Why? Goals are lofty and esoteric. We live with splits—how many calories did I consume today?—every day.

Bad metrics aren't the only reason seemingly fact-based, rational decision making can go very wrong. Tell a miler that his first quarter-mile was run in sixty-four seconds—say, the coach's stopwatch is broken—and he'll fly into an ill-advised mid-race sprint that's sure to destroy his race. If you are going to make good choices, to paraphrase Mom a bit, you've got to be discerning about the data you hang out with.

We live in an age of almost endless information, but more times than not, this confuses our thought process and does more harm than good. We all know we need to set goals, and we have all heard that laser-like focus is required to reach those goals. At least, that's what the late-night infomercial folks tell us. That's true, as long as the goals aren't too narrow, too stiff, or too artificial.

Knowing that you live in a hall of mirrors should help you shift your thinking about the splits and metrics you look at every day to judge success and failure. And here's the great news: It might mean you are already doing all the right things but simply not giving yourself credit for it. The scale stayed at 195 again this week? Wonderful! The rest of your body is now catching up with your improved body mass index.

Every day, we all make decisions that deeply affect our friends, our jobs, our lovers, and our futures. One could argue that choosing to learn to make better decisions might be the most important decision you ever make. So let's continue. Next up: fun with numbers!

Risk Miscalculation

"Shark attacks in 2010 rose 25 percent!" screamed one headline. Below it was a picture of a sign posted at a tourist spot in the United States: "WARNING: Recent shark attack. Beach closed."

In other words, Sharkmageddon had hit.

At least, that's what the data said, quite clearly. But as you should know by now, numbers lie. We dug into the numbers a little and performed some additional calculations on the shark attack epidemic. Here's what we found.

There were seventy-nine attacks in 2010, up from sixty-three a year earlier. That is indeed a 25 percent jump. But you really don't care what the number of attacks was. The real question is: What are the odds that you will get chomped? Are the world's oceans really 25 percent more dangerous? We'll ignore the fact that five of the attacks were the result of two angry sharks that had a human-eating orgy during a four-day stretch. Let's recast the odds a bit.

There are about three billion people on the planet. Let's say on any given day 1 percent of them swim . . . forget it, let's say in any given *year*, 1 percent of them swim in an ocean or body of water that might have a shark. That's thirty million people. Let's say these swimmers average five swims per year. That's 150 million treks into shark-infested waters.

2009: 0.0000042 attacks per swim (63/150 million)

2010: 0.0000053 attacks per swim (79/150 million)

In other words, 99.99958 percent of swims were shark-attack-free in 2009 versus 99.99947 percent in 2010. That's not *really* a 25 percent increase in risk, is it?

Let's get this out of the way: We've all heard that the definition of insanity is doing the same thing over and over but expecting to get a different result. Still, people constantly fall into this repetitive cycle trap. So, with all apologizes to Nietzsche, simply knowing this fact clearly isn't doing anyone much good.

There are plenty of reasons that people make ineffective choices over and over again. They get bad information. They get limited information—using only a weight scale to assess health, for example. Sometimes, they poorly weigh the information—a doctor says have surgery, a neighbor says try drinking herbal tea every night for a month, and they consider both these inputs equally. And then, there's the most common problem: People react poorly to information they receive. We choose to ignore critical information that tells us we'll likely be laid off within six months or that a new competitor has improved on our product and is stealing our customers.

We call this poor risk assessment because generally people in denial are really protecting themselves from fear of the unknown. Their mistake, however, is misjudging the risk of standing still. We start with the biggest measurement mistake of all: ignoring measurements.

If the stock market collapse of 2008 proved anything, it's this: We stink at assessing risk. Not just Americans, everyone. There's no more direct, comprehensive, or scientific experiment we could hope to conduct. Most of the world made bets, consciously or unconsciously, and most of us lost. In fact, we lost 45 percent of the world's wealth; countless trillions of dollars went *poof* thanks to the magic of Wall Street accounting. That's quite a doozy.

Of course, the world is full of proof that we are terrible at risk assessment. We fear sharks but don't wear condoms—or wash our hands. We're terrified of turbulence but drive drunk. We subject grandmas to full-body frisking at the airport but let terrorists listed on watch lists get onto airplanes. We buy lottery tickets, often described as a tax on the mathematically disinclined, despite knowing the odds.

Maybe you are above all that. And maybe you feel like you could blame all those market losses on other things—a lack of information, terrible advice, even criminal behavior. Those are perfectly good explanations, but they prove our point. We incorrectly assessed the risk that criminals giving bad advice and hiding data controlled the markets. We can do better. In fact, we have to.

Risk assessment is among the most important tools that humans—indeed, all animals—need to get through life. Sitting behind the wheel of a car, you trust that an oncoming car won't careen into your lane, so you drive, even though that is a distinct, if minute, possibility. You step in the shower assuming you won't slip and hit your head. You think better of flipping the bird to the six-foot-seven football player who just cut you off in the grocery store. You walk down a crowded, well-lit street at night but not a dark alley. People make risk assessments constantly.

These primal skills, sadly, have remained relatively primal. Brain studies show that when humans encounter risks, the "reptilian" portion of our brains, as it's now called in pop psychology, takes over. This reptilian brain—really the brain stem and cerebellum—controls base functions we have in common with most of the evolutionary world—fight-or-flight responses. It was designed to optimize our ability to run away from large, hungry animals in a crisis. Sadly, when faced with decisions about things like money and investing, many people's brains believe they are being chased by a saber-toothed tiger and act accordingly. That is, they run. Metaphorically speaking.

Our reptilian brains might be useful at assessing a trip down a double-black-diamond ski slope, but we're relatively awful at assessing the risk of a mutual fund, inflation, or trusting our current place of employment. As a result, many people are overly risk-averse, not realizing how risky that is.

The reptilian brain, as you might imagine, is about as good with subtlety as a Gila monster. It can muster two thoughts: BUY and SELL. QUIT or STAY. It definitely can't come up with the advantages of dollar-cost averaging in a falling market. OK, it usually comes up with one additional thought when it comes to money: PUNT! People find a money manager, and they say, "Please, Mr. Man in a White Shirt—take care of this for me so I don't have to think about it." (To neuroscientists, the technical term for *punt* is *freeze*, but you get the idea.)

And trust us: Mr. Man in a White Shirt is happy to take the money out of your frozen hands while making sure you can't live without him for the rest of your financial life. He's going to send you long paper statements you can't really understand. Sometimes, these statements will show your pile of gold is larger, and you'll be happy. Sometimes, the pile will shrink, and your reptilian brain will yell, "SELL!" You'll call, and he will calm down the reptile within you— that's his main skill, speaking to that part of your brain. And you'll decide to BUY again. You'll make that decision over and over, which really is the definition of insanity. It's also the definition of a plateau.

Or you'll do what most Americans do and simply stop opening the monthly statements. Somewhere, someone told you (probably that Man in a White Shirt) that the best thing to do with your investments is to ignore them, to "set and forget" the money you're putting in your retirement account. Sometimes, your retirement planning can be one of those background tasks we discussed in the introduction. But usually, it's not a good idea to punt on your future like that. But again, "don't worry about it, I'll take care of it" is a secret message aimed directly at your reptilian brain. Just ignore it and everything will be fine! Can you imagine the gall of this advice? Thank God our ancestors didn't fall for this trick. Imagine if no one ever checked to see if insects were devouring the winter grain stored in the grain elevators!

Back in 2008, a majority of US adults had put their money into set-and-forget mode. Clearly, that didn't work. But neither did the next-most-common strategy: putting money under the mattress.

How do you break free from this reptilian, all-or-nothing, buy-or-sell cycle? By measuring things and listening to what the measurements tell you. You've got to move the decision out of the part of your brain that made you decide whether you should or shouldn't jump off that high wall outside your elementary school when you were eight years old.

Billion-dollar industries exist that are based on nothing other than risk assessment—chiefly, the insurance industry. We promise to only mention the word *insurance* three or four more times in this chapter, but it's a really important concept here. Those nerds you knew in high school who actually chose calculus as an elective class (over, say, drama or advanced phys. ed.) have spent their adult lives coming up with complicated mathematical formulas that have one goal in mind: predicting the future. They can't *quite* accomplish that yet, but they can tell you with great certainty the odds that you will lose your right arm in a car accident during the next forty years, or the chance that a river near your home will wash away all your personal belongings. These are not Gila monsters. They absorb data from thousands of sources and create models that literally attempt to re-create the universe so they can run elaborate tests on it. If you played poker with them, you'd lose because they'd already know every possible hand that could be dealt. To the reptilian brain, risk offers two possibilities: "I'm safe" and "I'm in danger." To an insurance actuary, the future holds thousands of possibilities. A change in odds from 12 percent to 13 percent can mean millions of dollars to them, and that's a bet they win almost every time.

Opportunity Cost

If you think about it, that makes people who work in the insurance industry pretty optimistic, no? They aren't dwelling in the past; they live almost entirely in the future. And it's the future we want to concentrate on now, the stuff you can actually change. There are dozens of things to learn from people who work in the insurance business (last time!), but for the purpose of overcoming the Plateau Effect, we will focus on a single, vexing element of risk assessment: opportunity cost. It's a simple concept: With every choice we make in life, we pick against something else. Go on vacation in Ireland, and you're not going to the Caribbean. Buy this house, and you're not buying that one. Marry that man, and you're picking against a few hundred million others. Simple idea, hard concept to internalize. No one really picks one mate as compared to hundreds of millions of others. Humans are incapable of contemplating a gazillion potential future outcomes—too many options and the regret that might follow could create a condition called "cognitive dissonance," an unnerving feeling that we avoid at all costs. So we tend to burrow ourselves into a mental tunnel and self-limit our choices. But even then, we struggle mightily.

Here's the problem: Using current technologies, it is very, very hard to predict the future. Some would say impossible. As a result, people tend to focus much more on what they have right now, and what they can see now, than on possibilities they can't see. Known trumps unknown. Door no. 1, if it's open or transparent, is often favored over the mystery behind door no. 2. In a famous test, researchers found subjects would choose a known mildly uncomfortable outcome over an unknown outcome—one that could be either desirable or uncomfortable—nearly every time.

What we have here is a failure of imagination.

Nothing keeps people unhappy, stuck, underemployed, frustrated, and struggling like the failure to imagine other potential outcomes—or, more directly, the failure to see the opportunity cost of standing still. That might be the very definition of a plateau.

Opportunity cost is among the first concepts taught to budding economists during their freshman year. These future venture capitalists are being trained to pick carefully how they will invest $5 million in seed money when they have to pick only three of fifty potential projects. But, sadly, opportunity cost is among the last lessons that humans generally learn. So they keep dating their unsuitable mates, keep investing in their miserable portfolios, and keep working for their incorrigible bosses, not realizing the opportunity cost of doing so.

Of course, it's very hard to calculate opportunity costs; it's nearly impossible to measure things that haven't happened yet, or will never happen. (Here's a favorite sci-fi book idea. Someone invents a supercomputer so smart that it allows you to simulate all the billions and billions of permutations your life might have, the way supercomputers now run weather test models. It'd sure be spooky to see all those simulations and be able to pick the one that looks best. And, if weather forecasts are any indication, we feel pretty confident something unexpected would happen anyway.)

Faced with the unknown, the common response from the reptilian brain is straightforward—RUN or FIGHT! But the third possible response is perhaps even more common—FREEZE! Freezing is a bad idea if you are a deer being chased by a lion, and it's a bad idea if you're in a dead-end job, too.

Even if you move deeper into the more emotional side of your brain, the limbic brain, you aren't likely to find much help there. In fact, things get worse. When facing the reality of breaking up with a lover, most people can only imagine the future of singlehood surrounded by cats. Breakups hurt in a primal way, and are often accompanied by fight-or-flight impulses. Plus, they fill most people with a sense of dread for the future, a completely debilitating emotion reptiles don't experience. Logically, your friends will tell you, you'll find someone else. But in times of extreme stress, like a breakup or a reaction to a drastic market downturn, the reptilian and limbic brains have no trouble shouting down the logical neocortex. Jilted lovers just can't imagine that the next man or woman may very well be a far more suitable partner. Only the most optimistic among us can leave a job, a school, or a friendship feeling confident that the loss means the future holds far better things. Yet that is indeed nearly always true. You can measure that simply by counting the number of times someone around you says something like "Thank goodness she broke up with me" or "What a blessing in disguise that I was laid off."

Making matters worse, another oft-misunderstood economics principal is conspiring against people in this circumstance: the problem of sunk costs. You're heard this before but probably didn't realize you were dealing with sunk costs. You buy a stock at thirty dollars. It falls to twenty. You curse and swear. Then, you tell yourself you'll wait until it hits thirty again, and get rid of the godforsaken company. And slowly, the stock erodes your wealth even more—19, 18, 17, 13.5. . . . The market, sadly, doesn't care what you paid for the stock. It only cares what other people are paying for it at the moment you want to sell. When you are holding the stock formerly known as "thirty dollars" that is now known as "twenty dollars," your thirty dollars is a sunk cost. It's gone. It should have no bearing on your decision going forward. This is nearly impossible for mere mortals because of a related concept known as "anchoring."

You were the victim of anchoring the last time you were cheated by a car dealer when buying a car. (Think you're above being cheated? Then you're even worse off than most of us.) Anchoring is simple. The first number people hear when conducting a transaction forms a sort of calibration that's hard to get rid of. The car dealer says the car you want to buy is priced at $20,000, which makes you feel like you got a good deal when you pay $17,000, even if, without the anchor price, you wouldn't have believed the car was worth even $15,000. Anchoring gives people an unconscious reference point, and it keeps many salespeople in business. So when you buy a stock at thirty, you brain anchors the price there, making it very, very hard for you to sell at twenty.

This hold-on-till-it-recovers mentality severely exacerbated the great housing recession of 2008 to 2010 because many home sellers were stuck in denial over the sale price of their homes. You heard them. They were your neighbors. Maybe they were you. "But the Smiths' house sold for $425,000 two years ago. Ours has *got* to be worth at least $400,000. We need that to pay off the $350,000 mortgage!"

Home sellers, uniquely unqualified to be setting the price of homes, often cost themselves tens of thousands by holding out for mythical buyers based on out-of-date information—their anchor price, their sunk cost. A home is worth exactly what someone else will pay for it and nothing else. Two-year-old prices don't matter. And the market certainly couldn't care less about your mortgage payoff price.

Sunk costs are all about living in the past. The price you paid for a hundred shares of Corporation X at $30—$3,000—is sunk. The $350,000 you borrowed to buy that home is sunk. Each transaction forward is independent of those prior figures.

Of course, human beings rarely see things that way.

"I've been in this job for twenty years—that has to count for something!" Unless it helps grow your pension, it counts for nothing.

Neither does holding on to the mutual fund, sticking with that average music teacher, or dumping money into that failing business. Still, when you've already invested a lot in something, human nature seems to insist that you hold on until you get back at least what you've put in. It's nonsensical, but it's human. So people are bad at seeing the future and give too much credibility to the past. When posed with a question of risk, people usually fall back on their most base—their most reptilian—natures, and ignore the data that's presented to them. Instead of measuring the real risk—the risk of change versus the risk of standing still—they tend to see only half the story. Learning to automatically calculate both sides of the risk story is the first step in making decisions based on the right criteria.

But even when we are open to both data and change, like the airlines trying to game on-time arrival measurements, we often outsmart ourselves. Even if you have overcome your reptilian fight-flight-freeze impulses, even if you have mastered the limbic system's tendency for dread and believe you have great skill in measuring risks, you probably fall prey to one or more of the other choice-killing, data-twisting, light-bending hall-of-mirrors distortions that follow.

Magical Thinking

The Amazing Randi served as Johnny Carson's "house" magician in the 1970s and 1980s, appearing dozens of times on *The Tonight Show*. As he did, he grew increasingly frustrated with what he saw as abuse of magic skills by hucksters selling useless herbal cures or psychic powers on late-night television, and he created the James Randi Educational Foundation for the study and encouragement of healthy skepticism. He has since spent most of his late life teaching people how to avoid being fooled. His perspective on the real tricks of magic is eye-opening.

"It's not about the trick, it's about the target," he says. Magicians—and hucksters—need to have one skill above all others, he believes. It's not sleight-of-hand skills. It's not endless hours of study or a velvety voice.

"It is identifying those who want to be fooled," he says.

Everyone wants to believe in magic. Magic tricks got us through those first few traumatic years—first trip to the dentist, first airline flight, first sore throat. Magic made presents appear under the Christmas tree. So, yes, we want to believe. We want to believe that when we give $5,000 to a Man in a White Shirt, he can turn it into $20,000, tax-free. We want to believe that drinking this tea will cure us of cancer, or filling out that spreadsheet will get us noticed and win us a promotion.

The problem with magical thinking is that—lo and behold—it's sometimes right. Once in a while, a $5,000 investment really does pan out. For magical thinkers, that's enough to send them into years of futility. You've heard them. "But John did this and it worked!" they say.

A classic magical thinker is always late for meetings, movies, and dates—not because he is disrespectful but because he's overly optimistic. Here's a concrete example. Say a typical trip from home to the theater takes about thirty-five minutes, door to door. But once, our naive, magical-thinking movie-goer made it in twenty-six minutes! Through some wonderful gift of the universe, every traffic light was green, the usual road congestion had melted away, and there was a parking spot right by the door. For a magical thinker, that one positive experience provides evidence and a permanent marker for life about how much time he should leave for a trip to the movies—in this case, twenty-six minutes. Forevermore, he's panicked at every traffic light, befuddled by the delays that seem to attack him personally. He's usually about ten minutes late, for years, irritating friends and family until they stop inviting him. But every time, he expects to re-create that one magic moment, the one twenty-six-minute trip.

Magical thinking is big trouble. It leads people to sign bad mortgages or marry the wrong person, and it tricks companies into spending years headed in the wrong direction.

There is really only one cure for magical thinking: hard data. For that, we're going to turn to America's pastime.

Measurables and Unmeasurables

Brian Doyle was the brother of a relatively famous infielder for the Boston Red Sox, Denny Doyle. Brian was basically a career minor leaguer, struggling to follow in his brother's footsteps but not getting very far, when something suddenly happened during the crazy summer of 1978. As the New York Yankees faded deeper and deeper out of the pennant race—a staggering fourteen games back in mid-July—injuries ravaged the team. Still, as the dog days of August approached, the leading Red Sox faded, and the Yanks reeled them in. Brian was called up in September to provide backup defense, but in late September, Yankees All-Star second baseman Willie Randolph suffered a leg injury that ended his season. After five long years toiling in the minors, and only one year removed from spending his off-season selling hats at the Golden Farley haberdashery in Bowling Green, Kentucky, Brian found himself in the middle of the most intense rivalry in sports—playing against his brother. Brian would get only ten hits during thirty-nine games down the stretch. But miraculously, the Yankees caught the fading Red Sox, made the playoffs, and charged into the World Series. Then, the real miracle occurred. Brian hit .438 for the series, leading the Yankees in hitting—in sixteen at-bats, he had seven hits, nearly his total for the season. He tied the crucial Game 6 with his first-ever extra-base hit. He nearly won World Series

MVP. At the ticker tape parade in NYC, Doyle said he felt like Cinderella, and no one argued with him.

If you were a general manager in the winter of 1979, you might have been inclined to think Brian Doyle was a diamond in the rough, perhaps even a magical find who deserved a multimillion-dollar contract. If you had given him that contract, you'd probably have gotten fired within two years.

Brian soon joined the long list of flash-in-the-pan baseball sensations. In 1979, Brian mustered only four hits in twenty games; in 1981, he was shipped to Oakland, managed only five hits that year, and retired. If you were a GM and you signed a bunch of Brian Doyles, you would very likely have a very poor team, but one with a bunch of random magical moments somewhere in their past. You'd probably be the kind of person who is stuck chasing after last year's one-hit wonder, and last year's overperforming mutual fund, too.

Sometimes, everything just breaks right. Sometimes, baseball teams have a collection of players who have "career years," and they overachieve. But that never lasts. Athletes "regress to the mean." Coldhearted general managers in baseball today try not to be swayed by impressive playoff runs, or by the infamous "hot September" that seems to grace many free agents. They want large swaths of time to measure players. They want someone who's proven he can hit in May, June, July, and August. They want, as the saying goes, a player with proven years' worth of success on the back of his baseball card. They don't want magic. They want data. The critical question is: What data?

Michael Lewis, author of *Moneyball* and a host of other best sellers, has made an entire career out of telling general managers and American CEOs precisely what data matters . . . and perhaps, more to the point, how to find hidden value by using unusual data to outsmart competitors. For years, statistic-obsessed managers and owners judged hitters mainly on batting average, which is generated through a crazy, old-fashioned formula that actually penalizes hitters who make their way on base by walking. In a classic case of measuring the wrong things, most teams preferred a hitter who reached base 3.5 times per 10 at bats to one who reached base 4 times per 10 because of a bias against a hitter who got on base from a walk rather than a hit. That bias might make a little bit of sense at first glance, but in fact, when it comes to winning games, it makes no sense at all.

The Oakland A's, operating on the tightest of baseball budgets, were desperate to find and exploit undervalued assets, and with the aid of a new generation of data jockeys, GM Billy Beane settled on "on-base percentage," which truly says "a walk is as good as a hit." Beane's discount team routinely clogged the bases with runners and overachieved because he had a secret advantage.

Lewis had a great appreciation for Beane's strategy because he worked as a bond trader when he graduated from college. As a Wall Street outsider—his college major was art history—Lewis immediately saw the folly of bond trading, which has little, if anything, to do with the actual value of bonds and everything to do with finding pockets of overpriced or underpriced assets only a few moments before the rest of the Wall Street mob found them. This hidden-treasure model works in every industry. Note that it's not enough to simply generate spreadsheets and find the nation's top salesman or the player with the highest on-base percentage. After all, everyone knows they are valuable. The key to taking a real step beyond magical thinking is to look for true diamonds in the rough, such as talent in your company that may have been overlooked by previous managers or through inflexible review processes.

Can you create some advanced metrics at your company that would help flush out hidden treasures? Can you find ways to make room for introverts in decision making? How about random cold calls to clients asking for satisfaction ratings—not the squeaky wheels but everyone else? How about so-called 360 reviews, which give co-workers a chance to comment on one another and nearly always identify which employees people most enjoy working with?

Of course, good data is key in all these analyses. Not surprisingly, the discount-rack success of the Oakland A's led to immediate imitation around the league. Once other GMs learned of the value of on-base percentage, those hitters were no longer undervalued, and the on-base percentage discount rack was emptied. So scouts had to start looking for even more subtle traits. Defensive metrics were created, all with the ultimate goal of indicating how many runs a player saved or cost a team. Pitchers were no longer judged in win-loss records because that rough data point allowed too many externalities (it un-fairly penalized pitchers whose bull pens blew games, for example). Heat maps were invented that show inch by inch the location of pitch-es that batters are most likely to hit, and spray charts map precisely where balls put in play are most likely to land. Baseball stadiums are built to take advantage of this information now. The hunger for base-ball data became so extreme that suddenly, almost everything about players was measured. Almost everything.

On-base percentage was just a fleeting gimmick for the Oakland A's; the real revolution begun by Billy Beane was to tear down the good old boys' network in baseball. Before the *Moneyball* era, players were judged by a tiny cabal of scouts who used little but their consid-erable guts to make their decisions. They were convinced that players needed a "baseball body," and that every pitcher needed a ninety-five-mile-per-hour fastball. A fifteen-year-old high school player with a 12-0 record and pinpoint control would often be ignored if he didn't also possess a lightning-fast heater. The good old boys, as they often are, were wrong. But you couldn't just tell them; you needed proof. The Oakland A's provided that proof. Think of magical thinking as the good old boys' network stuck in your brain. Your guts get in the way of you reaching the next level. Sometimes, the only way for your brain to win a fight against your guts is to overwhelm it with data, like Billy Beane overwhelmed major league baseball. Good data is often the best tool for that.

But, as is the *Getting Unstuck* way, we're going to tell you that measurement also has its limitations. Those who are slaves to data ultimately fail, because contrary to popular belief, you can't measure affairs of the heart. Back to baseball for one more minute: Baseball nerds said for years that Derek Jeter was a simply terrible shortstop, something that just didn't pass the eyeball test. He made fewer errors than most, and always seemed to make an amazing play at some crucial time. In fact, it was Jeter's historic, game-saving "flip" play, in which he instinctively strayed far away from his normal position to throw out a runner at home to preserve a razor-thin 1–0 margin, that cost Oakland a series against the Yanks in 2001 and signaled the beginning of the end for Billy Beane's successful *Moneyball* run. Data can only take you so far. You gotta have heart, too.

Data Idolatry

The use of data to break through plateaus might be seen as a continuum. If you've used no data, you should start immediately. If you've adopted data, you should seriously question its accuracy. But even if you believe your metrics are sound and true, yet another trap lies ahead: data idolatry.

We live in a time when there is incredible bias toward data. Companies create goals for employees and force them to say that they are "35 percent complete" halfway through the year, which usually indicates no progress has been made. Cost cutters measure the price of office space per square foot and ignore the effects of longer commutes on performance that result from consolidating offices. Put simply, for many firms, if you can't measure it, it doesn't exist. That's *Moneyball* taken too far. Sales managers have known for years that the occasional free football ticket or pricey steak dinner is key to closing big sales. But which steak dinner got the signature on the check? No one knows. But everyone knows that if there's no steak dinner, there's no sale. How do you measure good will? Trust? Loyalty? These qualities are the backbone of any successful venture, but they have taken a severe hit during a time when many seem to hold measurement above all else. This is foolish, especially when data itself is often the problem. As you've no doubt heard many times, there's lies, damn lies, and then there's statistics.

What matters most, your best-selling product during the past month or your best-selling product during the past year? Who really has the most-watched show on television, the program with the most family sets turned on, the show with the most adults age twenty-five to fifty-four, or the show whose viewers have the highest per capita income? It all depends on what story you are trying to tell. Data can go very bad, very quickly if you don't watch it carefully. And in the hands of manipulative people, it can be used for pure evil.

One data crisis arises from something called conformance metrics, which simply means that companies tend to measure the exact same things that other companies measure because that is the only thing their tools are built to do. It's a bit like a game of copycat and a bit like anchoring. For years, websites published the number of "hits" they received, some bragging they'd been "hit" a billion times in a month. Ultimately, advertisers soured on this measurement because it had many flaws, like this one: Hits could represent the same person refreshing the same page over and over again. Next, unique visitors became the standard, with the thought that advertisers really wanted to get their material in front of as many people as possible. So all sites started bragging about visitors and doing all they could to amass as many visitors as possible. "But wait!" advertisers said soon. "Throwing ads at random millions isn't really that effective. We don't care how many millions of readers you have. We care how many people looking at your site are geared up and ready to buy our product. We want to target only those people." And so the cycle continues.

Meanwhile, even good data isn't always persuasive. While reading illiteracy is seen as a national scandal, worthy of the creation of large nonprofit foundations, an estimated fifty million US adults can't do something as simple as calculate a tip after getting a lunch bill. That's one reason data doesn't make its way into the workforce more; when people are afraid of something, they build false gods. When people don't understand numbers, they ignore them. "Just forget all the figures on this mortgage disclosure document," the mortgage broker said over and over. "Just concentrate on that first month's payment. That's all you have to worry about." That ended badly.

Take a workforce that's afraid of numbers and try to get them to use data to find undervalued assets, and you're likely to get the same response, something therapists have taken to calling "flooding." When hit with too much information, people's brains turn off. Then, they can be talked into almost anything, just to escape a stressful situation. Flood your employees with too much data at your own risk: You will create a high priest class of manipulative people who act like they know everything but really know just a tiny bit more than their innumerate counterparts. Some psychologists call this phenomenon "downshifting." When stressed, some people downshift from thoughtful, neocortex decision making to emotion-based impulsive choices. However you look at it, the result will be the same: You'll follow the bad data as it drives you and your business off a cliff.

Overweighting Grandma

Naturally, executives have this problem, too—many of them are equally bad at math and can also be persuaded by the right clever pie chart. Worse still, executives have an outsized voice inside virtually all companies—their opinions often trump the opinions of thousands of employees—which puts them in prime position to really screw up, or engage in something we call "overweighting Grandma."

There's an expression in journalism that rears its ugly head once in a while: "News is what happens to editors on the way to work." Should the editor drive through an annoying construction zone on his block in the morning, he'll march right to the transportation reporter and demand a piece about widespread problems created lately by excessive detours. Should he see a dog running loose around the corner, he'll demand a piece about enforcement of dog leash laws. There might be only one unleashed dog in all of Any Town, USA, but if the editor sees him, it's a trend, and it's worthy of a front-page story.

You know this happens in every business. The CEO goes to Thanksgiving dinner, and Grandma says at one point, "Sonny, I think that pink looks awful on your website," and by Monday evening, every designer in the company is working all night to remove all pink from the site.

We're not just picking on Grandma. Plenty of tests have shown that people are bad at weighting information correctly. It's often a problem of time, something behaviorists call "recency." You might read a three-hundred-page report on the benefits of integrating your company with Facebook, and prepare a memo to your troops mandating Facebook features. But if you hear someone complain about Facebook privacy on the Starbucks line right before you distribute the memo, odds are you'll cancel the meeting. The most recent input you receive often outweighs weeks and weeks of study.

Recency has taken on a powerful new place in bad decision making, as technology has made recency a fact of everyday life. As we discussed earlier, our brains are wired to notice change, a tendency that our evolutionary ancestors probably developed to help them spot mortal danger. An arriving e-mail that pops on top of your computer is almost irresistible, as is a new Facebook post or tweet. While the distraction this causes is one obvious and severe problem, the recency impact of such interruptions probably sneaks up on you. If you receive a tweet right before you enter a meeting about sagging sales, that could actually trump the hard data from the sales team presentation you heard this morning showing the bright side.

A similar bad habit, overgeneralizing, sees subjects take a piece of local information and apply it too generally to the world at large. So our editor above sees one loose dog and assumes canines are overrunning the town. Overgeneralizing is most obvious in the field of shark attacks. Ask anyone on a beach whether there's been an attack recently; they'll tell you shark attacks are on the rise (well, they're up 25 percent, right?). The problem here isn't ignoring data, it's simply seeing data out of context—which can be worse than having no data at all. If there was a shark attack yesterday, you could make the case that the beach is averaging one attack per day . . . but only if you haven't read *Getting Unstuck*. Picking an artificial start and end time can really screw with your data, but it's just a very simple form of overgeneralizing, or what mathematicians call erroneous extrapolation. The only thing it will really succeed in extrapolating is your plateau.

Bad Norms

Here's a quick experiment. Think of the five people you spend the most time with each week. How can we ask this politely . . . ? Are they, ahem, a bit larger than they should be? Have any of them gained weight recently? Pardon our brashness; we're just trying to help. According to a study conducted by two researchers at Harvard University, if your friends are getting larger, you are at significant risk of gaining weight, too. Researchers identified pairs of friends, picked out people who became obese during the study, and then had their friends step on a scale. Surprise: Friends of recently obese people are 171 percent more likely to become obese than others.

Perhaps at this point, something your parents may have said to you about choosing your friends wisely pops into your head, but that doesn't begin to describe the concept of conformity. Most people drift toward what they consider normal. This natural tendency can hold us back when "normal" falls short of our goals and potential. The pull of normal can keep us in an orbit of mediocrity and lead to a plateau. Psychologists call this behavior conformity—it's the act of adapting to fit your circumstances.

But what is normal? Normal to someone with a job in finance in New York is working fourteen-hour days, riding subways, and making several hundreds of thousands of dollars a year. Normal to a school teacher is having the summers off. Normal is defined by your local environment, not by averages calculated across the entire country or the world. *Local norms* can have a profound effect on the choices we make.

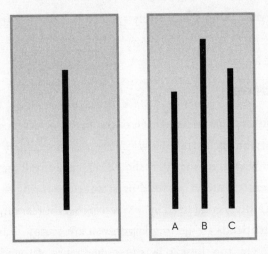

To understand the impact of local norms and conformity, take a look at the line on the left of the image above. Now take a look at the three lines to the right of it. Which one is the same length as the line in the first picture: A, B, or C? It's pretty obvious the right answer is C. But what if we gave you a bit more information before you made your choice?

In a landmark experiment by psychologist Solomon Asch, subjects were placed in a room with five to seven other people who were in on the experiment. We'll refer to these folks as "confederates." The confederates were told to answer in a particular way, so only the research subject had the free will to choose. Researchers would present a line comparison similar to the one above. The confederates were told what to answer before each trial. The researcher would go around the room, allowing each person to give his or her answer out loud. The subject of the experiment would always answer last or second to last so that he could hear the other responses before making his choice. In the first and second trials, confederates were instructed beforehand to give the correct answer, thereby building the subject's confidence in the group. On the third trial, confederates were instructed to all give the same wrong answer. There were eighteen trials in all, and confederates colluded to give the wrong answer in twelve of them.

The results were shocking. Research subjects began to conform to the "incorrect" answers given by the rest of the group. In fact, 75 percent of "real" subjects were cajoled, deluded, or "normalized" into giving the obviously wrong answer at least once. They conformed to the opinion of the crowd. To put these results in perspective, in a control group—where there was no conspiracy to influence choice and no confederates—only 3 percent of subjects ever gave an incorrect answer. Asch's results have been reproduced in many other settings with the same conclusion: Most people conform to those around them. We seek normal even if normal is wrong.

The desire for things to stay "normal" is rooted in biology. The human body will go to great lengths to remain stable and resist change; the medical community calls that phenomenon homeostasis. That's why we sweat when it's hot out; our bodies are hard at work trying to maintain an internal temperature of 98.6 degrees. When it's cold, we shiver to generate heat in our muscles for the same reason. But it's easy to see how homeostasis, your body's search for norms, can work against progress. For example, if you're overweight, the path to a better life is exercise, but the body tries to resist—you are moving in opposition to homeostasis.

It is important to realize our pull toward the normal, in our bodies and our lives. Conformity helps us blend. It also prevents us from achieving our best. Conformity has a big impact on our lives—personally and professionally.

Asch's experiment showed that a group of conspirators can induce someone to make a bad decision. This desire to conform leads people to bad decisions every day. You might know this as peer pressure, but there's a particularly insidious form of that pressure called "groupthink," where members of a group mold their opinions around the consensus of the group. Groupthink limits the exploration of ideas. The group becomes insular, closed, and resistant to viable new ideas.

Even families are hit by groupthink. Someone gets the idea that Grandma really likes snow globes and starts giving her one as a gift every Christmas. Other grandkids pile in. Years go by, and Grandma ends up with a closet full of the spooky things before someone finds out she secretly hated them all along.

On Christmas morning, groupthink can be funny. At your business, it can be fatal. Think back to the dot-com bubble, when everyone seemed to believe that normal rules of industry—that companies must earn a profit—had been suspended. If you didn't want in on the latest IPO, you were a fool. If you didn't take a low-paying, high-stock-option job with a start-up, you were missing out. Or what about the housing bubble? Back in 2005, you were crazy if you rented—at least, that's what all your friends said.

But it doesn't have to be that way. Understanding the pressures of groupthink can help you break free from them, or even use them to your advantage. There are encouraging results from the field of psychology that show we can pick our own norms by selecting the people we benchmark ourselves against. Perhaps one group of friends is your norm for physical fitness; perhaps another is your norm for career success. If you are selective in the people you associate with, the natural pull toward normal is working in your favor. Instead of keeping you contained and causing a plateau of conformity, defining a new norm can be a magnetic force pulling you toward a breakthrough. You have choices about where you spend your time, the relationships you invest in, and the interactions you have. If you direct those interactions and establish positive local norms, you can achieve greatness through the natural pull of homeostasis.

Accidental Reinforcement

That brings us to one of our favorite obstacles to corporate bliss: the random, early success. Nothing entrenches a company, or any adventure, deep in a plateau quite like beginner's luck. It's the star of bad decision making—a little bit magical thinking, a little bit denial, a little bit recency, and a whole lot of stuck.

Imagine you've put a rat in a maze. If the rat solves the maze, he gets a piece of food dispensed from above. The idea here is to teach the rat to solve the maze as quickly as possible. But let's say you work in a lab that's been particularly hard-hit by funding cutbacks, and your rat maze hasn't been updated since the 1960s. It's been acting up lately, but you have a test to run, so you drop the critter into the maze. He's skittish, and so the first thing he does is panic and bang into a maze wall. Your aging trap shakes, and your food dispenser erroneously delivers a food pellet right where the rat is now seeing stars.

What happens next? The rat jealously scoops up the crumb, devours it with satisfaction, and then starts banging his head into the wall, expecting more food. You try explaining, cajoling, begging, even picking the rat up and putting him at the end of the maze, where more food awaits. No matter. He learned quickly that banging walls equals food, and he's going to keep on trying that, again and again. This is the torture called accidental reinforcement.

If reinforcement—say, giving your dog a treat for sitting nicely— is the best teaching tool, accidental reinforcement is teaching's evil twin. Need proof? If you accidentally drop a piece of adult food off the dining table, how long does it take the dog to learn to hang out under the table while you eat? And how long does it take for the dog to unlearn this habit?

Unlearning something is a heck of a lot harder than learning something. That's why accidental reinforcement is learning's dark side. If you've ever had to teach a distracted group of adults how to fill out a form, you know the feeling that comes when you misspeak, and all twenty-three people ask you separately why you changed your mind about whether to include your middle initial in the box that says "first name." You feel like you're trying to get a litter's worth of puppies back into their box after you've accidentally tipped it over. But it's much worse than that.

As any sociologist will tell you, accidental reinforcement triggers superstitious behavior. We know, there was that one time when you sat in your favorite chair with your Dallas Cowboys sweatshirt inside out and Tony Romo threw a game-winning touchdown pass, but how many times has Romo—and your sweatshirt, and your Cowboys—disappointed you since? Fans of all professional sports teams are regularly seduced by young athletes who tear up the league early on but ultimately turn out to be flashes in the pan—which leads to a particularly cruel kind of magical thinking. ("But he was so good during that September call-up last year—he hit seven home runs!") Gambling pit bosses have known this trick for years. Let the novice win a hand of blackjack early on, and he will lose another ten hands before giving up, doubling or tripling his losses in the meantime. At some point in history, a sick person recovered after he or she was bled with leeches. Countless thousands had to die before we unlearned that strategy. How many places in your life are you bleeding from leeches?

Sometimes, getting an early taste of success can be your worst enemy. People rarely attribute success to good fortune (though strangely they usually blame failure on it). So the young executive tries something radical, like bringing in consultants who divide workers into personality groups, and sales rise 40 percent. But what if the increase is only casually connected or coincidental? No matter.

Years go by, and with every sales slump, a new set of personality consultants are brought in. How long does it take your company to stop banging its head against a wall, expecting food to arrive from above? What we have here is an overweighted voice who just can't imagine he's wrong. His firm is spinning in circles; he is lost in the Hall of Mirrors with no hope of finding the door. The Plateau Effect is in full force.

While there's nothing quite like accidental reinforcement to confuse a situation, a group, even an entire company, the Hall of Mirrors has an incredible array of deceptions that can cause all manner of distortions in your life. The flattening forces and mechanical factors that cause plateaus are everywhere, all around you, once you start to look for them. Identifying these nemeses is one thing; overcoming them, transcending them, is quite another.

We turn to that heady task now. The forces and mental structures we have described so far need to be understood for you to become adept at breaking through the Plateau Effect—but that understanding is useless without the personal execution we detail in the next part of the book.

If you're not paying attention, you might miss it.

PART THREE
THE
ACHIEVEMENT

Peak Behaviors

7. ATTENTION

The First Action

Or, Do One Thing at a Time and Listen

It is a hellish scene.

The slow, perilous drift across the dashed lines from one highway lane into another. The too-fast jerk back across the road. The sloppy turn, where the driver begins to bank too late and then jerks the wheel too quickly. We've all seen something like this and wondered: What the heck is going on in the driver's seat?

One morning not too long ago, Bob witnessed a particularly dramatic version of this scenario. A small SUV was right in front of him, swerving back and forth in the center lane. It looked like a deadly crash was imminent.

The car was drifting right, but an eighteen-wheeler had just passed Bob and was headed for the open lane next to the drifting car, readying to attempt a risky pass on the right. As the cab of the truck reached the car, its wheels slid over the dotted line. . . . three feet, two feet, one foot . . . seemingly mere inches away from the enormous wheels of the truck's cab.

Then, *swing*! The car lurched back to the center. Whew.

But as quickly as it did, it drifted back to the right again, this time toward the back of the truck! Center line, three feet, two feet, one foot, *swing*!

The truck sped up and passed. But Bob kept watching the erratic driving from behind out of a sense of self-preservation, and now realized that he had slowed down dangerously to keep a safe distance. He had to pass the car and planned to waste no time on the way by. He'd seen this behavior before—a drunk driver, drifting to the side the way a drunk might lean while walking down a sidewalk.

But this was eleven A.M., a very strange time for drunk driving.

So he decided to take his chances in the left lane, thinking the car would continue to slide right, and he gunned his Jeep to pass. On the way by, he stole a glance.

What he saw made him sick. The driver was a middle-aged woman with a smartphone on top of her steering wheel, typing what seemed like a novel.

Our world is in a great transition. A thousand years ago, brains were wired to recall entire thousand-line poems from memory. Sages sat around campfires and recited Homer's *Odyssey*. Then Gutenberg came along, and suddenly, our ability to spin tales that required repeating hours-long dialogues was all but gone. Memorization became unnecessary as books could tell stories now. This brain skill was replaced, however, by a newfound and powerful ability to focus for long stretches of time in solitary mental confinement, and to follow long, linear arguments. It's no mistake that thoughtful concepts like democracy spread through the masses as man's ability to think matured.

Today, our brains are being rewired again, in a way that is every bit as dramatic as the post-Gutenberg shift from memorization to solitude. Images from pictures and television have largely replaced reading as the main doorway into the brain—indeed, children spend nearly eight hours per day watching moving screens of one kind or another. Images are obviously more emotionally evocative, and result in more impulsive judgments, than reading. The consequences for our level of political discourse are equally obvious. But more to our point, our brains are losing the ability to sit in silent contemplation and follow a long, deliberative process. This skill has been replaced by a lie: multitasking.

In 1987, Microsoft and IBM introduced the first multitasking personal computer software. Commercials from that time seem quaint now, but they did stick. Wasn't it amazing? You could print a long document while still typing another one!

Soon after, man sought the ability to multitask the way he initially sought fire. In fact, as we saw at the beginning of the chapter, people are literally risking death in their quest to multitask. What e-mail is worth a close encounter with an eighteen-wheeler?

Multitasking, however, is a false god. It makes promises, and has consequences, that are akin to drug addiction.

Psychologist Susan Weinschenk talks about the random reinforcement that comes with the arrival of an e-mail or a text message—Is it a note from your new lover? Your boss saying you're fired?—and the dopamine the interruption releases into the brain. It's not unlike a swig of beer or a hit of marijuana. The effects start small, but frequent users know it's nearly impossible to ignore the beep of a text message while driving. It's only human: You're in what Weinschenk calls a dopamine-induced loop. You look at the phone, and maybe you even type a response . . . even if that means careening toward a tractor-trailer. That text means that much to you.

Plenty of studies make this technology-addiction connection, but here's a disturbing one: The Institute of Psychiatry at the University of London published a study on infomania that found checking your e-mail while performing another creative task decreases your IQ in the moment ten points. That's the equivalent of not sleeping for thirty-six hours—or double the impact of smoking marijuana.

Technology is making us dumb and reckless. Unable to focus our limited powers of attention on what's important, we get stuck in a plateau made of our own distractions.

The big lie, of course, is the ability to multitask. We are not IBM computers; we can't really parallel process most tasks. Smart people like Lord Chesterfield knew this and rejected this notion, even before the American Revolution. But we didn't listen.

Instead, today our brains switch from one task to another, to another, and back again. There is a cost, though. If you have four ten-minute tasks and you try to do them all at once, it will likely take you at least an hour to complete them all. In fact, many studies show that if you attempt simultaneous work on four projects, you'll probably only finish two of them.

Psychologists call this cost "context switching." When you go from writing a memo about a new advertising campaign to filling out an expense report and back again, you can't just dive right back into the project. It takes time to get your head about the ad campaign again. Where was I? What had I just said?

Jordan Grafman of the National Institute of Neurological Disorders and Stroke says multitasking is actually a misnomer. Instead, he calls it "rapid toggling" between tasks.

Rapid toggling is very expensive. One study showed today's office worker gets only eleven continuous minutes on a project before interruption. But much worse than that, it takes twenty-five minutes for them to return to the original project after interruption! You see, there's always another e-mail to read or a score to check. And often, we get a spare five seconds or so while we wait for a new spreadsheet to open or a friend to respond to an instant message. Many people believe that the solution to this problem is simple: start an e-mail while waiting. They just can't resist. After all, what's the harm? It can't be stated any plainer than this: Most of us cannot actually multitask.

In fact, most self-identified multitaskers are dangerously delusional, suggests another study conducted by Stanford University in 2009. In a series of cognitive tests administered under rigid conditions, multitaskers repeatedly fared *worse* than their counterparts. In one test, subjects were shown both letters and numbers, then given varying instructions—sometimes to decide if the numbers were odd or even, sometimes if the letters were consonants or vowels. Multitaskers often failed because they couldn't focus on the task at hand— the number seekers were distracted by the letters, and vice versa.

"They couldn't help thinking about the task they weren't doing," researcher Eyal Ophir told the Stanford University news. "The high multitaskers are always drawing from all the information in front of them. They can't keep things separate in their minds."

Another researcher, Clifford Nass, was more blunt.

"They are suckers for irrelevancy," he said. "Everything distracts them."

Another study offers even bleaker results. It found that following an interruption, such as an e-mail or phone call, participants get so distracted that they simply move on to something else—40 percent of the time! Perhaps not coincidentally, they also waste about 40 percent of their time.

And in the largest study of this phenomenon to date, a company named Basex found that its employees lose 2.1 hours per day to interruptions. That means the company is wasting 20 percent of its workforce. It pegged the cost of interruptions to the US economy at a stunning $588 billion annually, assuming an average employee cost of twenty-one dollars an hour.

But that cost only measures time completely *lost* to distraction. As we all know, distraction carries with it a more subtle penalty—doing less than your best work, missing out on the emotional content of your spouse's complaints about housework because you have one eye on the television, or missing the disgruntled sighs of customers as your service business slowly loses its edge. Distraction and interruption are the enemy of focus and concentration, and they attack with the force of addictive drugs, billions of dollars in new technology, biological rewiring of your brain, and seemingly inexhaustible resources—your cell phone can always be recharged, even when you can't. It's no secret that distraction is the enemy of every successful venture.

Before we go on, we'd like to fine-tune the definition of multitasking a little bit. People do two things at once all the time, of course. Any parent who's read to one child while putting pj's on another can attest to that. Proficient musicians bang on a kick drum while tapping a snare in different rhythm. Cooks sauté mushrooms while boiling pasta. Even Hugh has been known to walk and chew gum at the same time (Yes! Bob's jab got through editing). There is something in common with all these efforts, however: automaticity. When people do two or three things at once, all but one task must involve a level of proficiency so advanced that it can be done thoughtlessly, as if on autopilot. As all parents (and teachers) know, this is a life-or-death skill. All drivers know this, too. You can't (or shouldn't) drive while distracted by anything in the car, but of course, you often do. You talk to passengers, you listen to music, and you might even have to glance down to change the radio station. When you are driving along an empty highway, on your brain's version of autopilot, you can do all these things at the same time. But as you pull into a big, unfamiliar city, with lots of traffic and frequent lane-changing, you need to focus a lot more on driving. Have you ever turned the volume on the radio down in order to focus better on driving when traffic gets a little hairy? If you haven't, you should try it. You'll concentrate better. Because in truth, you can really only focus on one thing at a time, despite the false god of "efficiency" that is promised by gadget marketers.

The confusion about this critical topic starts at such a young age.

Ralph Nichols, a professor of rhetoric at the University of Minnesota, had a haunting feeling: His students weren't listening. So he did what any good researcher would do: He studied students' listening skills.

It was a simple test. With the help of school teachers in Minnesota, he had teachers stop what they were doing in midclass and ask kids to describe what the teachers were talking about.

You might imagine that wiggly, distracted first-graders had the toughest time with the test. That's precisely why you need to read on. Yes, turn off the TV and read on.

Surprisingly, 90 percent of first- and second-graders gave the right answer. But as kids got older, results plummeted. By junior high, only 44 percent answered correctly; about one in four high school kids succeeded. Clearly, they had better things to think about.

The truth is, the older people get, the more their listening comprehension sinks. Making matters worse, studies show that people wildly overestimate how good they are at listening. Now, do I have your attention?

Nichols, who died at age ninety-six in 2006 and is now considered the father of listening research, describes his study in his book, *Are You Listening?* If you think about it, the results make sense.

Plenty of studies examine this phenomenon. While listening is the core of most of our communications—the average adult listens nearly twice as much as he or she talks—most people stink at it. Here's one typical result. Test takers were asked to sit through a ten-minute oral presentation and, later, to describe its content. Half of adults can't do it even moments after the talk, and forty-eight hours later, fully 75 percent of listeners can't recall the subject matter.

Here's the problem: The human brain has the capacity to digest as much as 400 words per minute of information. But even a speaker from New York City talks at around 125 words per minute. That means three-quarters of your brain could very well be doing something else while someone is speaking to you.

This helps explain why little children are—or can be, anyway— better listeners than adults. Their brains are less developed, so they are much more likely to be completely engrossed in a topic. Adults, with all that extra brain power, are much more easily distracted.

The risk should be obvious. You might start out with all intention of focusing on your boss, or the useless sales presentation, or your spouse's frustrating work story. But soon, you hear a squirrel in the trees outside. You notice that the woman across the room has colored her hair. You see a tile on the floor that is cracked. You are tempted by the false god of multitasking. And you are lost.

These missteps have a variety of consequences, from a missed work assignment, to nothing at all, to a night sleeping on the couch.

By now, we hope you see the problem. Your brain is hungry for information, like a golden retriever puppy is hungry to chase a tennis ball. Important information, however, rarely comes as fast as your brain can take it, just as you can never toss the ball fast enough for your puppy. At the dog park, your baby Fido won't be able to resist if someone else nearby throws a ball . . . off he bounds, chasing after whatever is moving. And your brain, thirsty for data, with a whole bunch of seemingly spare time on its hands, can't resist the ping of a text message or the temptation of looking at YouTube videos of cats.

As a dog owner, you have two choices. Keep tossing the ball faster and faster and try to keep your pet at full stimulation at all times, or train you dog to shut out distractions and focus only on you. While entire TV shows are devoted to such crucial dog grooming, there is very little to help you with brain grooming. In fact, there's very little research into the real-life consequences of distraction and poor listening skills. So we decided to try some.

We wanted to find out firsthand about listening plateaus. So in a rather playful project conducted with researcher Larry Ponemon of the Ponemon Institute, we recorded three videos—a husband and wife's spat about painting the guest room, instructions for voting, and a reading of the privacy policy for Facebook—and tested a thousand adults for listening comprehension. While the Internet-selected sample of test takers wasn't scientific, it was representative of the US adult population, with test takers spread fairly evenly across the country, across income groups, and across genders. The findings are informative. Well, dismal.

For starters, of the fifteen simple questions we asked—such as "What color will the room be painted?"—only 18 percent got them all right. The vast majority of takers got somewhere between one-third and two thirds of the questions right. And while we didn't warn the test takers that this was a listening test, the tests were administered in a fairly unrealistic environment that should have made getting the answers right a layup. These middling results were incredibly consistent across regions of the country and income groups. Lower-income earners scored a few percentage points lower, but so did upper-class folks earning more than $250,000 per year. The difference of around 5 percent should be considered slight, however. There was only one finding large enough to peg one group as better listeners than another.

Women beat the pants off of men—at least, to a statistically significant degree.

Nationwide, women answered 66 percent correct, while men

scored only 49 percent. Again, this discrepancy cut across age, income bracket, and even education.

As two men, we'd like to remind you again at this point that the test was informative but unscientific. It's important to note, however, that men aren't kidding themselves about this listening gender gap. After we administered the questions, we asked test takers what they thought of their own listening abilities: Men consistently indicated they were average or below-average listeners. At least there's some self-awareness there. But men, look at it this way: If you are missing details on half of everything that's said to you, think how easy it will be for you to improve your lot in life, to break through plateaus, simply by focusing a little more on what speakers say.

(There's more on this study in the endnotes if you are curious.)

We wanted to go even deeper into this question of listening comprehension and distraction, so we partnered with Carnegie Mellon University to develop a distraction and listening test that was designed to be painstakingly scientific. More narrow in scope, but more convincing in its results, the test conducted by professor Alessandro Acquisti and researcher Dr. Eyal Peer is remarkable, eye-opening, and hopeful. We asked a simple question: Does the mere presence of a cell phone or any other "interruptive" gadget on your body decrease your basic cognitive skills, such as comprehension?

To simulate the magnetic pull of an expected cell phone call, we had subjects sit in a lab and perform a standard cognitive skill test. Precisely 136 subjects were asked to read a short passage and answer questions about it. There were three groups of subjects. One merely completed the test. The other two were told they "might be contacted for further instructions" via instant message. During an initial test, the second and third groups were interrupted twice. Then, a second test was administered, but this time, only the second group was interrupted. The third group awaited an interruption that never came. Let's call the three groups Control, Interrupted, and On High Alert.

Remarkable finding no. 1: Both Interrupted and On High Alert groups answered correctly 20 percent less often on the first test, showing the kind of brain drain that distraction takes on our everyday tasks.

Remarkable finding no. 2: During the second test, the Control group performed equally well. But here's the twist: Both Interrupted and On High Alert improved dramatically the second time around. Interrupted improved by 14 percent, scoring almost as well as the Control group. But even more stunning, On High Alert—which was warned but not interrupted—actually improved its results by 43 percent, far outperforming even the Control test takers. This unexpected, counterintuitive finding, which will be the subject of an upcoming paper published by Carnegie Mellon, requires further research, but Peer thinks there's a simple explanation that could lead to some powerful, practical tips for working in a distracting environment. Participants learned from their experience, and their brains adapted.

"[The first test] may have caused participants to pay more attention and invest more cognitive resources in the second task," he said. "[On High Alert] recruited more cognitive resources in order to overcome the expected interruption and when that did not come, they had more resources to devote to the actual task."

In other words, warnings about, and experience with, interruptions can help people marshal more brain resources and do better, perhaps the way athletes sometimes perform better when they are angry. Interruptions, it's clear from this test, can cause a dramatic decline in ability, but they don't have to.

We all agree distractions can have devastating consequences. Napoleon was distracted by Russia. Microsoft was distracted by the

government's antitrust lawsuit. The National Safety Council estimates that 1.6 million accidents are caused annually by cell phone use
and texting while driving. And we think we'd all agree that listening
and thinking are a good thing. And yet, when it comes to distractions, we are our own worst enemy. In the summer of 2011, *Mother
Jones* magazine put a face on something all Americans have felt since
the recession began in 2008: the "Great Speedup." Companies around
the country shed off millions of workers during the depth of the
downturn, but workers with "survivor syndrome" picked up the
slack. The end result: Productivity among US workers has skyrock-
eted. A generation of employees now fills what *The Wall Street Journal*
calls "superjobs," which are basically two people's jobs smashed into
one. Americans now work 378 hours more per year than their German counterparts. In hardly more than a decade, BlackBerrys and
other smartphones have completely violated any semblance of work-
life balance and work-home division. You are expected to answer an
e-mail on Saturday afternoon at three P.M. because if you don't, someone else at your office will.

Just try being the one person in your office who stands up and
says, "Let's think about this for a day." In fact, at most companies, try
being the one person who walks into the boss's office and says, "We
need to talk. I think we are really riding off the rails on this one."
Odds are high that you'll have trouble getting to the word *riding* before your boss looks down to check his e-mail.

All this productivity can really waste a lot of money. To borrow
a phrase, when you're going in the wrong direction, you should at
least take your foot off the gas pedal. Listening is one way to do that.

When we talk to Fortune 500 companies about business threats,
early on in the conversation we say something that no self-respecting,
profit-motivated consultant would say: "The solution to your problems
is probably already somewhere in the company. In fact, it may very well

be in this room." The problem is, most companies have long since stopped listening to the people who work there. They've stopped listening to customer service representatives on the front lines who know the product is slipping. They've stopped listening to midlevel managers who have ideas for breakout new products. The same bold self-confidence and drive—the same risk-taking, I-don't-care-if-everyone-says-I'll-fail personality that took the firm through its early start-up days—is now holding it firm on a plateau. A shock to the system will require someone new saying something new. If you are running a company, you won't hear it if you are busy noticing the cracked tiles on the floor or trying to throw the tennis ball faster and faster.

What do most firms, and families, do in this situation? They hire an outside expert. Now, if you get a consultant drunk and ask him for the truth, he'll tell you this: Most of the time, consultants are merely tiebreakers. One part of the company isn't listening to the other, so a third party is brought in to confirm one side's point of view. For some strange reason, people are often far more willing to listen to random strangers than close friends.

Here's how this same problem often manifests itself in marriage. (Without this phenomenon, financial planners wouldn't really have a business.)

In most marriages, only one partner cares about money and financial planning. That doesn't mean the other is a spendthrift; it just means that, in most cases, one partner pays the bills, stays up late looking at budget spreadsheets, and researches the 401(k) investments. For ease, let's say that in this case the woman is the "bill payer" and the man is the "distant executive."

Day-to-day financial operations chug along with ease. But when the time comes for a big decision—say, setting up a new IRA—the man inevitably gets involved and spits out random, often conflicting opinions.

That's when the couple goes to a financial planner. Usually a lovely man in a nice white shirt and tie, the financial planner takes 2 percent of the couple's money and tells them to do what the woman had recommended all along. This makes the man feel better, and the couple goes on its merry way. They have become numb—remember the power of numbness from Chapter 2?—to their financial future.

Better listening would have saved the couple 2 percent of their money!

So far, our examples have been tame—most families don't miss the 2 percent. But failing to pay attention to people around you can have devastating results, as any man who's heard only 49 percent of what his wife has said can attest. With organizations, it can literally mean the difference between hitting the iceberg and steering around it in the nick of time.

What makes listening *listening*? Let's agree for now that distraction is the enemy of listening. But as with all things, it's not quite so black-and-white. Attention and focus don't have an on-off switch; they work more like a thermostat. We are all slightly distracted at all times, with some part of our brains always scanning our surroundings for a bear that might be ready to jump out of the next bush or a car that's going to hop the curb and take us out. So attention, focus, and listening are a matter of degree.

Poke around, and you'll find plenty of schemata for describing this. One simple description: Stephen Covey's five levels of listening. The list begins with not listening at all and moves up to "pretending to listen," which we've all experienced before. Then comes selective listening, active listening, and finally full-fledged empathetic listening. This list is a bit negative for our tastes, but the five levels are very useful. Think of it this way: Sometimes, Level 2 is perfectly suitable, such as when your two-year-old is happily chattering away while playing and simply pleased to have you nearby. Talking to a cell phone customer service rep making an unwanted sales pitch requires nothing more than Level 3. Hearing a friend talk about his very sick parent clearly calls for Level 5. Understanding how you move in and out of these levels—and, heck, making sure you are able to call on all five—is a critical life skill. Without breaking through to Level 5, you'll always be missing critical information, critical connections, critical subtexts in conversations, critical unspoken words. You'll be like the pianist who plays the concerto perfectly but doesn't seem to move audiences because he doesn't feel the music. Without Level 5, you'll never reach your next peak.

But something critical happens between levels 4 and 5 that we'd like to dwell on here. Something amazing happens when you move from what might be called mere attentive data gathering in Level 4 and true empathy in Level 5. And we can learn a lot about this magic by learning about our century-long quest to teach robots how to listen.

Alan Turing was a British mathematician who, like many geniuses in the early 1940s, worked on military-grade cryptography and code breaking. He helped decipher secret messages created by the infamous German Enigma machine. But his work after the war places him on the Mount Rushmore of computer science founders. He largely invented the concept of sophisticated algorithms—large formulas that today control what results we get from a Google search and what books Amazon recommends to us. More to our point at the moment, he is widely regarded as the father of artificial intelligence. Back in 1948, he was among the first to ponder the implications of thinking computers in a paper titled "Intelligent Machinery." Then, in 1950, in a paper called "Computing Machinery and Intelligence," he laid out the framework for a simple test that has romanced, frustrated, and captivated nearly all computer scientists ever since: something known today simply as "the Turing test."

Turing's test has its foundations in a parlor game from the time called the Imitation Game. Two players would retire to a separate room and provide typewritten answers to a series of questions, trying to trick the remaining players into believing that player A was player B, and vice versa. Hilarity ensured as a man tried to sound like a woman, for example.

Turing twisted the rules. What if one of the players was a computer? Could a machine be created that would fool people into thinking it was human? This simple question, still very much unanswered, is now the impossible Gordian knot for nearly everyone who has ever attempted to program a computer.

But we sure try. Nearly every year since, with great fanfare, an international Turing test competition is held with programmers inching ever closer to tricking judges into believing a machine is a person. While the game was created to focus a quest on the creation of artificial intelligence, it has produced an even more powerful byproduct: an intense study of what it means to be human.

Writer Brian Christian took on the Turing test in 2009 as part of an international competition seeking the Loebner Prize, in which aspiring computer programmers attempt to trick human judges into believing they are communicating with people instead of machines. But Christian wasn't actually vying to be the first winner of the Turing test; instead, he wanted the consolation prize that's awarded to the chatter who persuades a panel of judges that he or she is the most convincingly human participant in the test. He chronicled his effort in a book called *The Most Human Human*. Preparing for the test required Christian to deeply examine the efforts of artificial intelligence creators, learn their weaknesses, and put the most human parts of his conversational skills on display. After a year of homework and practice, he had only one hour—a series of five-minute one-on-one online chats with twelve judges—to prove he was, in fact, not a computer.

Christian's deep dive into artificial intelligence unearthed dozens of key differences. For starters, people are very flawed, and so are their communication skills. Human conversation is full of mistakes. People say "um" and "ahh," for example—sometimes for no reason at all, sometimes to hold the floor during conversation while they think. This kind of imperfection is hard for a computer to imitate.

Computers can be very good at basic chitchat—"Rotten weather today, eh?"—but if you personalize such banter a bit more—"The gray clouds get me down in a hurry, I'm from Florida"—you get a leg up on machines. Computers also do a terrible job of appreciating the context of a conversation and tend to just answer one question at a time, ignorant of the past. They are unlikely to appreciate how asking, "What did you do on Friday night?" would sting a person who told you three minutes ago that he's recently been dumped by his girlfriend. In a beautiful explanation of this difference, Christian describes two friends sitting down to lunch, with one beginning immediately with the question "Did you tell her how you feel?" and the other needing no explanation for the pronoun. Computers also do a terrible job of something that good friends do routinely: finish each other's sentences.

Christian's most serious point, however, isn't that computers are getting better and better at imitating human speech; rather, it's that humans are becoming less and less human, and beginning to imitate computer speech. Back to Covey's five-level attention model: A friend who is stuck in Level 4 data acquisition mode probably *would* ask that insensitive question about Friday night to the suddenly single friend. Customer service workers are rewarded for living their entire lives in Level 3 or below, carrying on multiple chats at once and simply repeating different variations of "No, I can't give you a refund," no matter what the impassioned plea might be from the frustrated caller. Workers fill out spreadsheets in an attempt to quantify a day's effort with a single number. Spam filters confuse our e-mails to co-workers with messages sent by the millions hawking male enhancement products.

"Oxford philosopher John Lucas says that if the Turing test is passed, it will not be because machines are so intelligent, but because humans, many of them at least, are so wooden," Christian told an interviewer in 2011.

In the 1960s, robot wars offered endless fodder for sci-fi screenplay writers, as thinking machines waged battle against, and eventually enslaved, humanity. Nary a novelist had it right. The robots look like they have won without lifting a mechanical finger. We've volunteered to become robots.

What is lost when human beings robotize their listening skills? Marriage therapists spend much of their time dealing with exactly this problem. The husband says, "I was listening. Here's what you said! You said you want more help getting the kids ready in the morning." Still, the wife, on the verge of tears, knows her husband isn't really listening because he hasn't got the foggiest idea why she can barely suppress the urge to throw his cell phone out the window when he starts with conference calls at seven A.M. Stuck in Level 4, he has no ability to sense her feelings, and no idea how anxious this tension between them is making their five-year-old son. He'll be utterly shocked when the kindergarten teacher keeps sending notes home saying their boy won't stop pushing over other kids on the playground.

You might call all this nonliteral information a "sixth sense"; it's hard to disagree that this human ability to activate a sixth sense is fading in our data-oriented, distracted world. With no sixth sense, there is no respect for those mystery ingredients we discussed earlier. But for all you data huggers out there, consider this: 93 percent of all communication is nonverbal, according to some studies. If you are listening purely for data acquisition, you are missing a lot. Like an AM radio tuned to a staticky, faraway station that cuts in and out, you are going through life hearing the equivalent of only one of every fifteen words spoken to you.

Of all the things someone might say about your company, *wooden* might be the least attractive. And, yes, the least profitable. But how many companies put real effort into hearing the deeper message that their customers are giving them on a daily basis? When the video revolution hit, Blockbuster could have been the helpful local merchant who would happily recommend movies to you or who would break ties when couples argued over which flick to bring home for the night. Instead, Blockbuster meant one thing: a greedy company that couldn't wait to charge you four dollars for forgetting to drop off the movie on the way to work Monday morning. The moment they had an alternative, people bolted. Company brand managers could have learned in one day's worth of interviews that consumer loyalty was nearly zero, even while the firm was riding high.

Zappos.com, on the other hand, has always preached the value of customer happiness above all else. When its disaster struck, the firm barely missed a beat.

In January 2012, Zappos had to confess something that could have ruined lesser businesses: A hacker had stolen critical customer information—lots of it. In fact, the situation was so bad that security professionals advised the company to force all consumers to change their passwords. The firm sent out an astounding twenty-four million mea culpa e-mails. The "send" was so large the messages took several days to spool their way out of Zappos' servers. The response was so big that Zappos actually turned off its telephone lines, because they were about to become unusable anyway, with the firm expecting hundreds of thousands of customer support calls within hours.

Zappos CEO Tony Hsieh struck an apologetic tone in his e-mail to staff, which was made public immediately:

"We've spent over 12 years building our reputation, brand, and trust with our customers. It's painful to see us take so many steps back due to a single incident," he said.

But a funny thing happened on the way to brand disaster. Customers actually believed Zappos. They changed their passwords as told, and after a rough couple of days, Zappos went about business as usual. The firm had built up so much trust—had proven it could be empathetic—that customers cut it a break. All those free shipping upgrades and friendly phone calls were an investment that paid off.

The critical part of this story, however, is that Zappos wasn't simply pretending to listen: It really had listened to people. It had built up currency in the "emotional bank account," and when time came for a withdrawal, there was something to draw on.

The key, of course, is planning ahead. You can't wait for a corporate disaster to listen to your customers. You can't wait until your wife says "I'm getting a divorce" before you put down the phone, sit on the end of the bed, and hold her hand while she talks. You can't, God forbid, keep texting until you have a life-threatening car accident.

Every good business begins with extremely good listening. Someone somewhere notices a need that people have—perhaps even before they themselves know they have it—and races in to fill that need. People need a cheap way to entertain their families at home now that a night at the movies costs fifty dollars for three kids and two parents. People need a place to sit and relax (and, perhaps, sip coffee) that's not home and not work. People with increasingly diminished manual labor skills, and more money than time, need a quick way to get their car oil changed. And yet this spark of an idea, this entity that began with complete customer empathy, almost always runs into an unforgiving plateau when it stops listening to customers. Love affairs almost always begin with intense, all-night listening sessions where people are absorbed with each other's stories. They flatten out when that warm, enveloping attention disappears. And when you think about all the forces working against your attention—"mature business" problems like overexpansion or containing health care costs, or mature relationship problems like racing the kids to ballet and soccer—the pattern seems inevitable. Of course, the thesis of this book says it is. But now, we will tell you that the valleys need be neither deep nor painful, and the peaks don't have to fade away.

We will begin with an idea that might be a struggle for some, but it is the only path out of the distraction plateau. We call it *peak listening*. Here's what we mean.

If you try to improve your listening skills, you'll notice a lot of discussion about "listening with intent." That phrase means different things to different people, but here's how we will use it: Most people listen with intent to do something—usually to defend themselves or to solve a problem. Nearly everyone listens with the intent of having something ready to say as soon as the other speaker is finished. Have you ever wondered how crazy that is? Shouldn't there be a pause once in a while, as one of the speakers actually thinks about what to say or, even better, thinks about what has been said? Here's a phenomenon you'll observe repeatedly if you look for it: two speakers appearing to be carrying on a conversation but really just giving two monologues, split up by each other, each one simply waiting for time on whatever stage he or she imagines him- or herself to be on. Call it "talking past each other," if you like; it's clearly a cultural cancer that's been learned from the endless chatter on talk radio and cable TV, where you will never hear the following phrase from a talking head: "That's a good point; let me think about that for a moment."

There is no "thinking for a moment" on television; in fact, every pause is penalized.

Of course, if the speaker is saying something that might be hard to hear—"I hate your product" or "Why are you so selfish?"—all this goes double. Listeners usually can't wait to leap to their own defense, and spend their time thinking like an attorney who's planning a closing argument rather than hearing what's being said. You can imagine how ineffective this is.

We'd like to see you try something very different: listening with intent to agree. That's right: Before you offer an explanation or defense, just imagine that whatever the other person is saying must be true. That's radical. But it sure is the fastest way to get new ideas into your brain. That's peak listening. For the purposes of this discussion, we're going to divide the world into two categories: sociopaths, who lie without guilt and who really have nothing but their own selfish gains in mind, and everyone else. If you are in the presence of a true sociopath, then all bets are off. The advice we give here is useless. But after you've determined that your spouse, friend, coworker, or customer isn't a sociopathic liar, here's a thought that will short-circuit almost every fight you ever have.

The person you are listening to is right. Always. Your wife, your husband, your employee, your customers. They're right.

They may not be 100 percent right. But even if a person is hysterical and speaking in terribly ineffective language, perhaps even accusing you of things that on the surface are demonstrably false, *there is truth in what he or she is saying.* And rather than defend yourself by finding error in some details, challenge yourself to find the deeper truth of what's being said. Often, that will require you to dig deep into that 93 percent of nonverbal communication. It definitely will require you to drop all your defenses, and in some cases, it will feel like you are being forced to believe that black is white and the sky is orange.

Here's a simple trick you can apply today to take a step in the right direction. Ever wonder what keeps a great improv troupe from falling silent? It's simple. No one is allowed to say no. Anyone who has ever taken a class in improvisation has learned the "yes, and . . ." technique. Whatever is said, the other actors are forced to accept it and build upon it. As a conversational style, this same principle pays immediate dividends. Instead of creating blocks, or "stops," to the chatter, it allows group discussions to build on one another. Talking takes on a spirit that floats higher and higher when it isn't subjected to "conversation stoppers" thrown in by negative nellies. Such stoppers sound like "I don't believe that," or "What's your proof for that?" or often simply "No." Those stuck in a frame of mind that forces them to pick apart conversations piece by piece often miss the forest for the trees. You know them because they often leave people feeling like a balloon has just been popped and its remnants have drifted to the floor. Popping other people's balloons is a surefire way to discourage them from telling you how they really feel—and a terrible way to break out of plateaus caused by becoming stuck in a feedback-proof cocoon.

The more successful you are, the more important this becomes, as many people around you will begin to agree with you as a matter of deference. One beautiful interpretation you'll find of the Bible phrase "love your enemies" holds that your enemies are the only people who will be honest enough to tell you the truth about yourself. Loving what your enemies tell you about yourself might be the pinnacle of open-mindedness.

Often, the simplest way to do this is to be the bigger person. Companies (and we know that companies are people, too) have a very hard time with that.

For the past two decades, we've observed an increasingly disturbing trend in American commerce. Type the name of any company you can think of, then add the word "sucks" into a search engine, and you are sure to find dozens of webpages and comments devoted to attacking the firm and destroying its reputation. Some of this antagonism is well deserved, but much of it is not. Regardless of your opinion on that, it's undeniable that in general, consumers hate many big-name US brands: cable companies, airlines, cell phone providers, you name it—they hate it.

Talk to customer service agents for many of these companies, and you will hear the exact opposite tale. Typical customers, they say, are lying, cheating, stealing, unreasonable people who are constantly trying to talk their way into freebies and making impossible demands. In fact, exasperated telephone agents have a hangout where they swap stories: It's called CustomersSuck.com. They have a nickname for the rest of us: "SC's," which is short for "Sucky Customers."

Here's a typical story you'll read there:

> So I got a call the other night from someone complaining that their wireless network wasn't working. I said, "OK, first thing, go turn your wireless router on and off." His response? "I can't, it's in my neighbor's apartment." Typical SC.

It's true; they hate us, and we hate them. This is something we call, with apologies to C. S. Lewis, the Great Divorce. We don't know who started it. It probably has something to do with the mechanization and computerization of all customer interactions. It was hard to cheat the local butcher when he lived next door to you. It's easy to cheat an anonymous person who lives across the country, or across the world, and knows you only by a serial number. Whose fault is it? Who cheated who first? Who knows?

Who can stop it? Only you. The primary piece of advice given since the beginning of marriage counseling applies to every genre of interaction, and to ending the plateaus formed and hardened by poor listening skills and distraction. Someone has to make the first move to begin the healing . . . and nothing ramps up passion, sales, loyalty, and trust like an honest-to-goodness olive branch offer. Nothing breaks through a plateau like the freedom that comes from admitting you're wrong, and from seeing how the person on the other side of the conflict is right. Nothing teaches better than another person. Peak listening is the surest way to get the most out of the interactions you have with people, and the surest way to reach your peak. If you want to get to the next level with your customers, just tell them they are right. Give them what they want. Be on their side. Yes, of course, prune out the sociopaths, but don't let the rare liar control your policy in every interaction and hijack good business decisions with paranoia.

Another story about that:

There once was a man who walked to work every day with a friend. Each morning, on their way to the subway, they passed a bodega where they purchased coffee. Every day, the man gave a big, happy "Good morning!" to the bodega worker. Every day, he got back a blank, angry stare. One day, the friend asked, "Why do you bother being so friendly to him day after day?" Unblinking, he responded, "Because that's how I am. And I'm not going to let some guy at a bodega tell me how to act." Don't let your bad customers tell your company how to behave. Break through by honoring the good ones.

Of course, listening—real listening, with Level 5 attention and a focus on hearing and believing even the hardest things—is only the beginning of the solution to the problem of distraction in our time. Much of this advice you have heard in bits and pieces before. Everyone wants to be a good partner, a good parent, a beloved business owner. But something goes wrong along the way. The problem usually isn't a lack of desire to be fair and honest. It's probably the distraction. The most important factor is to be humble enough to acknowledge the problem—no, you probably aren't the one-in-a-thousand freak who can actually multitask efficiently. And once you are humble enough, the solutions start to become apparent.

In a world where it seems everything is conspiring against your focus and attention, where do you begin to regain control? It should come as no surprise that there's a profound and vigorous homespun movement to practice yoga. From 2002 to 2011, circulation of *Yoga Journal* soared 300 percent, at a time when virtually all magazine subscriber bases shrank. About 14.3 million people in the United States practiced yoga in 2010, up from 4.3 million in 2001. The number of certified yoga instructors has soared, too, partly energized by the recession and a desire for work-at-home jobs but mostly fueled by an unmistakable countermovement to the rise of BlackBerrys and the twenty-four-hour-connected worker. It's not just yoga. Churches report an increased interest in meditative prayer, such as the rosary. Sales for items that purport to offer relaxation, such as candles, have also soared. It's unavoidable; people are craving a shot at returning to their centers, even as they are being pulled apart.

One of our favorite expressions about work is this: "Type A personalities often mistake busyness for productivity." The key to beginning a culture of focus over busyness is similar to the key to listening: You have to be the bigger person. Busyness is like a virus that gets passed from one e-mail account to the other around the office, until it's impossible to be that one person who refuses to answer e-mail on a Saturday night. It takes a true leader to stop the madness. An organization that wants to regain focus needs a leader who can utter perhaps the most powerful phrase of our time.

"It can wait."

"It can wait" says so much in so few words. It says, "Relax." It says, "I can set priorities." "It can wait" says you have a sense of timing, a sense that it's important to do things with rhythm—recall the

"Bad Timing" chapter? Like picking blueberries at their ripest, acting at the peak time requires patience. "It can wait" also says, "I trust you." And most of all, it says, "I care about you." And it carries with it a truly meaningful action. Watch what happens to your employees when you tell them directly that you care about them, and you show them you mean it. Watch what happens when you have the courage to tell them to let some things go and focus only on what really matters. If you stop the e-mail pass-off madness, watch what happens when there's a wee bit of digital peace. Watch the real work slowly rush in and fill up all the free time that's been created by the end of endless e-mail chains.

"It can wait" says you have patience. "It can wait" says you have integrity. "It can wait" is the antidote to the digital age. It also brings up the possibility that we can return to one of the most powerful phrases of the last century, "Let's sleep on it." Good decision making involves quite a magic formula that includes both data collection and raw instinct. When there is no time to wait, there is no time for the unconscious to deliberate on accumulated information; there is no time for hunch. Most important decisions—who to marry, when to quit, whether to send that angry e-mail—are better made after a good night's sleep. Unless you can say, "It can wait," you'll never be able to sleep on it. As we learned back in the "Timing" chapter, bad timing—refusing to sleep on decisions—can literally mean the difference between freedom and jail for parole applicants. Nearly all good decision are made early in the day, when self-control and willpower are at their best. The simple phrase "It can wait" tells people they can structure their lives accordingly and gives employees the ability to think clearly and make better choices.

Some companies are instituting e-mail-free hours or meeting-free days. In his runaway best seller *The 4-Hour Workweek*, Tim Ferriss advises managers to check e-mails only twice a day . . . and describes a consistent phenomenon that reveals how often conflicts arise and are solved without management intervention during the four-hour spans of time this creates. Companies such as Intel and Deloitte & Touche have experimented with "no e-mail days" which they have named, affectionately, "Quiet Time."

When Intel instituted "Quiet Time" for four hours on Tuesday mornings at two locations involving three hundred engineers, the result was a resounding success. More than 70 percent of employees recommended the program be extended, according to posts on Intel's website.

An interesting finding is that Quiet Time is useful to different people for different reasons. Some people need it to concentrate on creative tasks, as we had predicted, but even people whose work involves ongoing interaction with others found the periodic "breathing space" beneficial in restoring balance and getting back in control of an otherwise hectic work routine. One should, we learned, let each person decide how to use the quiet hours to best effect. A key success factor, however, is that people must realize that the "quiet" requirement is not absolute; when an urgent situations requires it, interruptions are permitted. Communicating this clearly was necessary halfway through the pilot.

"No e-mail day" is now a movement headquartered in the UK, getting people across the world to disconnect from the grid for specific twenty-four-hour periods ranging from "Leap Day" 2012 to clever calendar happenstances such as 12/12/12. While the movement is small, to our knowledge it has not caused any planes to fall out of the sky or any patients to die on the operating table. But it does create some empty space for peak behaviors to take hold.

What if technology didn't just cause the problem with attention but could provide a solution, too? This was precisely the work of Mark Weiser, who was chief scientist at the famed Xerox PARC lab during the 1990s, and back then quite accurately predicted the explosion of gadgets into our lives. He helped popularize the ominous-sounding phrase *ubiquitous computing*. Imagine a kind of Orwellian world where computers and sensors are so tiny and powerful that they are literally everywhere—in our clothes, in our food, floating in the air—and fully networked. This world makes humans just another component of the Internet. And while this vision is scary, Weiser saw a way out of the Orwellian future. He called it "calm computing."

Bob conducted extensive interviews with Weiser back in 1998.

"Attention is the most valuable commodity on Earth," said Weiser, who had the glow of a brilliance and emitted none of the stress we normally associate with techno-geniuses like Bill Gates. He was more like a bemused uncle who saw computers as charming nieces and nephews.

"You don't want personal technology; you want personal relationships," Weiser said. He complained that, at the time, "smart" devices such as pagers, cell phones, and even computers usually added to our general sense of panic. "In the next age, how do we make technology help us be calmer, how do you change that equation? The basic way is you have to make it more invisible. You have to get it out of the way, out of your face, and into the environment and into your pockets, into your clothing."

If his goal sounds lofty, wait until you hear his space-age path for getting there. Weiser demonstrated repeatedly that there are ways into the human brain that don't require full attention. When you wake up after sleeping, you have a sense of whether it is morning or still night based on the light that's coming through the window. You might even get a sense that it's sunny or raining, warm or cold, without thinking about it. If you're lucky, an odor might tell you that the coffee is ready or the bacon is cooked. Weiser wanted to design computers that were capable of communicating with humans on this same semiconscious level. Imagine, for a moment, that instead of your reading an e-mail that told you to pick up the kids after work, a small smart computer could slip that news into your subconscious without interrupting the memo you were writing.

"Right now, all these devices are constantly beeping, popping up on your screen, and grabbing at you," he lamented. All these interfaces were terribly designed. This robbed people of their precious attention. He hopped around the Xerox facility—the place where the computer mouse and several other fundamental PC technologies were born—demanding that coworkers only invent devices that made the world a calmer place to live.

Calm computing, in Weiser's mind, could give humans their humanity back. Well-designed ubiquitous computing didn't have to be scary at all. It could be relaxing. He thought the age of distraction was merely a phase humans had to go through. When you heard him say it, you believed him. You left conversations with him somehow calmer—at least until you checked your e-mail.

In 1999, when Weiser was forty-six, he was diagnosed with stomach cancer and given six months to live. Xerox PARC raced to set up special dictation technology so he could write the book he'd never had time to write, but he never even penned a paragraph. The cancer progressed with vicious speed, and he died three weeks later, leaving the rest of us on our own to figure out how we'll find calm in our technology storm.

8. AGILITY

The Second Action

Or, Failing Slowly and the Just-Noticeable Difference

K ent Beck was an outcast. Some might even have called him an anarchist.

Had he lived in the sixteenth century, perhaps he, not Copernicus, would have taken up the "earth moves around the sun" cause. When Hugh first heard him speak, the sheer escapism of his philosophy and the brazenness of his assertions were so jarring that they demanded attention. He might as well have been saying bridge builders should just make it up as they go along. Actually, that's almost exactly what he was saying. And people seemed to believe him.

Like all successful revolutionaries, he sought allies. They met, sometimes in secret cabals, and shared plans to overthrow the establishment. It was at a small gathering in Snowbird, Utah, that Beck, along with sixteen other people, signed the Agile Manifesto. It was one of the most heretical documents in the field of software development. The year was 2001.

Beck is the creator of an approach called Extreme Programming, and the beginning of his book *Extreme Programming Explained* reads more like a political doctrine than a technical text for software developers:

> Extreme Programming (XP) is about social change. It is about letting go of habits and patterns that were adaptive in the past, but now get in the way of us doing our best work. It is about giving up the defenses that protect us but interfere with our productivity. It may leave us feeling exposed.

"Exposed"? Heretical? What could be so radical about the way someone builds software? Beck turned the fundamentals of computer engineering inside out, but his newfangled methods—really a new way of thinking—can be applied in all areas of life.

Before Agile, most big software development projects were rigidly structured and followed a model known as "waterfall." In waterfall, development occurs in a few monolithic stages, where one stage flows to another in sequence. It's an approach that structural engineers might take when they design and build skyscrapers—design, build, test; very structured, very methodical—and like a skyscraper, the software could take up to several years to complete. Committees would meet and agree on all the features a piece of software would need while programmers twiddled their thumbs. When the feature set was finished and set in stone, the "blueprints" would be given to programmers, who slogged through lists of tasks while testers twiddled their thumbs and the committee's collective blood pressure rose. When programmers finished, their code was handed off to testers who probed for bugs, and everyone else twiddled their thumbs. At this point, almost certainly eighteen months or so after the committee first met, someone would mention that Netscape had been invented, or Facebook had been invented, and so whatever the committee had wanted at the beginning had become totally irrelevant. Of course, with the features set in stone, there was no going back. Finally, some programmers would quit in frustration, and the marketing team would join in the discussion and figure out how to lie about what the software could actually do.

The needs of a software product change quickly. New technologies emerge, and yesterday's design can become outdated—fast. Features that users once demanded become useless before the product is even shipped. These dynamic systems, where things are constantly changing, mean that the stable course originally set by software designers was leading projects into irrelevancy.

By the time most waterfall-developed projects were actually finished, they were either irrelevant, or they had to be completely rebooted. The result was delays, exploding budgets, and some of the most expensive plateaus in modern business. A survey of IT development efforts at the time found that a third of business software projects were canceled before they were completed, and just more than half of those that made it to completion cost twice as much as their original estimates. The industry needed to change.

The model used to build software was rigid, but needs were dynamic. When we have a rigid model for something that changes often (and quickly), we end up in chaos.

Beck's approach was to abolish structure and the imagined stability that came with it; his mantra was two words: *embrace change*. Agile is, by definition, nimble. If you've ever been a part of software design, or really any large project, you will understand how rebellious Beck's ideas are. With agile development, new software is built in small, self-contained pieces. Developers must produce working projects they can share with stakeholders in—get this—not years, not months, but weeks! In fact, Agile's "timebox" requirement means that programmers design, code, test, and share working models of their subprojects within one to four weeks. Meanwhile, the Agile

Manifesto set out what seem like impossibly accommodating principles, such as "welcome changing requirements, even late in development." And Agile allows managers and sales staff to assess the market and make course corrections. If something is headed toward
failure, Agile makes it fail fast instead of prolonging the inevitable.

Beck describes the process like driving a car:

> I can remember clearly the day I first began learning to
> drive. My mother and I were driving up Interstate 5 near
> Chico, California; a straight, flat stretch of road where the
> highway stretches right to the horizon. My mom had me
> reach over from the passenger seat and hold the steering
> wheel. She let me get the feel of how the motion of the wheel
> affected the direction of the car. Then she told me, "Here's
> how you drive. Line the car up in the middle of the lane,
> straight toward the horizon."
>
> I very carefully squinted straight down the road. I got the
> car smack dab in the middle of the lane, pointed right down
> the middle of the road. I was doing great. My mind wandered
> a little . . .
>
> I jerked back to attention as the car hit the gravel. My
> mom (her courage now amazes me) gently got the car back
> straight on the road. My heart was pounding. Then she actu-
> ally taught me about driving. "Driving is not about getting
> the car going in the right direction. Driving is about con-
> stantly paying attention, making a little correction this way,
> a little correction that way."
>
> This is the paradigm for XP. Stay aware. Adapt. Change.

Most of us live our lives as waterfall, but modern life increasingly demands an agile approach. If we don't stay aware and adapt,

we fail slowly—we eventually run off the road. We fail to notice the changing winds that indicate a storm is brewing. We continue to hope that a bad relationship or horrible job will somehow get better. We continue to invest our time and energy, to persevere, when deep down we know that we're headed toward an unrewarding plateau. Change feels decisive; drifting off the road might seem like the result of failing to make choices, but in reality, it is a series of incremental choices of stop versus continue, where we pick the latter. Stopping would be to admit failure, and most of us have a deathly fear of failure.

Failing slowly is natural because it's difficult to tell that a situation is incrementally getting worse. If you toss a frog into a pot of boiling water, it will immediately jump out. But if you put it in the pot a few minutes earlier, while the water is still cool, it'll ride it out as the temperature climbs. As things get just a little warmer with each passing moment, it never notices when it crosses a dangerous threshold—and neither do we. Science has a lot to tell us about this type of incremental failure and why we have such a hard time noticing it.

The answer sits at the intersection of psychology and physics in a concept known as the *just-noticeable difference*, or the JND. Psychophysicists define it as the amount of change in something it would take for us to notice the change. The just-noticeable difference has its own law: It takes a specific *percentage of change* in the intensity of the stimulus for someone to notice, and that percentage is constant for a given stimulus. It's the word *percentage* that's important here. For example, if you stared at a pile of four rocks, walked away for a while, and then came back and saw that there were five rocks, you would likely notice the difference. That's a one-rock change, but it's a 25 percent increase in the number of rocks. Now let's do that mental experiment with a bigger pile. What if someone added one rock to a pile of a hundred rocks? You're unlikely to notice the difference as that's only a 1 percent increase—well below the *just-noticeable difference*.

The just-noticeable difference is why parents don't realize how much their newborn has grown in a week until a friend comes over and says, "I can't believe how big she's gotten!" To the friend, a week's worth of growth came all at once. To the parents, who see the baby every day, all that incremental hourly growth fell short of the *just-noticeable difference*. Marketers are experts at using the just-noticeable difference to their benefit. If they reduce the number of crackers in a box just a little, nobody notices. It's under the radar of the JND, and it lets the company increase profits. If they then introduce a "jumbo pack," they make sure that the perceived increase is above the just-noticeable difference. You can only perceive incremental change when there is some point of comparison, some marker—like a friend coming to visit, or an outfit that just doesn't fit the baby anymore. Without these markers, we're sitting in a pot of warm water, staring at a frog.

The just-noticeable difference helps explain why we continue forging ahead when we're stuck on a plateau—we just don't realize how much less we're getting for our efforts. Once you understand the *just-noticeable difference*, however, you can counteract its effects. By setting clear, objective markers, you can see how you're progressing, figure out what's working and what's failing, correct it, and move on. If the frog had a thermometer, he'd have known to jump ship and head to another cozy spot (a sink, perhaps?). It's when he boils slowly—and finds out too late—that you get green soup. Without objective markers, changes may happen slower than the just-noticeable difference, and what was a good model yesterday will become outdated. Conventional wisdom becomes bad advice.

It was the unquestioned conventional wisdom of the twentieth century that owning a home was the American Dream. And from the

Great Depression all the way to the Great Recession of 2008, the percentage of adults who owned their homes in America climbed with steady predictability—from 44 percent in 1940, through a post–World War II boom, through urban decay and suburban sprawl, all the way up to 69 percent at the height of the housing bubble. Every one of the 70 million American families that purchased homes had been told over and over and over: Buying a home is the key to financial stability. It means you're an American. Heck, it means you're a grown-up.

As we now know, everything these families were told about stability was wrong. They applied an old model to a situation that had slowly but meaningfully changed, and the American Dream became the American nightmare. With rare pockets of exception, nearly everyone who bought a home from 2002 through 2010 made a "wise" but ultimately financially painful choice. By 2010, eleven million US households were "underwater," meaning they owed more on their mortgages than their homes were worth. That's not just a paper problem; it limited their agility. Homeowners who are underwater generally can't relocate for better jobs because they can't afford to sell their homes and take the loss. They can't refinance to take advantage of lower interest rates. And they can't take out home equity loans to buff up finances dragged down by high-interest credit card debt or student loans. They are the opposite of agile; they're stuck.

Following conventional wisdom made their life situation incredibly perilous. Why? Because the real nightmare was inflexibility. Being tied down by an onerous thirty-year loan is a disaster in an economy where the average worker changes careers five times during a lifetime. Losing your job is one thing. Losing your job and being unable to move to improve your prospects is quite another.

At this point, if you are one of these underwater, unemployed consumers, you are probably thinking of your annoying friend, "the renter." She decided not to jump into the housing market during the bubble and heard one catcall after another during its glory years. "You're missing out," all her friends warned. "You've got to grow up."

She's sitting pretty now. She can sleep at night, knowing she doesn't have to figure out how to come up with $2,800 every month for the next twenty-eight years. She can take that job offer in Boston when her New York PR company folds. She can even move in with family without ruining her credit. She's flexible. Her agility turned out to be the most stable thing about her.

Let's go back to the housing market and look for some objective markers that might have alerted us that we were creeping toward danger, perhaps just under the just-noticeable difference. A funny thing happened in the second quarter of 2007, right around the apex of the housing bubble. Almost no one noticed at the time, but the Federal Reserve collected some startling data that it would soon release: The percentage of equity US homeowners held had slipped below 50 percent. For the first time since the Fed had begun collecting the data in 1945, Americans collectively owned less than half of the homes they had purchased. That meant the banks owned more than half.

In other words, these "homeowners" were really renting anyway. By the end of 2007, the figure had dropped to 47.9 percent, making it even more clear that consumers weren't really homeowners at all—banks were. Add in the rabid growth of designed-to-be-temporary mortgages such as five-year adjustable-rate loans, interest-only loans, and negative amortization loans, and it should be clear that people who moved into those six million homes bought every year from 2002 to 2010 were never really homeowners at all.

We often get stuck in old models. We need a way to recalibrate, a way to test whether the model still works or whether it's leading us toward a plateau. We need to be more agile. To understand how agility works in practice, we need to revisit the world of high-tech.

———

Kent Beck helped ignite the field of agile software development, where businesses can adapt quickly and make small course corrections before their efforts lead to an expensive and often terminal plateau.

Other agile models emerged around the same time as Extreme Programming. One is called Scrum—a term borrowed from rugby, referring to a way of restarting the game. Instead of the marathon of waterfall software development, Scrum is organized into *sprints*, short bursts that last two to four weeks as the team builds a working piece of software, demonstrates it, and recalibrates as necessary.

Agile took the software development industry by storm. Surveys estimate that, by 2010, nearly a third of software development projects used agile methods as opposed to waterfall. Agility, it turns out, was the key to avoiding monumental, slow, and expensive failures. Projects could be recalibrated and refocused before they went too far down the wrong path. The process results in a large set of fast, small failures instead of one giant, monumental, and slow failure. Some of the smartest people in America, charged with solving our most vexing problems, now use this fast-fail approach. It's true: Even the government can change!

When the US Department of Defense needs to solve a big problem, the agency hands the issue over to its crown jewel, the Defense Advanced Research Projects Agency, or DARPA. If you're not familiar with DARPA, we think you might know some of its creations, like the Internet and GPS. DARPA is a rarified atmosphere and soaked in Ph.D.s from some of the most prestigious universities on the planet. These program managers, shepherds of innovation, seek solutions to the most challenging research problems on earth. So-called DARPA-hard problems include things such as cars that drive themselves and invisible walls. DARPA solicits proposals from companies, professors, and individuals who might be able to help.

Hard problems need big solutions, and when DARPA believes in something, it tends to bet big. But the typical process to get approved for a DARPA grant is rigid and slow. Research awards for small businesses usually involve a hundred thousand dollars and a year to prepare a design, and then a million dollars and another two years to build a prototype. In some areas, such as biochemical engineering, three years is a pretty short period. In others, like technology, it's an eternity. The people creating most of the technology problems that DARPA is trying to solve—hackers—tend to innovate on a much quicker timescale. So in the spirit of innovation, DARPA hired one.

Peiter Zatko has a conflicted relationship with US government. In the late 1990s, he was part of hacker groups with names such as Cult of the Dead Cow and the L0pht. Back then he went by the name Mudge. Mudge caused quite a stir in 1998 when he testified in front of a Senate committee and told them that he could bring the Internet down in thirty minutes. After that he worked for a few computer security companies, some of which did government work. Then, as perhaps his greatest hack, he started working for DARPA.

He's an odd fit with his peers: Most of them have Ph.D.s from places such as MIT and Carnegie Mellon. Many have published tens or hundreds of academic papers in their fields. They oversee core research in areas that might help the DoD, but not till years later. Before Mudge got to DARPA, research proposal approvals alone took two months—and that was just the beginning. Typically, three years and seven figures went by before the awardee could deliver a fully functional prototype. That's a major investment in something that might not be of much use, and one seriously expensive potential plateau.

Mudge figured out how to hack the system. Here's his offer to top researchers: I'll give you $50K and six months to build a fully functional prototype. No need for red tape—if a good proposal comes in the door, he can get it approved in seven days.

Instead of investing big in a few slow but promising projects, he stress-tests ideas, and if they fail, the cost is minimal. If they work, he has something tangible that can be used immediately. More important, he now knows where the government can make bigger bets. This ability to fail quickly is key, especially when the problems are changing quickly.

In 2011 Mudge gave a DARPA colloquium presentation titled "If You Don't Like the Game, Hack the Playbook," where he outlined his radical approach to core government-funded research: "The key to a good strategy is to have multiple options."

Multiple options let you roll the dice of life more often. Multiple options give you flexibility. The key is to prune the bad options quickly and find the one that will lead you to success. Good entrepreneurs do this naturally. They are more willing to take risks, fail, and then take risks again. To find these people, hungry for the fast fail, we travel to Silicon Valley, where fortunes can be earned or decimated at unfathomable speeds.

"I said to myself, Hey, I am *good!*" Alberto Savoia told a class at Stanford, reflecting on his mind-set back in 2002. Who could argue with him? He'd sold his first Silicon Valley start-up for $100 million in 2001. Then he joined Google, a small but growing Internet search company (perhaps you've heard of it?), as engineering director in charge of a little project called AdWords. What followed will likely be fodder for business school lectures for decades to come. AdWords was a huge hit, and a decade later, it accounted for most of Google's $37.9 billion in revenue.

But somewhere between starting a revolution in 2001 and his lecture at Stanford in 2012, Alberto Savoia hit a plateau.

Hugh first met Savoia back in 2005. He'd left Google to start a venture-backed software company called Agitar that helped businesses build more reliable software. The office was typical for a start-up—long desks sprawled out in a massively open space, and lots of smart people writing software. Every day the company brought in a free lunch for its employees, a habit Savoia picked up from Google. With Savoia's track record and $25 million in investment funding, it almost didn't seem to matter what the company did. Principals at the firm were headed for another revolution and a huge payday—or so they thought.

But a funny thing happened on the way to the bank. After two years, Savoia wasn't generating piles of cash. Agitar plateaued.

"We spent twenty-five million dollars of venture capital to sell twenty-four million dollars' worth of software. And, you know, that equation doesn't quite work," Savoia said. He had misjudged the market and ended up building a great piece of software that very few people actually needed.

"It seemed so easy; I thought I was just born to do this," Savoia said as he reflected on his experiences at a talk at Stanford back in 2012. It turns out that plateaus hit even the most ordained of entrepreneurs.

In 2008, Savoia left Agitar and went back to Google, this time with a different mission: to study failure. In fact, among his accomplishments there was the creation of a "Law of Failure," which simply says: "Most new ideas fail even if they are well executed."

Statistics back him up. On average four out of five start-ups fail. Most books don't earn back the author's advance (present book excluded, of course). Most new restaurants fail in their first few years of operation. Many new ventures, ideas, and creations stagnate; they plateau. Some of it can be chalked up to bad execution: Even a great idea can't survive poor implementation. But precise execution can't protect against a fatal flaw: A good idea might not be a good business. Savoia puts it a slightly different way: "Make sure you are building the right 'it' before you build 'it' right."

Savoia believes that his Law of Failure is inescapable. If that's true, can we use it to our advantage? Instead of avoiding failure, is there a way to *fail faster*? The real disasters are slow failures—where you continue to put more time, more money, and more energy into something that just won't work. The quickest way to the top, to the peak, is often to reach the bottom first. The faster you fail, the faster you can move on to something that will work. Savoia might have a way to make this happen.

You've heard of prototypes. They're an important part of the development process, used to show investors or others how a product might work without having to manufacture on a large scale. Prototypes, however, are generally fully operational. That means they can still take years to build. Savoia prefers what he calls the "pretotype." As we'll see, a pretotype could be as simple as a drawing of a website that you imagine is fully functional, which you allow others to "test." The advantage is enormous: While a test website might take weeks to build, a pretotype can be drawn in Photoshop within a few minutes. With pretotyping, you never have to say, "Sorry, it's not worth experimenting with that idea," because there are hardly any barriers to entry.

"[Pretotyping involves] testing the initial appeal and actual usage of a potential new product by simulating its core experience with the smallest possible investment of time and money," Savoia says.

As we mentioned, every respectable revolution needs a manifesto. Pretotyping needed one, too—with one exception: It's subject to change. Alberto Savoia's Pretotype Manifesto reads more like a poker newbie's cheat sheet that shows a full house beats a flush. Here it is:

innovators beat ideas

pretotypes beat productypes

data beats opinions

now beats later

doing beats talking

simple beats complex

commitment beats committees

Savoia believes that it is the innovator, not the idea, that is the key currency in invention. His reasoning is that innovators, the great ones, are willing to allow their ideas to be exposed to the world, get feedback, go through a perhaps large set of failures, and then repeat the process till something hits. He talks about innovation as more of a discipline than a bolt of lightning. The discipline of innovation demands failure. It's as fundamental to innovation as spreadsheets are to accounting. Failure is inevitable. The question isn't "How do I turn this idea into reality?"; it's "How can I find out if my idea is a bad one without committing too much time, money, and resources to it? How can I avoid working my way up to an expensive plateau?"

When Savoia founded his first technology start-up in 1999, the world was full of bad ideas. Hugh was in graduate school around that time and remembers day-trading Internet start-ups like Pets.com before getting to the grind of his dissertation. Bob was writing a column called "Not So Fast," which poked fun of silly dot-com start-ups like Pets.com. In those times, there wasn't really a question about whether a particular Internet stock would go up. The question was: Is there another stock that you're missing out on that might go up faster? Silicon Valley was drunk with optimism. When the hangover came in 2001, lots of those ideas had disintegrated. They weren't based on data; they were based on a sense of unchecked optimism. Venture capitalists were willing to ignore their most stereotypical question: How is this thing going to make money? Some companies were saved by online advertising. Others were able to build up a big enough user base that they convinced someone else to buy the company and figure out how to make money off of it (most never did).

After the dot-com bubble burst around 2001, the model for investing in these types of companies changed. Instead of the old model, in which would-be founders handed a napkin with an idea on it to venture capitalists and got a check for $20 million, the notion of a "lean start-up" formed, where founders would build version 1.0 on their own dime or go to the community of wealthy individuals—angel investors—for hundreds of thousands of dollars (sometimes just tens of thousands) to turn their concept into reality. No longer could a website that showcases cats that look like Adolf Hitler (that site exists by the way) get $20 million in funding. If, however, you built something inexpensive—a pretotype, in Savoia's parlance—and proved viability, there was still a lot of money on the table.

Some of the biggest dot-com failures came from ideas that got heavy investment but little validation. Pets.com, the online shopping destination for pet needs, lost $147 million in the first nine months of 2000 before finding out its business model was unsustainable and had to be shut down. The grocery delivery company Webvan went all in, making a one-billion-dollar investment in warehouses before it realized that actual demand for grocery delivery was nowhere near forecasts. The company filed for bankruptcy. But failure can also happen when the environment changes but the business model does not. Remember Blockbuster? Brick-and-mortar video rental stores were a good idea until the environment changed and people could get their videos sent to them (either by mail or the web). Constantly looking for signs of trouble is the hallmark of innovation. Pretotyping might be the answer—just ask Jeff Hawkins, a man who once held the world in the palm of his hand.

In 1992, Jeff Hawkins, one of the world's leading technology designers, was headed toward a plateau. He'd founded the company Palm with the mission to build a tablet computer that would set the world on fire. Its first release, the Zoomer, was destined for success. Hawkins got all the right people together, and he had a plan. He and Palm would build software applications to run on the device; another company, GeoWorks, would build the operating system; and Casio would manufacture it.

The Zoomer debuted in October 1993. It tanked.

The device was slow, the handwriting recognition didn't work very well, and it was just too big. It cost millions of dollars and several years to bring to Zoomer to market. In modern times this might be referred to as an "epic fail." Instead of closing up shop, though, Hawkins went back to the drawing board. This time, as Alberto Savoia might say, he pretotyped it. He went to his garage and built a prototype of what the device would look like out of wood. He fashioned a stylus out of a chopstick and then started to walk around with it. When he needed to make an appointment, he'd pull the wooden device out and imagine that the appointment would be made. Hawkins carried it around for months, making fake appointments, reimagining the button configurations, identifying design failures, and then correcting them—cheaply. He lived with the product, put it through real-life paces, and all it cost was a slab of wood.

The rest, as they say, is history. The Palm Pilot was one of the most successful devices in history. Hawkins had learned a huge lesson from the Zoomer—adapt, and don't fail slowly. With his wooden pretotype, he could make revisions as quickly as he could get his hands on a hammer and some nails. After lots of fast failures, he reached one of the greatest successes in technology history.

———

In the spirit of pretotyping, Alberto Savoia left his executive job at Google in 2012.

"I felt like I was plateauing. I felt I've proven I can do software, I've proven I can manage software," he said. With a pedigree like Savoia's, undoubtedly he could name his price at almost any firm in Silicon Valley. It would have been easy, safe. But Savoia chose a different path. A few months after leaving one of the best jobs in technology, Savoia cofounded Prototype Labs. "My mission is to help people find the right 'it.' I'm also going to expand 'it' in the future to personal lives: finding the right job, making sure you get the right major, and all of those things because the lessons are all very similar." It's a very different path for Savoia. But who says successful people don't hit plateaus, too? "Now I'm being a coach, a public speaker, and if that's not a way to break out of an engineering plateau, then I don't know what is." Savoia could fail, but that doesn't seem to bother him. He's got a secret weapon. "Just so you don't think I'm crazy, I did pretotype the idea of making a living with pretotyping. I created a brochure for a one-day seminar. I know I could build the material if I needed to, but I just had the brochure. I went to people and said, 'Would you sign up for this one-day workshop at Stanford?' And then I went to Stanford and said, 'There are people that would sign up for this workshop,' and then I made it happen. It was a pretty hectic month, but I am living my life by pretotyping everything."

The willingness to try when failure is likely is a distinct character trait. We all seem to have it at birth, but for some, it dissipates later in life. To see that trait in action, just watch babies trying to crawl. They push themselves up in a yoga-like position with their arms outstretched and then, under the weight of their own torsos, they collapse back to the ground. Hugh watched his daughter do this for weeks. Sometimes, her little legs would kick back and forth behind her, trying to get some sort of traction. He'd crawl next to her, showing her how it's done. She'd look and smile, try again, and fail. Eventually, she tried other techniques to move around the house. For a while, she engaged in what Hugh called "creative rolling" to get where she wanted to go. He once clocked her moving at one body revolution per second (these are the kinds of statistics Hugh's wife has to put up with, being married to a mathematician). Later, his daughter was able to do a seated shuffle. It's hard to really describe this move to someone who hasn't seen it, but think of an agitated chipmunk that is inching toward its target. Her whole existence was about trying, failing, and trying again.

"All babies are eager to learn," said Carol Dweck, professor of psychology at Stanford, in a lecture there. "You never see an unmotivated baby." Dweck believes that this is a *growth mind-set*—babies believe that they can do something today that they couldn't do yesterday. People with a growth mind-set see success as an outcome of their efforts, not an inherent quality of who they are. They are willing to try and fail, and learn from that failure to improve. Sadly, like the baby elephant you met at the beginning of this book who confined himself to the bonds of a weak chain and a small radius, many people grow out of this growth mind-set.

"Some people have a *fixed mind-set*. They believe that their basic intelligence is just a fixed trait. They think they have a fixed amount [of intelligence] and that's that," she said. Dweck believes that this makes people with a fixed mind-set very concerned about the intelligence they have. Someone with a fixed mind-set is afraid to hold a mirror up to his own abilities. He sees failure as a reflection of who he is as a person. The result: People with a fixed mind-set don't try. "They think, 'Am I going to look smart, am I not going to look smart?' And they base their activities on whether their intelligence will be show in a positive light." Since they believe that their skills are finite,

how they do today is who they are. People with a fixed mind-set pro-
crastinate. They also tend to be perfectionists, never wanting to "finish" something for fear that it will be judged—and, by extension, that
they will be judged.

"There is a danger of reaching a plateau because you're not willing
to see that you're fallible," Dweck told us during an interview at her
Stanford office. A fixed mind-set is a scary place to be. If you're judged
poorly and you think that your talents are fixed, you believe you can't
improve. Criticism cuts to the very core of who you are as a person.
It's like the cruel schoolyard barbs traded among kids: "You're fat!"
says one. The other child responds: "I may be *fat*, but *you're ugly*, and I
can lose weight." Someone with the fixed mind-set thinks that if she
holds her intellect up to a mirror, she'll see an ugly fool. Someone with
a growth mind-set doesn't mind appearing foolish.

Carol Dweck believes that people who have a growth mind-set
are much better equipped to handle the twists and turns of life. They
see failure as a reflection of their efforts, not the essence of who they
are.

"Growth mind-set people are tuned into mistakes," Dweck told
us. "They look for them, they use them. When they study, they have
yardsticks of comprehension; they validate their learning against
other sources." Dweck's research points to how one fosters this
growth mind-set in children and adults—or how parents can create
monsters. Parents, she says, often mistakenly praise a child instead
of praising his or her efforts. They say, "Look at what you've done,
you're so smart!" Or, "You are brilliant." It's hard not to effusively
praise your small children when they accomplish even the most trivial things: figuring out how to open a bottle, pulling up on the couch,
or learning a new word. Dweck's research shows that this type of
praise gives children a sense that their worth comes from who they
are, not how hard they try. Children start to believe that they have

a fixed capacity to achieve. In one study, Dweck looked at the influence of praise for intelligence versus praise for effort in a group of 128 fifth-graders. Each child was asked to spend four minutes solving a set of medium-difficulty puzzles. After they were done, a female researcher spoke with each child individually, scored their results, and no matter how they did, the researcher told the child that they had performed well, like this: "Wow, you did very well on these problems. You got [number of problems] right. That's a really high score." Regardless of what their actual score was, each child was told that he or she had solved at least 80 percent of the problems correctly. After that initial praise, about a third of the students were also praised on their intellect: "You must be smart to solve these problems," and so on. Another third of the children were praised on their effort: "You must have worked hard at these problems." The final third, the control group, were given no additional feedback. Children were then given four minutes to work on a harder group of puzzles. This time each group was told they did "a lot worse" on them and were informed they had solved no more than half of the problems correctly.

What happened next was shocking.

All three groups were then asked to solve a third set of puzzles, similar to the first set. The control group improved slightly on this third trial, by about 3 percent. What about the group that had been praised for their intelligence on the first go-around?

They plateaued. Their scores dropped by 18 percent.

Those children saw failure as a reflection of their innate ability to solve these kinds of problems, of who they were as people.

But what of the children praised for their effort? Those told, "You must have worked hard at these problems"? To them, failure was a reflection of their effort; their response was to work even harder. The effort-praised group increased performance by 23 percent!

Similar results have been reported across a very diverse set of scenarios and age groups. Dweck's research shows that people who believe they have a finite set of talents and abilities see failure as a reflection of their fundamental core being, their essence—who they are—and not simply what they've done, or the results they've seen in the past. In one case, Dweck and her colleagues studied freshmen at the University of Hong Kong who had a deficiency in English. The students who had a fixed mind-set were reluctant to take a remedial course. They didn't want to expose their deficiency—even though English is the dominant language in Hong Kong. The result is a plateau of self-preservation, where people avoid risky endeavors that might expose how limited they truly are.

"The fixed mind-set has so much fear of humiliation and so much, maybe, remembered humiliation that it stops you from growth," Dweck said.

Fixed mind-sets can also cause people to misjudge others, making them miss out on potential friendships. People with a fixed mind-set tend to put others in categories.

"Is this a smart person or not a smart person? Are they a winner or a loser?" Dweck says. "Then, because you think these things are fixed, you don't revise readily. You know, that person is not as smart as I am, I don't have to worry about competition from them."

On the other hand, those who reshape their lens of self-reflection look at failure for what it truly is—a combination of effort and circumstance—and can hone their habits into peak behaviors and achieve greatness.

"There is a voice in your head from the fixed mind-set and a voice in your head from the growth mind-set. The fixed mind-set voice will tell you, 'Don't try that, it's too hard, you'll look stupid.' If you make a mistake it'll say, 'See, I told you, there's still time to get out.' You need to answer it back with the growth mind-set," Dweck told us. But what if the voice of the fixed mind-set persists? "Do it. Execute. Take that risk. Hear the criticism. Feel bad for a day or two. Use the criticism."

If you're still held captive by a fear of failure, you've hit perhaps the most toxic plateau cause of all: perfectionism.

9. APPLICATION

The Third Action

Or, Blowing Away the Dull Fog of Perfectionism

One more story of a classroom prank pulled by the teacher is in order. Bob, more than a decade ago, was teaching junior-level editing at the prestigious University of Missouri School of Journalism.

You could say Bob totally freaked out his students. He might have gotten himself into some hot water with the administration, too, if any of the students had blabbed about it. There he was, telling these future Bob Woodwards and Katie Courics something they'd never heard before, and something they really didn't want to hear.

"What's the most important task of a newspaper editor every day?" he asked them and then began logging their answers on a chalkboard.

They treated every class like a press conference. He loved that. Answers were shouted with abandon.

"To break news stories."

"To get everything right, to be accurate."

"To be fair."

And since they had been focusing on copyediting in recent classes . . .

"To make sure there are no typos."

Through each answer he drew a line.

"Wrong. Wrong. Wrong. And wrong," he said.

They shouted a few more guesses. He shot those down, too. Finally, when their guesses were exhausted, he gave his answer.

"It's simple. It says it right here on the front page." He then picked up the newspaper and pointed to a small word under the masthead. It said simply, "Daily."

They were completely confused. Exactly the plan.

"Daily. It means you promise this paper will be there every morning at six A.M. when people wake up. Daily. That's the biggest and first promise you make to readers. That's the one thing you can't compromise. And if any of these other things get in the way of that," he said, and pointed to their rejected answers, "they have to go."

Anticipating their next question, he continued.

"And, yes, that means some nights—in fact, many nights—you will knowingly send the paper out the door with mistakes. You want to minimize them. You want them to be small mistakes. But there will come a time—many times—when you will have to pick between 'daily' and 'perfect,' and every time, you must pick 'daily.'"

As he expected, the students now thought that Bob was the new Richard Nixon, and they were going to expose "Mistakegate." These bright young twenty-year-olds spent most of their time in the journalism program learning about First Amendment law, Marshall McLuhan, hidden biases in journalism, and how they were going to change it all.

He was giving them a much more "earthy" lesson. They didn't like it.

"Look, it doesn't say, 'Daily, except when we have to go back and re-edit a few stories,' or 'Daily, except when our basketball writer thinks he has a good scoop so we waited and waited and now, sorry, there's no paper.' It says, 'Daily.' "

Then, he made his final point. "And so your job as a journalist is this: You are not supposed to put out the best paper you can put out. You are supposed to put out the best paper you can *in the time you have*. There's a big difference."

The argument continued for the rest of the class period. He didn't convince a single student, but before the semester was over, not one had failed to see his point. They had learned it all firsthand. These bright kids were part of a special program that took them from this editing class right to a copyediting job at the *Missourian* newspaper, a for-profit rag owned by the school. Very soon, they would be on the front lines of the daily paper, jamming to send the camera-ready pages to the printer by midnight, and they were in for a shock.

No matter how well you have paid attention, no matter how agile you remain, as midnight approaches, it is still shockingly difficult to keep on applying your best judgment in real time.

Perhaps the most insidious of all human imperfections often lies hidden in the weeds most of our lives. But it rears its ugly head and screeches for our attention in an environment of intense deadlines. It kills all learning and dooms us to a life of plateaus: the desire to be perfect.

You probably won't be surprised to learn that the hardest thing for a twenty-year-old journalist to do is to write or copyedit on deadline. When you are having those first heady experiences of seeing your work in print, and knowing all your peers will see your work in print, and thousands of readers will see your work in print, you are pretty darn worried about making very public mistakes.

For many students, this is almost crippling. They spend two hours poring over a story that really should take fifteen minutes to edit. They scream when they see the camera-ready version of their pages and notice typos. They beg, always, for more time. The single hardest lesson for young journalists to learn—harder than learning about subtle racial prejudice or how to write clever headlines—is how to throw tasks overboard when the hour grows late. There's never enough time to finish what really needs to be done to make a newspaper.

"Do I really need to make that extra phone call? Do I really need to listen to the mayor's lengthy conference call? Do I really need this paragraph? Can't this lead be better?" These are the impossible questions that get asked every day in every newsroom. Every one is a judgment call. Putting together a newspaper—really, putting together anything with a deadline—requires constant reassessment of progress toward that deadline, and a constant willingness to throw tasks overboard if you are falling behind. For many people, performing this kind of daily life triage is a perfectly impossible task—a rigid, unforgiving plateau.

Do you dwell on small mistakes for hours, days, or even weeks after they occur? Are you crushed when someone points out a small flaw in your work? Have you ever spent four hours fine-tuning a task that could have been completed in ten minutes? Are you haunted by uncertainty when you finish a task, so nothing ever feels finished? Have you ever hidden mistakes to avoid hearing one nagging comment from a friend or coworker? Can one negative comment from your boss or mother-in-law throw you into a tailspin? Do typos in e-mails or sloppy grammar in speech bother you so much that you can't even see or hear the meaning of the words being used? Do the words *good enough* make you cringe?

Then you're likely engaging in a form of self-torture that many psychologists now recognize as a modern-day epidemic—

part obsessive-compulsive disorder, part overbearing superego, part digital-age narcissistic nightmare, and nearly always on the edge of miserable. You are a slave of success but focused on failure. Some therapists will tell you that you're doomed to a life of self-doubt and depression.

We'll tell you that perfectionist behavior leads directly to plateaus. The quest for perfection is the enemy of improvement. At its worst, perfection is the ultimate weapon wielded by that great cosmic enemy of plateau-busting: procrastination, which we'll examine deeply in a moment. But we're going to show you that perfectionist tendencies can be curbed, slain, even harnessed and put to good use. We'll show that it's better to be better than perfect. We're going to show you the power of the words *"good enough."* And we're even going to reveal how procrastination, once mastered, can be a great ally in everything from cleaning your bathrooms to writing that great novel. But first, we're going to be perfectly clear about what perfectionism is.

Life as a perfectionist is like living in a constant state of Olympic competition. Nothing is done for fun. A ski weekend turns into a quest for the over-forty World Cup title; a weekend stroll in the woods becomes a foot race, or a chance to burn 663 calories. An echo of that quality we so admire in our professional athletes, perfectionism is not settling for second place, whether in child rearing or stacking rows of toilet paper in the store. The pressure is always on.

The constant questing means perfectionists only take on tasks when they know they can be champion; for them, it's first place or bust, it's all or nothing.

Perfectionists lead rigid lives; they avoid tasks that might expose any inadequacies. Life in this mistake-free cocoon eventually turns into an echo chamber, where sufferers never try anything new, never get any critical feedback, and never receive new information needed to break through plateaus. Many perfectionists end up ferociously concealing their mistakes, the way a bulimic conceals trips to the bathroom—a tactic that ends the critical life feedback loop altogether. As we learned from Carol Dweck in the previous chapter, perfectionists have that classic fixed mind-set. As a result, they see any negative feedback as an attack on their very souls. So they avoid it at all costs.

When psychologists Paul Fitts and Michael Posner wrote their groundbreaking book on learning, *Human Performance*, they described a three-stage process for acquiring any new skill: the things-are-new cognitive stage, when it takes focused effort just to get by; the associative phase, when things start becoming easy; and the autonomous stage, when you can do things without thinking. Of course, there is a fourth phase that athletes and world-class performers know about—beyond automatic lies "expert." As you might guess, Derek Jeter didn't join the three-thousand-hit club by going through the motions. It required focused practice to slowly eliminate flaws in his game and any vulnerabilities in his swing. You might think of focused practice as going back through that three-stage process over and over: finding a weakness, forcing yourself to awkwardly reform that weakness, and slowly turning it into strength. To put a positive spin on it, some therapists talk about finding your "growth edge" and constantly pushing your boundaries. No one can get to such a place without expert coaching, without outside feedback—and, in fact, without particularly expert feedback in precisely the right areas, something Fitts and Posner call "augmented feedback."

Perfectionists stink at this process. They avoid all situations where anything but positive feedback might arise. They are blind to their blind spots. They refuse focused practice. And they certainly aren't willing to dive back into the awkward, cognitive-heavy learning phase over and over. They kill the feedback loop and, with it, any chance at overcoming plateaus. In one of the great ironies of the universe, perfectionism is perhaps the biggest obstacle to peak behaviors.

Perfectionists focus on one point in time: the end. Graduation. Wedding Day. The perfectly clean house. They get no joy from the journey or the process. They can't imagine what happens *after* things are perfect. The second day on the dream job, or the second day of the marriage, is often cause for a descent into depression. The house with the impeccable carpet and plastic-covered furniture is a museum, not a place where people live. Perfectionism is the search for an ending that doesn't exist.

Perfectionists are so busy fiddling with fonts that they never get credit for the big ideas in the PowerPoint presentation. They live out a terrible version of the 80-20 rule, spending most of their energy trying to perfect that last 20 percent of any task. They get caught like a needle in a scratched record on fine details while neglecting the essence of a task. They dither; they endlessly debate. They fail to recognize one critical element of the just-noticeable difference we discussed earlier—they don't realize that if they are struggling over fine details that are below everyone else's noticeable threshold, the struggle isn't worth it. As a result, they are often tremendously unproductive in the workplace.

As coworkers, or in groups, they are often that person who throws a monkey wrench into discussions just as a group is about to reach consensus. Their obsessive insistence on minutiae can turn a one-hour meeting into a two-hour meeting, or make a one-hour meeting entirely unproductive.

Examples are easy to come by; here's one. Consider the plight of the frantic amateur choir director who has sixty minutes to rehearse five songs before a church service. One insistent tenor demands to practice the tricky key change in the closing song over and over, which the director unwisely allows to consume the first forty-five minutes of practice. The end result is disastrous: five seconds of music occupies the whole group for 75 percent of rehearsal time, leaving precious few minutes for everything else. Perfectionists are incapable of seeing the forest for the trees, and their neurotic desire to get things right blinds them to the needs of friends, colleagues, and even fellow choir members. The perfectionist is out of balance, stuck, and has no sense of the bigger picture or the consequences of "getting it right."

When perfectionists are managers, they are unreasonably demanding micromanagers who irritate employees by obsessing over nonessential details. Because everything is important, they are terrible at prioritizing, perhaps the most important task of a manager. They can't trust others to "get it right." And they can't leave anything misplaced, be it an eyebrow hair or a slightly crooked picture on a wall.

There is nothing wrong with straight pictures, of course. There's nothing wrong with personal grooming or the quest for self-improvement. But perfectionism is another thing entirely. The spirit behind it is not the joy of excellence; it is an absolutely deadly fear of failure. Therapists have developed extensive diagnostics to identify the different types of perfectionists, and you can get a sense of where you fall right now from this simple test: How do you treat mistakes? Are they learning experiences, or are they hateful events to be avoided at all costs? Can you name the last five big mistakes you've made and what happened as a result? Your emotional reaction to mistakes says much about you, and about your ability to break out of whatever plateau you are in.

It's always been this way—"Learn from your mistakes, or you will be doomed to repeat them," your mother or father said. But today, there's a difference. Modern society is more critical, and self-critical, than at any other time in human history. Our faces and voices are recorded constantly and played back for us in countless forms of indignity. "The hair looks bad, the gut's sticking out, and oh, that voice!"—we assure you, a caveman never uttered those self-conscious words. Neither did an eighteenth-century tobacco farmer in Virginia. Things are much worse in the age of Facebook. Some people are literally "life-casting" their entire existence to the world in video on the Internet; thanks to Facebook and incessant status sharing, many of us effectively do that anyway. Your bra strap might have been showing inappropriately at that party last week, but now, there's a critical difference: The chance that this exposed bra strap will be made immortal, to be dwelled on and Googled forever, is greater now than it's ever been.

Meanwhile, the art of color commentary that once might have been limited to a sidekick in a baseball announcer's radio booth is now a national pastime. Workers get extensive reviews; kindergarteners receive five-page narrative report cards; and, of course, every photograph posted online now comes complete with dozens, if not hundreds, of commenters. If we live our lives like an Olympic contest, the competition is broadcast on live TV, with our friends providing constant commentary in a hellish version of talk radio.

That's why perfectionism is at an all-time high. Gordon L. Flett, a psychology professor at York University in Toronto, says more than 50 percent of today's Western school-age children exhibit the perfectionist traits described above. And most high-achieving women suffer from some form of it.

"[If] we rounded up 100 creative, career-oriented women, it is likely that perfectionism would be rampant, especially if we measure the pressure to be perfect that we have called socially prescribed perfectionism, and the need to seem perfect when presenting the self in public," Flett told us during a summer Sunday morning e-mail chat. Even though his morning coffee had yet to kick in (he was sure to tell us that), he made nary a typo during our extended electronic dialogue. Our highly knowledgeable society produces this ugly by-product—rather than seeing people's achievements holistically, we live in an era of rampant picking apart. We break things into little pieces, finding more and more ways to "improve" each piece. Everything deserves criticism. How dare your eyebrows be so far apart/so close together! Whole milk in your latte? That's nuts. And it's simply indefensible that you haven't laser-whitened those teeth yet.

Women are particularly susceptible, of course—just look at the magazine covers on display near any supermarket checkout counter and you can see the punishment for being less than perfect in public. That message is internalized at a very young age.

"We know the immediate and widespread reaction that follows when a major celebrity does something wrong. So . . . people can see the price that is paid for making mistakes in public," Flett says.

Flett is perhaps the world's leading researcher on the subject, though he would object to that style of ranking. For him and other researchers, all perfectionism is not the same—and, of course, depending on the meaning you ascribe the word, all perfection-seeking behavior is not bad. He offers three types of negative perfectionists.

- Self-oriented (those who expect perfection of themselves)
- Other-oriented (those who demand perfection from others)
- Socially prescribed perfectionists (those who think others expect perfection from them)

Perfectionists often manifest their condition in one of three ways: The self-oriented have an irritating self-promotion style that involves constant attempts to impress others by bragging or displaying their work publicly in an endless quest for compliments; the self-oriented gyrate madly to avoid situations that might reveal imperfections; and the socially prescribed have a tendency to hide problems and an inability to admit failure.

Flett's 10 signs your a perfectionist*

1. You can't stop thinking about a mistake you made
2. You are intensely competitive and can't stand doing worse than others
3. You either want to do something "just right" or not at all
4. You demand perfection from other people
5. You won't ask for help if asking can be perceived as a flaw or weakness
6. You will persist at a task long after other people have quit
7. You are a fault-finder who must correct other people when they are wrong
8. You are highly aware of other people's demands and expectations
9. You are very self-conscious about making mistakes in front of other people
10. You noticed the error in the title of this list

In one fascinating test of perfectionist tendencies, children were given a computer test rigged to fail. The perfectionists couldn't stop trying and exhibited elevated levels of anger and anxiety while taking the test. They waited much longer before crying uncle; some never did. These poor kids have been robbed of the critical words "I can't do it."

Being a perfectionist can often manifest in an equal but opposite reaction, too. Young adults who seem proficient at a skill suddenly quit when they realize they've reached the apex of their natural abilities and the competition gets tough. They can't win all the time—oh no! A seemingly promising high school football player will suddenly

abandon the sport when he rises to the level of equal competition—
and take up bowling.

Dwelling on mistakes can produce a seemingly identical result.
A perfectly good major league second baseman like Chuck Knob-
lauch will make a mistake on a simple throw to first base, and then
be so consumed by the horror of the error that he will make another,
and another, and another, and ultimately become so disturbed that
he loses his million-dollar job due to his inability to perform a task
that was easy for him even when he was nine years old.

The ability to quickly forget a mistake—to have a short memory, many athletes say—is an essential element of succeeding at a
high level. In fact, in a sport like baseball, where hitters fail more
often than they succeed, success is defined by how players react to
failure.

Perfectionism can also be used to conceal a lack of competence—
such as an ineffective marketing manager who spends all day copyediting a one-page press release in an effort to avoid placing phone
calls needed to pitch the company's news.

The intersection of housekeeping—perhaps the greatest source
of domestic strife—and perfectionism is instructive. Witness the rise
of the ragingly popular FlyLady, an online character who acts as a
cheerleader for web users who feel overwhelmed by housework. Fly-
Lady attracts millions of users; she says that during a recent fifteen-
minute "fling" event, she coached users to toss 104,000 pounds of
clutter from their homes in one quarter-hour. The main philosophy
behind her site: Most homes are cluttered and dirty, ironically, because their occupants insist on perfectly clean rooms. When 100 percent cleanliness proves to be impossible, an endless task of keeping
up with dirt, the perfectionist housekeeper within us despairs and
simply gives up. Why wash the living room rug if the kids are just
going to track in mud after the next rain anyway? This silent despair

overwhelms perhaps millions of families, often making their homes nearly uninhabitable.

The solution, says FlyLady, is a new way of thinking.

"You're not behind. Just jump in wherever you are," she says, over and over. Her favorite kick-start: No matter what the condition of your home, your bathroom, your kitchen, go "shine" the kitchen sink. Make it the one sanctuary, the one cleanliness victory, in your house. This make-a-beachhead technique is a real-time solution just as is her other main technique: Don't try to clean the entire house at once. Just set a fifteen-minute timer, do what you can in those fifteen minutes, and stop.

Where has this obsession come from? How did it creep so neatly into modern culture? Housekeeping is not a uniquely modern-day malady—but stress about keeping bacteria-free kitchen floors no doubt is. Swiffers clearly wouldn't have worked well on the dirt floors of log cabins in the 1880s. The ancients surely suffered from perfectionism—can't you imagine Alexander demanding that every book in his library be lined up in the same direction?

"There are historical accounts of perfectionists that go back many centuries," Flett says. "When I visited a museum last year in Boston, I stumbled upon the concept of perfection, which was de-scribed on an Egyptian sarcophagus from the tombs, so it is a theme that goes back thousands of years."

Many historical examples of perfectionism are celebrated. We consider the obsessive work ethics of artists such as Van Gogh to be poetic.

Flett says perhaps the best example in Western history is his wife's ancestor John Harrison, who invented the chronometer. A clock maker, Harrison set about solving perhaps the biggest techno-logical problem of his time—letting a captain know where his ship was at sea. In his thirties, Harrison invented a very precise and sturdy clock that could determine exact longitude at sea during long voyages; the chronometer changed long-distance travel forever. It also consumed the rest of Harrison's life; he fiddled with the gadget for the next fifty years until his death in 1776 at age eighty-three. In 2002, Britons polled by the BBC named him one of the top hundred Britons of all time. Harrison's hard work is universally recognized; the internal misery created by his obsessive-compulsive tendencies comes across as a fun quirk in biographies. Nearly every biographical description of him has the word *grumpy* in the first few paragraphs.

Perfectionism isn't entirely a modern-day creation, but it's fair to say that it's been democratized in our era. Today, nearly anyone can have a library, and nearly anyone can obsess over which direction the spine is facing. Anywhere there's time for leisure, there's time for perfectionism.

The study of perfectionism arose in parallel with the study of psychology, and it seems to be part of what drove early patients into therapy. As such, it's reflected in most classic personality theories, according to Flett: The famous Austrian psychotherapist Alfred W. Adler wrote about striving for perfection to overcome the inferiority complex, Freud's superego was governed by the perfection principle, and German psychoanalyst Karen Horney aptly described neurotics as striving for perfection.

The crazed quest for perfection can even be cited as a cause of some of mankind's darkest hours—Hitler's views of Aryans as the master race, for example.

Before the 1950s, life was still too hard for most Westerners to obsess over minutiae, however. Blue collars are usually dirty, too. The rise of a comfortable middle class, and the switch to a white-collar economy, leads directly to the next logical question: Is that white collar white enough?

Flett has an interesting theory about the arc of perfectionism in modern times.

"Because perfectionism is central to eating disorders, it has occurred to me that perfectionism might follow the same course as anorexia, which was detected in the late 1800s, but seemingly grew exponentially in prevalence in the seventies and eighties," he said.

But how is wanting a perfect body, or a perfect bathroom, or a perfect PowerPoint presentation connected to plateaus?

Directly. Perfect, you see, is the enemy of good.

Recall all the techniques we've described for breaking through situations where you're stuck—stuck at work without a promotion, stuck in your marriage, stuck in your piano playing. If the goal is to improve in all these facets of life, trying to make things perfect is probably your worst enemy, just as counterproductive as trying to have a perfect bathroom or PowerPoint presentation. Of all the things you might think of to try to improve your marriage, your career, or your musicianship, doing the same thing over and over is probably nowhere on your list. Yet that's precisely what the perfectionist is programmed to do. Perfectionists ignore the law of diminishing returns and play the same piece over and over and over again, each time focusing on tiny mistakes—but eventually, as musicians in the trade will tell you, they are merely "practicing the mistakes" over and over. Recall from the discussion of Ebbinghaus and memorization earlier in this book how repetition runs into the law of diminishing returns—plateaus—faster than most realize. Well-timed practices that are consciously spaced out bring much better results. Sprinkling a bit of diversity into practice accelerates success even more. The best way to finally conquer that complicated section of music is to learn some new pieces, and learn some new skills, which in turn can be transferred to the troublesome piece. Just as a new pair of shoes can wake up an old dress, new pieces help a musician play old, familiar pieces anew. But perfectionists hate trying new things. Their ability to take risks is severely diminished, if it survives at all. And thus perfectionism reduces creativity and innovation—precisely those qualities most needed to adapt in the global marketplace. Perfectionists never get the magical, key piece of advice that suddenly busts their paradigm and changes everything. They are like the friend who walks around all afternoon with lettuce in her teeth because everyone is too afraid to say anything to the easily embarrassed woman. The cocoon has killed her feedback loop.

"All right," you might be thinking, "enough bashing of neat freaks." And, by the way, we imagine you also might be thinking that there are plenty of situations where perfectionists are awfully handy. Brain surgery comes to mind. If we've really irritated you, you're probably hoping that the next time Sullivan or Thompson end up in an emergency room, the perfectionist doctor is off duty. Heck, you probably know that perfectionist accountants, lawyers, and secretaries can be awfully handy, too. And you're right, of course. Perfectionism has a place. We're not arguing against doing things right. We're arguing against misplaced efforts. It's easier to show than tell, though, so let's do that now.

As you might imagine, corporate America has caught on to this growing obsessive perfectionism among the masses and turned it into a way to make a lot of money. The perfection business is worth at least $6 billion per year, masquerading as the "organization industry," embodied by companies like the Container Store. "Professional organizers"—folks who tell you how to make the most of your closet space—even have a powerful trade group now, the Association of Closet and Storage Professionals. Barry Izsak is its head.

Izsak uses a simple card trick to convince skeptics that perfect organization is worth every penny, a story told with deft elegance in the book *A Perfect Mess*, penned by Columbia professor Eric Abrahamson and journalist David Freedman.

Izsak gives a deck of cards to two people. One is randomly ordered, as if shuffled well; the other is lined up in perfect order. He asks each deck holder to find four cards within the deck. Each time, of course, the person with the ordered deck wins the race going away. Perfect order, then, is clearly superior to chaos, runs the argument.

Not so fast.

Izsak leaves out one important consideration in his card trick—the time it takes to line up the cards in order. The natural state of a deck of cards—and, in fact, many things—is disorder. Setting this into perfect order can take a lot of time and, in fact, is often a huge waste of time. Abrahamson and Freedman perform some alternate calculations and discover that if the card trick is run fairly—if the 140 seconds or so it takes to line up the cards in perfect order is included—the holder who seeks out the four cards from the shuffled deck wins easily.

The case for perfect organization is not nearly as clear as some would make it.

We're sorry to all those perfectly organized folks who feel utter glee the one time each month that someone asks for a file and they can pull out the receipt in a moment or two, but the truth is this: It's quite possible that you'd be better off leaving those receipts in a big messy pile on your desk, attacking it only in that occasional moment when someone needs something.

Wait, wait, before you start jabbing at us with hanging file folders, the story doesn't stop there. And all you slobs in the world who are smirking at your allegedly anal-retentive companions, you have another think coming, too.

Just as there is something practical between messy and clean, there's more than one way to organize a deck of cards. What matters is not neatness or messiness but rather *application*. If you had to look up a card in a pile every five minutes for forty hours per week, you're darn right it's worth taking two minutes to line the cards up in order. If you only need to perform the card trick once in a while, then ordering is a waste of time. But there are a few lovely options other than these extremes. What about spending fifteen seconds or so to pile the cards in batches by suit? Even if you didn't do it perfectly, you'd lower the search time through a random deck by roughly 75 percent while avoiding the large up-front cost of creating a perfect deck. Or what if you simply piled red cards here, black cards there—or face cards here, numbered cards there? Can you imagine some others? Again, in these scenarios, what matters is application; it will dictate the right size for your up-front work effort. The answer, like so many others, can be found in calculus. You can gradually lower the search cost by adding to the organization cost. Where's the right point for you in your current project? We can't tell you. But we can say that the right answer lies somewhere in between black and white, between messy and clean.

Perfectionists who can't live with their deck of cards batched in rough order will waste a lot of time on unnecessary up-front costs—for the rest of their lives. They'd also never be willing to even experiment with a looser form of organization such as what we've suggested—it's too risky, too outside the program.

By now, we hope it's clear why there's such a tight link between perfectionism and plateaus. Perfectionists are incapable of the kind of gray-area compromise required to takes things to a new level. They isolate themselves from new ideas and criticism, eliminating any chance that something new might arrive—even a happy accident—that could offer a breakthrough. Perfectionists live lives of sameness, wondering why new things never come. Perfectionism is the enemy of good, and good enough. But in an elemental way, perfectionism is the galactic enemy of action itself. If you believe in such things, as we do, it is the main tool of a demon whose existence has only one function: to stop the world from becoming a better place. This demon has many names. Here, we will use one that's probably new to you: procrastination.

Recall the last time you sat down to write a paper or an important e-mail. Chances are something like this happened next: You noticed that you suddenly had to pee, and then stopped by the fridge on your way back to the computer, and then chatted up a colleague about the kid's soccer team, until you finally decided it really was lunchtime. Don't feel guilty; everyone does it. Stop for a moment and pick your favorite forms of this kind of inaction. Golf? Changing the oil in your car? Twitter? Cleaning your room? Shopping? Obsessing over the kids/parents/neighbors?

While we're not about to let anyone off the hook by saying people have a biological disposition toward procrastination, or this negative force can be caused by a chemical imbalance, both those things are, in fact, true. From an evolutionary standpoint, humans need rest. Clearly, you can't spend all day running after buffalo or throwing spears. Moreover, while at rest, we often think our bodies have recovered sooner than they really have—any middle-aged man who volunteers for a second game of pickup basketball at the gym knows what we mean. So procrastination lets our minds tell our bodies, "No, wait a little longer." Four thousand years ago, the force was well-balanced by its opposite—"But I'm hungry" or "But a lion is chasing me"— which let people know exactly when break time was over.

Today, there is no such balancing force. For most of us, there is no direct relationship between being hungry and going to work. In fact, there isn't even a direct relationship between time worked and pay. Not long ago, a farmer's earnings were tied directly to how many wheat seeds he could sow and reap. In the salaried world, some people work seventy hours, and some work twenty and goof off for twenty, but they are paid the same amount. Even among hourly workers, some produce two or three times more than others but are paid at the same rate. It's strange and new, this idea that work and effort aren't tied directly to reward. It also means the impulse to rest often goes unchecked. That's why bodies at rest tend to stay at rest. Getting up always involves at least a small kick in the butt.

This same effect occurs in both our bodies and our minds, new brain studies show. In fact, intense mathematical computations can actually be more exhausting for the body than physical labor, and require more recovery time. Resting washes our brains with much-needed dopamine, which renews the synapses and prepares them for a new round of hard work. The problem is, there's rarely a lion chasing your brain around, forcing you to snap into action.

So the world's most powerful force of evil, if you believe some writers, is sitting right there on your shoulder, offering you a Garden of Eden's worth of temptations to distract you. And your own biology is working against you, too. How can you get off your duff and do the things that will break you out of a plateau-induced funk?

One way is outwit procrastination.

Stanford philosophy professor John Perry is a confessed procrastinator. In fact, he might be considered world-class. His website even contains a picture of him exercising at the beach, with the caption: "Author practices jumping rope with seaweed while work awaits."

Perry has noticed that procrastinators, such as authors, only have clean toilets when a book deadline looms, and he's decided to make that principle work for him. He calls it "structured procrastination." We chased him down by offering to distract him from the book he was working on by making him discuss plateaus with us.

Imagine a rotating to-do pile on top of your desk. On top is the business plan you must provide your investor before he will give you the money you need to quit your job. Below that is a poorly written draft of a book proposal that you know needs major work. Under that is an apology letter you need to write to your kid's fifth-grade teacher for missing the student-teacher conference. Then come cleaning out the garage, working out, changing the oil, and rebalancing your 401(k) investments.

If you think about it, all those tasks are pretty important, and every one would be worthy of a Saturday afternoon. Perhaps the most important thing for you and your family would be completion of that business plan. But the minute your brain focuses on that task, the welling force of procrastination rises up in your throat. Let it. Pretty soon, anything will be more appealing than that most dreaded task, and you'll gladly reach for no. 2 in that pile. Use the repulsion energy from the most dreaded task as a slingshot to another important job.

Of course, the problem with our model here is that you might never actually get to that business plan. Perhaps. But no doubt scheduling a week's vacation with your mother-in-law will eventually arise, and the business plan will get started in earnest.

It's shocking what seems appealing when there's real, hard work to be done. When there's a book chapter to be written, for example, Bob cleans. There is never anything so appealing as scrubbing the toilet when writing must be done. Yes, sir, the smell of bleach and the twisting of a Johnny Mop can be so, so much more appealing than sitting down with butt in the chair, doing work someone is paying for.

It's essential for anyone who plans to take on the battle of distraction to know this: The temptations never go away. Not after the six books and thousands of articles both of us have written. Not after your twenty-sixth piano concerto. Not after the first billion. Understanding the powerful inescapable forces arrayed against you—together with good habits, a good approach, and loving support—can make paying attention, remaining agile, and applying yourself easier. But every person who has ever done anything worth a damn has encountered relentless temptations to be lazy. Nothing good is ever effortless, even if movies like *Amadeus* portray Mozart's compositional process as a walk in the park. No one sits down beneath a tree and enjoys easy-street inspiration from muses. It is always a struggle.

This point is essential for those who are stuck in a plateau. We are often surprised by this battle, and we dupe ourselves into thinking that struggle itself is a sign that we should give up. It's not. It's a barrier, designed to derail you. Expecting the fight is half the battle.

While there are probably hundreds of causes of procrastination that we could name right now—perhaps even reading this book is procrastination for you!—there is one particularly devious cause we already know well: perfectionism.

A friend we'll call Peggy is like many of your friends, no doubt. She hates her job, has long since outclassed her boss, and feels her skills—and her life—are wasting away. She has a great idea for a small business, and she's spent years researching her product. She's even earned an MBA, partly so she can feel qualified to launch her business.

If only she could get that website finished. She paid the twenty-something programmer from work months ago to do it as a side job, but he keeps making excuses. Sure, there's a skeleton page up now, but it's nowhere near good enough. The fonts are wrong; the art is ugly. She's requested the changes repeatedly, but her programmer friend never seems to prioritize the project. And so Peggy's idea sits and waits. And waits.

It's a refrain we hear all the time—can't take that new job until I get a new wardrobe; can't go back to school until I get a new boss; can't write that novel until I finish remodeling the study. After all, who can write a novel in a study with orange walls! In fact, wall paint colors have probably been the death of great novels, new businesses, exercise programs, and all manner of personal growth projects all around the planet.

Have you ever stood frozen in the toiletry aisle of the grocery store, paralyzed by trying to decide what brand of toothpaste to buy? So has everyone else.

There's a very good reason for this. Deciding which toothpaste to buy is hard. Very hard! You barely know the truth about fluoride and whitening agents, let alone how to pick between a paste and a gel. Then there's the size consideration—is larger really cheaper? The math alone would stump most calculus students. And will this large tube even fit on your bathroom sink? What about those tubes that stand upright—are they better? Argh!!!!

Many life decisions follow this same route. Need to buy toilet paper? There are fifty choices. Need a toothbrush? There are a hundred choices. Need a hotel room in Manhattan? Expedia.com offers 542 choices. Need a flight from San Francisco to Chicago? There are nearly infinite possibilities, if connecting flights are included.

Welcome to Decision Quicksand. Life in the twenty-first century offers nearly boundless options for everything . . . and we humans hate it.

In a groundbreaking study on this uniquely modern malady called "Decision Quicksand: How Trivial Choices Suck Us In," marketing professors Aner Sela and Jonah Berger offer a good explanation of why otherwise capable adults seem overwhelmed by the tiniest of choices. They say that humans frequently confuse hard with important. Something deep inside us is triggered the second that a decision seems hard—psychologically, we begin to overestimate the importance of the choice. That's why, we're sad to say, you might have spent more time dithering over the shade of white you painted the bathroom woodwork than you spent deciding to buy this book. In fact, it's likely you spent more time on paint color than you spent picking mutual funds for your 401(k).

In their clever experiment, Sela and Berger tricked people into spending more time waffling between airline flights simply by making their fake airline websites harder to read. Even after controlling for all other factors, the slightest artificial hurdle that makes a choice hard puts people into a Decision Quicksand frame of mind. Because the process is difficult, people are tricked into thinking the decision is more important that it really is.

This Decision Quicksand leads to unnecessary emotional angst, and probably more than a few unnecessary domestic squabbles, but the consequences are even more dire than that. The researchers found a correlation between time spent on decisions and on dissatisfaction after the choice. The more deliberation on small choices, the unhappier the picker is.

The irony, which we've already hinted at, is that people spend far too much time on trivia and far too little time on the important stuff—deciding what mortgage broker to use, or who to marry, or when to change careers. Either problem leads to the same result: The final, most direct cause of a plateau is failing to decide to do anything at all.

For smaller choices—which gym should I join?—there are some pretty established rules to escape Decision Quicksand. Set a time limit for deciding that's commensurate with importance before your deliberations start. For example, give yourself only fifteen minutes to book that next flight. Delegate small decisions—"Honey, will you get the toothpaste?"—and live with another person's choices. And breaks are an important tool for breaking free from an obsessive-compulsive loop. If you find yourself trying yet another website after already considering 542 hotels in New York City, watch ten minutes of a baseball game to shock your brain back to center.

But often freeing yourself from a serious plateau at work, at home, in meditation, or in love requires something far more substantial. A commitment. Taking a stand. Trying something you've never imagined before. We've already discussed the importance of multimodal treatment in medicine—doctors give drug cocktails to minimize side effects and plateaus—and in life. We've given you eight areas to focus on when reaching for a breakthrough. Now comes the most important step: How do you decide what to do?

There are so many decisions to make, and so many ways decisions can go wrong—it's enough to make you think about avoiding choices all together. That's also a bad choice. (Just ask a perfectionist . . . well, on second thought, ask someone else.) You can't worry about getting everything perfectly right before you take the first step, but you also can't take the next twenty steps without honestly evaluating whether you're going the right way. You've got to allow for course correction, as we discussed in Chapter 8.

But how?

Fortunately, there is an entire field of study devoted to helping you make better decisions. It's called decision science. The name perhaps implies a little more than it can deliver—good choices are still a mixture of research and gut feelings—but there's an awful lot you can learn from the data that's been unearthed about good and bad decisions.

It is perhaps the paradox of our time. We have more information than any other generation, by far. When you get prostate cancer, when you buy a car, when you pick a college, when you pick a mate—there is nearly limitless information you can examine to help you predict the future and see if you are making the right or wrong choice.

Sadly, all this information is making us terrible at making decisions.

Huh?

Study after study shows that our brains are poorly equipped to consider dozens of data points while making up our minds. Even the smartest among us can only handle four or five. In fact, when confronted with too much information, many of us simply punt. Here's one test of this theory.

Sheena Iyengar of Columbia University found that when 401(k) plan participants were give two choices, 71 percent participated. Given fifty-nine options, participation fell to 61 percent.

Information overload isn't an academic phenomenon. A similar study showed investors who were given one hundred stock choices invariably made inferior picks than those given only a few. It's been said over and over that financial advisers rarely provide consumers with any real market advantage; in fact, nearly all managed mutual funds perform worse than index funds with stock chosen by computer. So why does the financial advice industry still survive? People see immense value in having someone else make decisions for them. Without information overload, the personal financial industry wouldn't exist.

So not having data is bad—you're a fool who lives as a magical thinker. And having data is bad—you can weigh it incorrectly, analyze it wrong, and let it overwhelm you. If you're ready to throw your hands up and cry uncle, good. Now you understand the depth of the problem and why you've been struggling to get past the artificial barriers set in front of you by bad decision making. Now it's time to solve the problem.

Let's wrap up all these techniques we've been talking about in a nice, pretty bow. Actually, to be more practical, let's make it an elastic band.

Elastic band decisions are the antidote to plateaus.

Picture now a thick rubber band, the kind that might have been snapped around a thick Sunday newspaper when it was delivered to you. What's the best way to get the band around the newspaper, which seems three times its size? Simple. You pull one direction—say horizontally—until it seems like the band will break. You anchor that on the edge of the paper. And then you pull the other direction, vertically, until the band is just the size you need. You take a little of this and a little of that. You employ nuance. You make one move until it no longer seems effective, then you take the opposite move.

What would happen if our rubber band stretcher was stuck in an accidental reinforcement cycle? He'd stretch the band so far horizontally that it would break, never reaching the necessary size. All the while, he'd be saying to himself, "But this worked before!"

Elastic band decisions recognize that life is a series of plateaus, and that one technique might work for a while, but then stop working. Sometimes, its opposite is precisely what's needed to solve the puzzle.

Or what if you picked up the rubber band and just began stretching it in all directions, hoping that you could somehow magically create the size you need to roll up all the papers? Decision science research tells us that our twenty-first-century digital world has done a great disservice to us and our need to simply mull over problems and let our unconscious have a go at them. As we said in the Greedy Algorithm chapter, a false god of immediacy leads to a scattershot approach to many issues. People are reluctant to "sleep on it," even though studies show sleeping on choices is remarkably effective.

Waiting to let choices stew a bit is related to the problem of having too much data, which acts as crack for the analytic side of your brain. Good choices are roughly half data, half hunch (again, imagine the rubber band), but today, data often crowds out our ability to make hunches informed by our unconscious. Feelings shouldn't be your only guide, but they certainly can serve as an excellent guide. Studies show that too much data suppresses the powerful unconscious, gut-level feelings we need to make good choices. In a classic experiment, subjects were asked to state preferences among a set of strawberry jams, and their results were compared to those of professional tasters. The subjects did nearly as well as the experts—who could be bad at tasting jam?—until they were asked to write detailed essays about their preferences. Then, the subjects' taste buds seemed to go kaflooey.

Shutting out your emotions is one sure way to make all your decisions half-bad.

On the other hand, too much information can also cripple the more logical parts of your brain, leading to a condition known informally as "information overload."

Angelika Dimoka, director of the Center for Neural Decision Making at Temple University, is one of numerous brain researchers taking full advantage of functional MRI machines to unlock the mysterious of our minds, and she's shown that information overload can force the sensible part of the brain—the dorsolateral prefrontal cortex—to "take five." During intense auctions she rigs to overload participants, she watches as that part of the brain lights up, blinking like a Christmas tree—and then at a certain point goes dark, as if a breaker were tripped. That probably happens to you every time you click on one more Google search link while researching a new school, or a potential vacation hotel, or another possible online dating prospect.

You need both your logic and your feelings to make good choices.

One way to think about it: Let your feelings imagine the solutions, the way Congress proposes legislation, but let your mind retain full presidential veto power. The creative and the analytic will always be in tension, like the tension along Pennsylvania Avenue. But used effectively, that's a good balance of power.

We've all known people who don't do so well in that veto department—the friend who believes the drug dealer she's dating will change, the investor who felt like it was a great idea to plunge into dot-com websites in 2001. On the other hand, we've all known people who seem crippled by decisions partly because they just can't go with their gut; every choice requires more and more information. That's why you won't see any one-size-fits-all advice here. Some people need to go with their gut more; some should give their gut a few years off while they reenter the dating scene. It depends. But here's one good guide—you probably already know which side of this continuum you're on. The fastest way to plateau breakthrough is to try the other side, to do what comes unnaturally to you.

There is a better answer than that, however. Psychologists have known for decades that the torment that often accompanies decisions is usually unnecessary. In fact, studies show people often need less than five minutes to assess even complex situations. How can this be? Those who study decision science have found that at the razor's edge of research and instinct is a critical skill that's the perfect tool for integrating your mind and heart. It's called "thin-slicing."

Whether you are trying to acquire a company or pick a salad for lunch, there can be nearly infinite variables to consider. And as we know, we usually overweight the data point right in front of us (say, the picture of the juicy hamburger beckoning us away from the salad). People who make good decisions don't even try to get all the information they can before pulling the trigger. First, they conjure up the three or four most significant variables and focus only on them. Perhaps only one data point matters—such as number of calories. (Remember, your mind can't hold more than four or five factors at a time, anyway.) Then, they weigh that very small number of factors efficiently, and they choose. Simple.

How do you perform this thin-slicing? How do you decide to

actually limit the information you receive? That's precisely where your gut comes in. Consider this: When a decision is made, what are the one or two things that will really matter later? Take picking a college, for example. Do you want a college that has sports teams you can root for? Do you want a school with a high job-placement rate? Do you want a pastoral campus? Is there one teacher in particular you hope to work with? Pick your top two, and go from there. That's thin-slicing.

There are more radical ways to thin-slice. Billy Beane, the *Moneyball* GM, doesn't actually attend Oakland A's baseball games. Why? He doesn't want his emotions influencing his decisions. If you think about it, there are plenty of ways you could say yes to some inputs and no to others. That's the quickest way to narrow down your decision into manageable nuggets. Naturally, some people are better at thin-slicing than others, and it takes practice. But it may very well lead to surprisingly good decisions that break you out of the plateau.

Among the most powerful decisions you can make is *not* to do something. Say you're offered a promotion. Who doesn't want a promotion? And that extra $12,000 a year sounds great. Perhaps. But really, the promotion means just $1,000 extra per month, or $500 per paycheck, or around $180 a week after taxes—maybe $30 a day. What if that promotion means you're going to have to stay at work until seven or eight P.M. every night and miss putting your kids to bed? Or that you will have to travel so much that you'll have to quit doing the charity work you love? Your gut will guide you, and thin-slicing will make it easy: If you really feel a need to move up and see the promotion as a step on a ladder to better things, you'll probably feel like you have to take it. But if you feel trepidation about the new job, you should probably take a hard, analytical look at the additional income and see if it will really help.

Most of all, you'll want to make an elastic decision. It's not all about the family, and it's not all about the career. At some points in your life, you should pick the title and the prestige; at others, you should find a way to be happy with the lower salary. Stretch the rubber band one way, then the other, never too far in either direction. Elastic band decisions are the antidote to the plateaus of life.

Surely, you've already seen through our simple metaphor of stretching a band one direction and then the other to secure a newspaper. In truth, the band is stretched roughly in a circle, snapped on the paper, and then rolled into place until it fits just right. It's not either/or, or horizontal/vertical. It's a 360-degree proposition, fitting that elastic band, requiring that it be stretched in all directions. At each point of the process, in all 360 degrees, there's a growth edge that needs stretching to fit neatly around the new goal. That's the only way you'll ever navigate the realities of a rich life, and the only way you will consistently break through.

Of course, deciding to act is just the beginning. Here's a proverb you might have heard before: People who have finished 90 percent of a task should think of themselves as half done. We call this "finishitis." The closer that you come to launching any new adventure, the more your demons will try to stop you. It's the way the universe works. It's homeostasis in action. Try to make a change, and you've disturbed the balance in the world; the universe will fight back. People will question your sanity. The demon will throw relationship drama at you. You'll get sick. You'll suddenly decide to take up skydiving. You'll rewrite that cover letter over, and over, and over, and never send it out. Perfectionism, most agree who examine it, is merely an excuse for procrastination, an excuse to not try after all.

But however insidious this enemy is, there are plenty of grand solutions. Structured procrastination, which we've already seen, is one. Here's another: Stop researching! In practical application, perfectionism often takes this one manifest form: It kills beginnings.

The next time you want to start something new, don't attempt comprehensive planning. Learn just enough to get started, and then get started. Then, learn how to do part two. If you're trying to replace the toilet in your bathroom, don't read up on the forty-seven ways the project can go wrong (plus, there's really only one—the new loo might spring a leak). Read up on how to pull out the old one, then bend down and start yanking. After you get the sucker out, go back to Home Depot and ask them how to drop a new loo on a wax ring properly.

Of course, this learn-as-you-go strategy isn't appropriate for every task. (Please, brain surgeons and pilots, as you were.) But you'd be surprised how much easier it is to begin a task—and to kill procrastination—by jumping into step one and taking a leap of faith that steps two, three, and four can be learned later.

As we have discussed in various ways already, you can start with a very, very rough approximation of what your idea is—remember the wooden Palm computer?—and just launch into a project. If everything Google does is beta, then everything you do can start in beta, too. Not all jobs or adventures require superior attention to detail. There is an inflection point we must constantly apply ourselves to judging: the moment at which continued efforts produce little or no added benefit. Learning when such points have occurred is a magic trick, a skill that goes along with becoming mature, we'd say. But here's one hint that you've arrived: When you feel yourself caught in a circle, trying the same thing over and over, writing that e-mail over and over, it's time to just hit send.

Learning to let go of self-defeating, repetitive behavior has a slogan in the recovery community: "If it's worth doing, it's worth doing badly," a twist of phrase usually attributed to Catholic writer G. K. Chesterton. Of course, somewhere drilled into your head from your childhood days is the more common phrase: "If it's worth doing, it's worth doing well." That's exactly the kind of programming that sends our minds down a destructive rat hole. The obvious conclusion to be drawn is "don't do it if you aren't great." Thank God most dancers in the history of humanity haven't thought that way. Replace that defeatist notion with this: "If it's worth doing, you should get started right away. And even if it's less than perfect, it's certainly worthwhile." If you must, think of it this way: "If it's worth doing, it's worth doing badly (at first)."

And here's another shocker for perfectionists: There may very well be more than one way to do things "perfectly." Real life is a lot more like a live blues jam than a recording—and any real blues fan will tell you that recordings are kind of dull compared to the real thing anyway. Every Grateful Dead performance was "perfect," but different. Jerry Garcia never played it wrong. Movies like *Amadeus*, and visions of poets sitting under trees praying to muses, have done a disservice to generations of creators who feel they are supposed to wait for communication from a god to write or sing or build in some perfect, preordained way. One concept that's very hard for young authors to absorb is that writing is a lot less like painting by numbers, where you are supposed to find the exact word and phrase in every place, and a lot more like bailing water out of a running river. You just take the words that are going by when you need them and write them down. There is no "right" way to communicate, no script from the heavens that you must capture. If we were to write this paragraph tomorrow, it would no doubt look substantially different. That's why it's fun. When you realize that your task is not to be perfect but merely to communicate, your communication improves immensely—as do your sleep habits.

And that brings us to the final, and most important, concept that will serve as your antidote to the plateau of perfectionism: satisficing, a combination of the words *satisfactory* and *suffice*. With every task you undertake—raising children, painting a Starbucks window, writing ad copy, making dinner—your goal should be to do *satisfactory* work that is satisfying to you and its consumers but at the same time is just enough to be *sufficient*. Satisficing takes much more into consideration than results: It weighs equally the pain and the process that are required to achieve a result. Search costs, for example: You might want to make the best salsa you've ever eaten, but that would require acquisition of the freshest vegetables. If the farmer's market doesn't open until tomorrow morning and the guests are coming tonight, then you'll have to make do with the more pedestrian tomatoes from the corner grocery store. Modern economists and behaviorists sometimes call this more realistic decision-making process "bounded rationality"—because a "fully rational" decision-making process that considers all options is impossible in the real world, decision makers simplify by self-limiting, or creating a boundary around, their options.

We just call it one of the keys to breaking through your plateaus.

Here's a better example. Say you need a new roommate for a year—your old roomie has suddenly announced she's leaving. So you place an ad on Craigslist and receive 150 responses. You might be tempted to interview all 150—after all, you want the best roommate possible. But if you tried that, a year would pass before you'd pick someone, and you'd end up eating an awful lot of rent. The more practical question to ask is, what number of potential roommates would you have to meet to pick a satisfactory replacement? Probably more than one, and certainly less than 150. Many factors might contribute to the number you consider: If you need help with the rent by next week, and you have to work late all this week, you might see only two or three. If the opening luckily falls during a two-week vacation, and you're not too worried about covering one extra month's rent, perhaps you'd interview twenty or even thirty. But you'd stop there. Satisficing weighs all these factors while helping you make a good enough choice. Feel free to change this mental exercise to a job candidate, to house hunting, even to dating, and you'll see. Satisficing isn't perfect, but it's pretty good. It's sufficient. You can easily see how perfectionism and satisficing are like oil and water. You perfectionists out there, you know you are wondering if candidate no. 31 would have been "perfect," but the odds that the thirty-first candidate is substantially better, or different, from any of the first thirty are quite low. Meanwhile, the costs of insisting on a perfect process are incredibly high—as we mentioned above, they could equal a year's rent. The mistake people make is by overestimating the potential improvement of a more thorough search, while underestimating its cost.

The same is true when writing a cover letter to apply for a new job, or when starting a website for a new business. Sure, you can write and rewrite the letter, but at what cost? Perhaps a poor font choice on a website will hurt sales, but more than a vacant website? We're not saying mistakes don't matter: Of course they do. Again, you brain surgeons, we're not talking to you. But with each task you begin, satisficing dictates that you must force yourself to analyze the costs and benefits of doing a less-than-perfect job, and act accordingly.

Surely, we've done a less-than-perfect job of convincing you that perfectionism is rampant, and may very well be the block that's keeping you from following your dreams. But if we've failed in some way, perhaps this last point will be good enough to convince you.

So much of Western culture and, yes, even Western guilt and perfectionism, can be traced to the Hebrew portion of the Bible—Christianity's Old Testament. As it happens, the Hebrew word for perfect is. . . . well, it isn't. There is no direct translation of the very English word *perfect*. Despite what you may have heard about obligations to offer a perfect sacrifice or to be perfectly free from sin, scholars now agree that those very Western turns of phrase have long been mistranslations of the Old Testament. In fact, there also are plenty of abuses of the word *perfect* in English translations of the New Testament from the original Greek, too. Even if you aren't religious, these long-held traditions are deeply ingrained in our Western culture and affect you every day—and it's time to expose their false origins. For example, the original Hebrew word used in many familiar Bible phrases such as "perfect sacrifice" is spelled in the Western alphabet as *tanam*. It's more appropriate translation is "healthy," or "whole," or even "as it should be." Jews understood that they lived in a world of motion, a world of change, and there simply was no concept of human perfection. *Perfect* implies complete, which also implies death. There is no such thing as perfect in this life, and there is no Hebrew word for it. No more than there is a perfect glass of water somewhere in that stream flowing by in that nearby park. The Bible is really telling people to be "whole as they are," not to be perfect. And so are we. Only then can you start to get better. Learning to live a life where all these costs are properly balanced and weighed is the very stuff of maturity, but it is also incredibly liberating. Free from the need to find the perfect roommate, you'll find something much more valuable:

A breakthrough.

The paradox is clear: Accept yourself as whole, and you can begin to change bad habits into peak behaviors. Instead of being stuck on a series of plateaus, you'll find yourself scaling mountains that always seemed far out of reach. And when you reach the peak, as all mountaineers know, you'll see there are always new mountains to climb. This time, however, you won't feel like you're going in circles. You'll be going up, and up, and up. You won't be perfect. You will be great. And, as Paul McCartney said, you will be getting better all the time. That's the power of understanding plateaus.

THE ENDING

Ever had someone say to you, "You don't have problems—you have opportunities"? So have we. And, yes, we've wanted to punch that person dispensing the cheap refrigerator-magnet advice, too. We're going to give you a turn of phrase that genuinely helps.

You don't have problems in your life. You have plateaus.

Plateaus rob you of early successes. They make hard work worthless. They turn beginner's luck into sophomore slumps. They can even make you look lazy, dumb, careless, or unloving. You aren't any of these things. You've just been fighting an invisible enemy. Now, you can see it.

You don't have to be a professional athlete or a billion-dollar company preying on a weak competitor to benefit from understanding the Plateau Effect. As we've said, plateaus are a part of everyday life, a part of mathematics, physics, and biology. Anything you want to do better—play guitar, make friends, relate to your children—you can get there faster by understanding the Plateau Effect.

You might find that one strategy or the other seems most attractive to you in your situation, and that's good. But remember our basic principle: Things work, until they don't. What works today may very well stop working tomorrow, so it's important that you understand the fundamental flattening forces, the mechanisms of flow and distortion, and above all the three key actions you must take.

Understanding plateaus might improve our nation's problem-solving skill set, too. It would help immensely if America's leaders learned how to stop jerking our nation one violent way or the other, acting like two-year-olds who haven't really learned spatial reasoning yet. Plateaus offer a helpful new way to think about political problems. What's right today is wrong tomorrow, and that's why intractable political parties that offer the same solutions year after year just don't work. Perhaps it was a good idea to cut back on taxes and regulation in the 1970s, but how does it end? With a crippling financial disaster that brought the world to its knees. Perhaps increased government spending is a way out, but when does that end? When all the world's money isn't worth the paper it's printed on. You've heard the phrase: "When all you have is a hammer, everything looks like a nail." Abraham Maslow, of Maslow's hierarchy of needs fame, was unknowingly talking about plateaus when he popularized the "Law of the Instrument" expression in the 1960s. He was also talking about the way society now approaches many of our thorniest problems.

The word *diversity* has gotten a bad rap during the past half-century, evoking notions of racial tension and inequality and affirmative action. Forget all that. Many plateau solutions can be characterized as exercises in embracing diversity. If you have plateaued as a rock and roll guitar player, a few classical lessons are often the fastest step toward a breakthrough. Studying so hard that you aren't remembering the things you are learning? Read some sports for a while. Is your company stuck, unable to get past some vexing problem? Tell the type A's in the room to be quiet for a while, and seek out some frontline introverts and ask for their advice. Giving voice to the quietest person in the room might be the most unique exercise your firm undertakes in an entire year. That's the power of real diversity.

One friend boiled all these strategies down to a simple phrase: If things are stuck, shake it up. This simple truth lies at the heart of the Plateau Effect. Trying new things literally rewires your brain, forcing it to open up long-closed neural pathways. Embracing diversity is such a profound concept that it actually can be, along with laughter and love, the best medicine. Elderly folks who learn a new language are less likely to suffer from Alzheimer's disease. This same approach—shaking up your mind—can work across every single human endeavor you might undertake. More push-ups not making you stronger? Muscle confusion from lifting free weights, or simply resting, can lead to a breakthrough. Angry at your husband? A night out with the girls often, somehow, makes things better.

You don't have to be religious to understand the notion of a guardian angel. Heck, if you've ever had a mother stop you just as you were about to crawl onto a dangerous flight of stairs, you've had a guardian angel.

The concept of little devil sitting on your shoulder is a little harder to imagine. Maybe an older brother once lured you into throwing an unsanctioned and unwise party at your parents' house, but that's not the little devil we are talking about. We're not dragging up some horror story about evil beings who seduce humans into committing awful crimes against humanity, either. The vast majority of people encounter the little devil in a more subtle way. We've spent twenty years each talking to people for a living, people from all walks of life, and without hesitation we can say this—most people are lonely, and then desperately happy when someone asks them a question and truly listens for the answer. And most are living a little bit of a lie: They struggle through the daily reality of what they are doing with their lives, and they secretly hold on to dreams of what their life could be. They imagine writing novels, opening coffee shops, starting businesses, working with children. But they soldier on in sanitized cubicles, wasting time on Facebook and hoping to win the lottery.

Why the disconnect? Often, it's one or more of the demons we have identified in the preceding chapters. There is always someone, or something, ready and willing to talk you out of taking a big, bold step. But understand that this enemy is rarely obvious and overt. Almost never will you talk to a friend who says, "I just decided I'd rather watch TV every Saturday than do market research for that company I want to start." The little devil is much, much craftier than that. His plan to derail you from your life's dream is a slow, steady bleeding of time and attention rather than a single, bloody blow. So twenty turns to thirty, thirty turns to forty, forty turns to fifty, and fifty turns to early retirement.

Talk about a plateau!

C. S. Lewis, probably the most famous Christian writer of the twentieth century, fought in World War I, so he understood evil in its most stark form. But he also understood the kind of evil that most people face in their daily lives—petty complaints about the way the your husband chews, about the Smith family's perpetual tardiness for church, about the neighbor's child running across the front lawn. He knew that humans have an amazing ability to rise up in the face of stark, dramatic evil—courage, in times of crisis, is their best quality. But he also knew that humans have an Achilles' heel. When the pressure isn't on, they are prone to laziness. The husband is quick to buy flowers after the wife threatens divorce but not before. The student studies all night before an exam but goes bar-hopping every other night of the semester.

Evil, in Lewis's estimation, has discovered this weakness and changed its strategy. A simple distraction is all that's needed to turn a loving heart slowly cold, to turn admiration into jealousy.

Writing in the post–World War II era, Lewis was primarily concerned with what he saw as breakdown of families, relationships, and Christian values. Here, we are concerned with this same devil's impact on success, the pursuit of dreams, and your ability to break out of the plateau.

The arsenal available to this evil force is many and varied. In the appendix that follows, we've summarized the eight devils of plateaus so you can easily recognize them, and begin to attack them, in your life. You ultimately have only one weapon: the constant application of willpower. That might not seem like a fair fight until you open your eyes and look around. Every songwriter who has even finished a song, every entrepreneur who has ever created a profitable business, and every man or woman who has ever formed a happy marriage has faced down this enemy. The world is full of songs, businesses, and love. You can win this battle.

APPENDIX

The Eight Elements of Plateaus

When you were (supposed to be) reading the classics in high school, CliffsNotes were bad. In fact, Bob recently met an employee of a company that makes animated versions of CliffsNotes—which apparently aren't Cliffy enough for today's students.

But when you're trying to improve your life and move past those plateaus that hold you back, CliffsNotes are great. They are efficient; they give you more results for less work—two of our main goals for teaching people about the Plateau Effect. So here we give you our version of CliffsNotes. If you're stuck, one of these devils is probably to blame. Remember, what helps you break out of your plateau today will one day stop working—and you'll have to try another method. Breaking through plateaus, as you've seen, requires constant recalibration—it takes a little of this and a bit of that. In the list that follows, we show you what "this" and "that" really are for you, today and into the future. These solvents produce solutions.

Element 1: Immunity

People, relationships, businesses, and even physical processes become immune to the same techniques, the same approaches, the same solutions. Immunity is perhaps the most basic force of the Plateau Effect. Everybody has experienced what it's like to become immune to something: Maybe it's the compliments of your spouse, the smell of garlic at an Italian restaurant, or the effects of your second beer. Immunity can be frustrating—what worked so well yesterday just won't work today.

SOLVENT: DIVERSITY

Immunity's Kryptonite is diversity. You've got to shake things up and be radical. Trying different approaches, techniques, or procedures can shake you out of an immunity plateau.

Element 2: Greedy Algorithm

The greedy algorithm is a concept borrowed from the field of mathematics. Here's how it works: You always pick the best short-term solution and ignore the long-term outcome. As it is in mathematics—and in life—the best short-term solution hardly ever leads to the best long-term outcome. The greedy algorithm always finds the locally optimal solution but ignores the globally optimal solution.

SOLVENT: EXTEND YOUR GRATIFICATION HORIZON

Short-term greed is bad, but long-term greed is actually good. To get beyond the greedy algorithm, you need to think about solutions on a bigger timescale. Someone following the greedy algorithm (driven by short-term greed) would never go to medical school—the student is building debt with no income year after year. Someone who's thinking about a ten-year horizon instead of a one- or two-year horizon sees the six-figure checks that will eventually start coming in.

Element 3: Bad Timing

If you're working hard but you're stuck in a plateau, maybe it's as simple as taking a break. When you do something—and, more precisely, when you don't do something—is critical. The key is to take control of when you apply effort, not just how much effort you apply.

SOLVENT: WAIT

If bad timing has you stuck in a plateau, remember, periods of rest and inactivity are just as important as periods of great effort, just as the silence between the notes is part of the music. If you use time as a tool, you can literally wait your way out of a plateau.

Element 4: Flow Issues

When things seem to be sailing along, sometimes the engine just breaks down. Specifically, you can run into one of four dysfunctions:

Erosion: Sometimes, we deplete the resources that we need to be successful. Maybe we run out of capital, or time, or skilled workers. When you hit an erosion plateau, progress tends to degrade slowly as some critical resource is gobbled up over time.

Solvent: Find a counterbalance, something that replaces the resource you consume. If you can't find a counterbalance, you might not be in a plateau at all. You may have reached a terminal point.

Step Function: Sometimes, you want to add just a little more of something, but that thing is only available in bundles. The result is a jump in cost, effort, or benefit. We call these things "step functions." If you aren't aware that something you need follows a step function, you can hit a plateau because incremental investment won't lead to incremental improvement.

Solvent: Try to smooth out your step function. Sometimes this can be done by identifying some other person or business that has *complementary peaks* to your own. If you can pool your resources, you can share the cost of the step and make it look more like a comfortable ramp.

Choke points: A choke point is the part of the system that breaks first and slows everything else down. Failing to identify a choke point can bring a gushing flow to an unexpected trickle.

Solvent: The trick is to find out where the choke point is and creatively route your way around it.

Mystery ingredients: The defining characteristic of a mystery ingredient is that even the chef doesn't know what it is. The mystery ingredient could be changing market conditions, interpersonal issues between coworkers, or just a team member with a can-do attitude. It's the elusive catalyst that makes things work.

Solvent: Mystery ingredients often can be hard to find but seem obvious in retrospect. Often, it's just important to recognize that a mystery ingredient might exist, that what you see isn't the whole story.

Element 5: Distorted Data

We often react based on distorted data. It's like walking through a hall of mirrors and basing a major decision on the crazy fat (or skinny) image you see. Sometimes we measure the wrong things or inappropriately assess risk. In other cases, we fall victim to common psychological errors with data, such as overweighting the most recent piece of information we've received, getting hung up on sunk costs, or conforming to what other people say the data is telling us.

SOLVENT: RECALIBRATE

The Enlightenment brought us the scientific method because smart people realized that they couldn't trust their own eyes. The key is to boil impurities out of the data and recognize that you are looking through a lens that might be deceptive. Each type of distortion has its own remedy, but the commonality that binds them is to look for a ground truth of data amid the chaos.

Element 6: Distraction

It's easy to fall victim to the illusion of multitasking and become distracted. Distraction is the enemy of adaptation and can lead you straight toward a plateau. How do we know when and what we need to change in a world of unrelenting distraction?

SOLVENT: PEAK LISTENING

If you take a page from improv comedy—where you look for the truth in what others are saying and build on it through the "yes, and . . ." strategy—you get to a skill we call radical listening. It's a mode of active engagement, where you are attuned to your surroundings, listening, and adapting.

Element 7: Failing Slowly

Failing slowly is natural because it's difficult to tell that a situation is incrementally getting worse. Often the incremental worsening of a situation happens slower than what psychophysicists call the *just-noticeable difference*. The just-noticeable difference helps explain why we continue forging ahead when we're in the throes of a plateau—we just don't realize how much less we're getting for our efforts.

SOLVENT: FAIL FAST

Once you understand the *just-noticeable difference*, you can counteract its effects. By setting clear, objective markers, you can see how you're progressing, figure out what's working and what's failing, correct it, and move on. It's important to realize if your efforts will eventually fail by *accelerating failure*. This ability to fail fast is key, especially when the problems are changing quickly.

Element 8: Perfectionism

Perfect is the enemy of good. The desire for perfection kills beginnings—it's never the right time to start, and even if you do, a task is never complete because it is held up to an impossible standard. A plateau of perfection is similar to a plateau of inaction.

SOLVENT: FIRST STEPS, ETC.

Accept that perfection isn't achievable. Focus on taking the first step, and then the next step. There are some tricks that can help, such as structured procrastination and setting hard (but liberating) deadlines.

NOTES

THE BEGINNING

Page

ix **"three thousand pounds of garlic":** That's a lot of garlic! The restaurant itself says so on its website: www.thestinkingrose.com/about.htm.

xiii **5 percent of their body weight:** Authors' research, calculations. The various results for all participants are available on the show's website (www.nbc.com/the-biggest-loser) and several fan pages. We plopped them all into a spreadsheet and did the math.

xv **"natural movements that hunter-gatherers did":** John Durant, interview on *The Colbert Report*, February 3, 2010.

xx **"Trainers once kept baby elephants in check":** We were unable to identify the origin of this story, but it's retelling appears in many places. Gavin de Becker used a version of the story in *The Gift of Fear* (New York: Little, Brown & Co., 1997).

1. DO THE MATH

3 **"concept of tolerance spreads far across . . .":** The authors would like to thank Robert Ang, a former surgeon and director of medical affairs at Cadence Pharmaceuticals, for his help with tolerance in medicine.

6 **a pen for your doggie:** You may be wondering how we got Fluffy so much space in that dog pen. Hugh thought we should go through the full math. Bob said, "Nobody likes to read equations." So we agreed to put the proof in the footnotes.

To recap, we have fifty feet of fence to build a pen for your dog, Fluffy, where one edge of the pen is the side of your house.

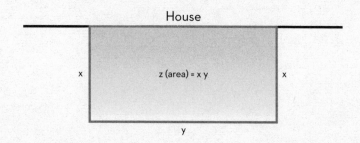

We also have one more constraint, the sides of this fence add up to fifty feet. So in mathematics terms this means:

$2x + y = 50$

In this situation, the algebraic approach might be to simply make all three sides equal:

$x = y = {}^{50}\!/_{3} = 16.67$ ft

That would definitely give Fluffy some running room. The result is a square with area:

16.67 ft $\times\ 16.67$ ft $= 277.89$ ft^2

But if we used calculus, we could get Fluffy much more room. First, let's rewrite our constraint as:

$y = 50 - 2x$

Now let's put that into our area equation:

$z = xy$
$z = x(50 - 2x)$
$z = 50x - 2x^2$

If you graphed this function, it would look like this:

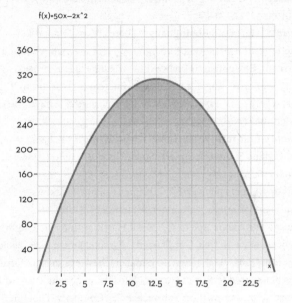

f(x)=50x−2x^2

Does that first half of the curve look familiar?

Now, we differentiate the function with respect to x. If you've never encountered differential equations before, you'll just have to trust us on this one. This gives us an equation for the slope of the curve. When the slope is zero, that means we've reached the top of the graph. This point is what in mathematics we call the *maxima* of the function. Here's the math:

$z = 50x - 2x^2$

$\partial z / \partial x - 50 = 4x$

If we set the derivative equal to zero we get:

$0 = 50 - 4x$

$x = {}^{50}\!/_4 = 12.5$

And there you have it. If $x = 12.5$ ft that means $y = 25$ ft and the area Fluffy has to play in is 12.5 ft $\times$ 25 ft = 312.5 ft^2. That's a lot more space for Fluffy.

12 **"formula that has been understood for decades":** To find out more

about spaced repetition, we'd recommend you read this paper: Paul Pimsleur, "A Memory Schedule," *The Modern Language Journal* 51, no. 2 (February 1967): 73–75.

13 **"In 1879, Hermann Ebbinghaus":** There are many good sources for biographical information on Ebbinghaus. Here are two we found helpful: Hermann Ebbinghaus, *Memory: A Contribution to Experimental Psychology,* trans. Henry A. Ruger and Clara E. Bussenius (1885/1913). R. H. Wozniak, *Classics in Psychology, 1855–1914: Historical Essays* (Bristol, UK: Thoemmes Press, 1999).

16 **"twenty-four million customers worldwide":** Michael Liedtke, "Netflix Regains Some Customers; Stock Up 16 Percent," Associated Press, January 27, 2012.

16 **"fell to 4.1 cents per share":** Caroline Humer, "Blockbuster Seeks Turnaround in Bankruptcy," Reuters, September 23, 2010.

16 **"rented the movie *Apollo 13*":** Reed Hastings, interview by Alyssa Abkowitz, "How Netflix Got Started," *Fortune*, January 28, 2009, money .cnn.com/2009/01/27/news/newsmakers/hastings_netflix.fortune.

17 **"Netflix soared to $169":** Humer, "Blockbuster Seeks Turnaround."

18 **"more than one million subscribers":** "Company Timeline," Netflix, accessed October 8, 2012, signup.netflix.com/MediaCenter/Timeline.

19 **"forty million users by 2013":** Jeanine Poggi, "Netflix Subscribers to Top 30M by 2013: Poll," *The Street*, May 9, 2011, www.thestreet.com/ story/11110093/1/netflix-subscribers-to-top-30m-by-2013-poll.html.

20 **"He gets far more girls. . . .":** Nate DiMeo, "Derek Jeter vs. Objective Reality," *Slate*, July 14, 2008, www.slate.com/articles/sports/sports_nut/ 2008/07/derek_jeter_vs_objective_reality.html.

21 **"world class scientists to prove":** Matt O'Donnell, "Science Proves It: Jeter Sucks," *Fenway West*, February 17, 2008, www.fenwaywest.com/ 2008-articles/february/science-proves-it-jeter-sucks.html.

21 **a new trainer, Jason Riley:** Ian O'Connor, "O'Connor: How Jeter Got Younger at Age 35," *Hackensack (NJ) Record*, October 6, 2009.

21 **"2.7 million times":** The authors' very rough calculations. We guessed that Jeter has swung an average of 250 times per day since he was a small child (250 swings × 365 days × 30 years). We gave him no vacations—he's obviously a hard worker—but if you figure he took a month off every year, he probably took twice as many swings during intense practice in March or April . . . well, you get the idea.

2. GOING FLAT

24 *American Idol:* Quotes taken from Season 10 of *American Idol*, episode 25, which aired April 7, 2011. If you watch the video be warned: It's a tear-jerker. (Note that Bob is baffled by Hugh's obsession with *American Idol.*) And don't worry about Pia Toscano. She still managed to sign a deal with Interscope Records a few days later: Megan Angelo, "Pia Toscano Gets a Record Deal with Interscope—So What's the Point of Winning 'American Idol' Again?" *Business Insider,* April 10, 2011, articles.businessinsider .com/2011-04-10/entertainment/30014648_1_jimmy-iovine-contestants-idol-winners.

25 **"cantankerous judge Simon Cowell left":** Simon Cowell left *American Idol* at the end of Season 9, but not without skewering a few contestants first. You can find some of his more inflammatory comments here: Joyce Lee, "Simon Cowell Zingers; 10 of the Best," *CBS News,* May 26, 2010, www.cbsnews.com/8301-31749_162-20005994-10391698.html. And these days you can find Cowell (and his cantankerous wit) on another popular show, *The X Factor* (www.thexfactorusa.com).

25 **"Craig Berman summed up the problem":** Craig Berman, " 'Idol' Judges Berate Fans for Sending Pia Home," *Today,* April 8, 2011, today.msnbc .msn.com/id/42484717/ns/today-entertainment/t/idol-judges-berate-fans-sending-pia-home.

26 **"99 percent of alarms were false":** There are quite a few interesting studies on car alarm ineffectiveness. We'd recommend reading this first: Aaron Friedman, Aaron Naparstek, and Mateo Taussig-Rubbo, "Alarmingly Useless: The Case for Banning Car Alarms in New York City," *Transportation Alternatives,* March 21, 2003, www.transalt.org/files/news room/reports/caralarms/08ineffective.html. Some other sources are listed below: Kim Hazelbaker, "Insurance Industry Analyses and the Prevention of Motor Vehicle Theft," in *Business and Crime Prevention,* eds. Marcus Felson and Ronald V. Clarke (Monsey, NY: Willow Tree Press Inc., 1997), 283–293. New York City Police Department, *Police Strategy No. 5: Reclaiming the Public Spaces of New York* (New York: New York City Police Department, 1994), 6, 11, and 20. Brian Anderson, "Let's Ban Car Alarms," *City Journal* 12, no. 1 (2002).

27 **"-16,022 votes for Democratic candidate Al Gore":** Electronic voting machine vulnerabilities are one of Hugh's favorite hobbies. He appeared

in the Emmy-nominated documentary *Hacking Democracy*, which aired on HBO and looked at the technological flaws in these systems. Find out more about the film at www.hackingdemocracy.com. Also see: Dana Milbank, "Tragicomedy of Errors Fuels Volusia Recount," *The Washington Post*, November 12, 2000.

28 **"calls this the Pesticide Paradox":** Boris Beizer, *Software Testing Techniques*, 2nd ed. (London: International Thomson Computer Press, 1990).

29 **"Fuzzing embraces the odd and unusual":** For a great technical reference on fuzzing see: Ari Takanen, Jared DeMott, and Charlie Miller, *Fuzzing for Software Security Testing and Quality Assurance* (Norwood, MA: Artech House Inc., 2008).

29 **"Hugh's first experience with fuzzing":** For a detailed technical write-up on the soda machine bug (and software fuzzing in general) Hugh invites you to read an article he wrote: Herbert H. Thompson, "Secure Software Needs Careful Testing—And Lots Of It," *Information Week*, November 28, 2009.

31 **Hugh learned this firsthand:** To read Hugh's original account of this adventure, check out: Hugh Thompson, "How to Crash an In-Flight Entertainment System," *CSO Online*, February 9, 2007, blogs.csoonline.com/how_to_crash_an_in_flight_entertainment_system.

31 **"call it a boundary value":** Good textbooks on software testing cover these issues. This is a particularly good one: Cem Kaner, Jack Falk, and Hung Q. Nguyen, *Testing Computer Software*, 2nd ed. (New York: John Wiley & Sons, 1999).

31–32 **"A common programming mistake":** Ibid.

33 **remember the Y2K bug?:** Richard Lacayo et al., "The End of the World as We Know It?" *Time*, January 18, 1999.

34 **often called "exploratory testing":** For a good treatment of exploratory testing see: James A. Whittaker, *Exploratory Software Testing: Tips, Tricks, Tours, and Techniques to Guide Test Design* (Boston: Addison-Wesley, 2009).

35 **"some of the most dangerous bugs":** It's actually even more severe than this. Fuzzing has become the dominant method for finding security flaws in the software industry. Every year, thousands of bugs are found using these techniques.

36 **competitor Andi Bell:** Bell set the record for memorizing a shuffled deck of cards at the World Memory Championships in London in 2006. He was able to commit the deck to memory in 31.16 seconds. (See World Memory

Championship 2006 speed cards results at www.world-memory-statistics
.com/competition.php?id=wmc2006&discipline=spdcards.) Bell's record
has since been broken multiple times. Quotes taken from the BBC documentary *Get Smart*, in which Bell was interviewed about his techniques:
"World Memory Champion Andi Bell's Card Technique [1/2]," YouTube
video, 4:58, from the BBC documentary *Get Smart*, posted by "Equivicae,"
December 10, 2006, www.youtube.com/watch?v=X-xl7_hdWZo.

37 **the method of loci:** Frances Yates, *The Art of Memory* (Chicago: University of Chicago, 1966). You may also enjoy the narrative journey Joshua
Foer takes as he competes in the USA Memory Championships: Joshua
Foer, *Moonwalking with Einstein: The Art and Science of Remembering Everything* (New York: Penguin Press, 2011).

40 **"impious because it calls up absurd thoughts":** This quotation is attributed to William Perkins, a Cambridge Elizabethan Puritan in 1592. See:
Yates, *The Art of Memory*.

42 **the world of CrossFit:** We spoke to several CrossFitters in preparing this
book; the quotes came from notes and comments left on the CrossFit
website. Bob and Hugh are almost convinced to start an exercise program. For more information on CrossFit see: www.crossfit.com. For
more information on P90X see: www.beachbody.com/product/how
-p90x-works-muscle-confusion.do.

43 **a deceptively highbrow restaurant called Moto:** Moto will have you
second-guessing your senses. Hugh thanks Homaro and Ben for the great
Caesar salad soup, the tour, and, of course, the dessert nachos. Many
quotes taken from notes. You can make a reservation here: www.moto
restaurant.com.

44 **"a kitchen that was more like a mechanics shop":** Homaro Cantu and
Ben Roche, "Cooking as Alchemy," TED talk, 9:34, filmed March 2011,
posted December 2011, www.ted.com/talks/homaro_cantu_ben_
roche_cooking_as_alchemy.html.

44 **"When you see a tomato . . .":** Homaro Cantu and Ben Roche, "The
Future of Food," TEDx talk, 18:09, posted November 3, 2010, www.you
tube.com/watch?v=Qk52Yk5V8PE.

45 **"an expedition to West Africa":** The history of miracle fruit can be
found here: Adam Gollner, *The Fruit Hunters: A Story of Nature, Adventure,
Commerce and Obsession* (New York: Scribner, 2008).

46 **a phenomenon known as "flavor tripping":** To see how the other half

lives read: Patrick Farrell and Kassie Bracken, "A Tiny Fruit That Tricks the Tongue," *The New York Times*, May 28, 2008.

46 **"reads like a John Grisham novel":** It may be more like a Dan Brown novel. For the sordid history we invite you read: Adam Fowler, "The Miracle Berry," *BBC News*, April 28, 2008, news.bbc.co.uk/2/hi/7367548.stm.

47 **"Cantu was asked to help":** Information from an interview on CNN's *The Next List* that aired on February 5, 2012. See: transcripts.cnn.com/TRANSCRIPTS/1202/05/nl.01.html.

48 **"straightens out their taste buds . . .":** " 'Miracle' Pill Takes the Bitter with the Sweet," *CNN Eatocracy*, November 28, 2011, eatocracy.cnn.com/2011/11/28/miracle-pill-takes-the-bitter-with-the-sweet. For additional information on Cantu's work with miracle berries and chemotherapy patients see this interview: Peter Smith, "Miracle Berries, Chemotherapy, and the Future of Food," *Good*, April 1, 2011, www.good.is/post/miracle-berries-chemotherapy-and-the-future-of-food-a-conversation-with-homaro-cantu.

48 **"the response to the MF fruit":** H. P. Soares et al., "Treatment of Taste Alterations in Chemotherapy Patients Using the 'Miracle Fruit': Preliminary Analysis of a Pilot Study," *Journal of Clinical Oncology* 28 (2010): abstract no. e19523, www.asco.org/ascov2/Meetings/Abstracts?&vmview=abst_detail_view&confID=74&abstractID=51247.

48 **"this idea of tricking your taste buds":** Cantu and Roche, "Cooking as Alchemy."

3. THE GREEDY ALGORITHM

51 **called the "greedy algorithm":** Greedy algorithms always look for the locally optimal solution. Computer scientists use greedy algorithms all the time when there is no ability to look out into the future and see what's ahead. For a more technical treatment of greedy algorithms see: Thomas Cormen et al., *Introduction to Algorithms*, 3rd edition (Cambridge, MA: MIT Press, 2009).

55 **the problem of making change:** To find out more about the optimal denomination problem, we encourage you to read these: Leo Van Hove, "Optimal Denominations for Coins and Bank Notes: In Defense of the Principle of Least Effort," *Journal of Money, Credit and Banking* 33, no. 4 (November 2001), 1015–1021. Mark A. Wynne, "More on Optimal Denominations for Coins and Currency" (working paper, Federal Reserve

Bank of Dallas Research Department, February 1997), dallasfed.org/assets/documents/research/papers/1997/wp9702.pdf.

57 **he toured Bing with Jennifer Winters:** From an interview conducted at Bing in July 2012. Our thanks to Jennifer Winters for showing Hugh around at Bing and for her insightful comments.

58 **you would have found Dr. Walter Mischel:** Jonah Lehrer gives a good account of Mischel's background and work in: Jonah Lehrer, "Don't! The Secret of Self-Control," *The New Yorker*, May 18, 2009.

59 **"Mischel would put a marshmallow":** Here are several of the fundamental papers from Mischel and his colleagues detailing their work with children and delay of gratification: Walter Mischel et al., "Delay of Gratification in Children," *Science* 244 (May 26, 1989), 933. Walter Mischel, "Processes in Delay of Gratification," *Advances in Experimental Social Psychology*, vol. 7, ed. Leonard Berkowitz (Waltham, MA: Academic Press), 249–292. Walter Mischel, "From Good Intentions to Willpower," *The Psychology of Action: Linking Cognition and Motivation to Behavior*, eds. Peter M. Gollwitzer and John A. Bargh (New York: Guilford Press, 1996). B. J. Casey et al., "Behavioral and Neural Correlates of Delay of Gratification 40 Years Later," *Proceedings of the National Academy of Sciences* 108, no. 36 (2011).

62 **discounting follows a hyperbolic curve:** Shane Frederick, George Loewenstein, and Ted O'Donoghue, "Time Discounting and Time Preference: A Critical Review," *Journal of Economic Literature* 40, no. 2 (2002), 351–401.

63 **"each additional ten seconds of delay":** Note that subjects took the SAT in the mid-1980s; the test has changed somewhat since then. Here is the paper that describes their results: Yuichi Shoda, Walter Mischel, and Philip K. Peake, "Predicting Adolescent Cognitive and Self-Regulatory Competencies from Preschool Delay of Gratification: Identifying Diagnostic Conditions," *Developmental Psychology* 26, no. 6, (1990): 978–986.

64 **affectionately called Beast Barracks:** Information from the West Point website: www.usma.edu.

65 **"acceptance rate at West Point":** "Top 100—Lowest Acceptance Rates," *US News & World Report*, accessed April 30, 2012, colleges.usnews.rankings andreviews.com/best-colleges/rankings/lowest-acceptance-rate.

65 **"Duckworth epitomizes success":** Background on Angela Duckworth from her TEDx Blue talk—highly recommended. Angela Duckworth, "True Grit: Can Perseverance Be Taught?" YouTube video, 18:37, from a

TEDx Blue talk on October 18, 2009, posted by "TEDxTalks," November 12, 2009, www.youtube.com/watch?v=qaeFnxSfSC4.

66 **she founded Summerbridge Cambridge:** It has since been renamed to Breakthrough Cambridge.

66 **"I didn't feel like I had that abiding commitment":** Author interview with Duckworth conducted July 2012. Many thanks to her for her time and insights.

66 **"a test for grit":** Here is the twelve-item grit scale from Duckworth's website at the University of Pennsylvania: www.sas.upenn.edu/~duck wort/images/12-item%20Grit%20Scale.05312011.pdf.

67 **Beast Barracks took Duckworth's grittiness test:** Angela L. Duckworth et al., "Grit: Perseverance and Passion for Long-Term Goals," *Journal of Personality and Social Psychology* 92, no. 6 (Jun 2007), 1087–1101, www.sas.upenn.edu/~duckwort/images/Grit%20JPSP.pdf.

69 **wondered if there was a direct connection:** Mischel explained his hope for the research: Mischel, "From Good Intentions to Willpower."

69 **"character measured across seven domains":** You can find out more information about KIPP and the Character Point Average here: www .kipp.org.

69 **"how KIPP integrates lessons on grit":** Presentation by Michael Witter, teacher at KIPP Infinity Middle School: www.scribd.com/doc/38244064/ Dual-Purpose-Experiences-Presentation-MWitter. See also: K. Anders Ericsson, Ralf T. Krampe, and Clemens Tesch-Römer, "The Role of Deliberate Practice in the Acquisition of Expert Performance," *Psychological Review* 100, no. 3 (July 1993), 363–406. Paul Morris Fitts and Michael I. Posner, *Human Performance* (Oxford: Brooks/Cole, 1967).

71 **"current thinking is actually quite mathematical":** Author interview with Johannes Eichstaedt, March 2012. Our thanks to Johannes for his enlightening perspective.

74 **"a combination of persistence and resilience":** See this inspirational video on KIPP featuring cofounder Dave Levin: "Incorporating Character into Your Classroom," Vimeo video, 12:13, posted by KIPP Foundation, February 2012, vimeo.com/36802654.

74 **"students' scores and report cards":** To see KIPP's report cards, go to: www.kipp.org/reportcard.

4. BAD TIMING

76 **"it's time to introduce Wozniak":** The authors learned much about Wozniak from Gary Wolf's excellent *Wired* magazine article: Gary Wolf, "Want to Remember Everything You'll Ever Learn? Surrender to This Algorithm," *Wired*, April 21, 2008.

77 **"I was collecting all knowledge. . . .":** This interview appears on Super-Memo's website: Jaroslaw Mlodzki, "From an Idea to an Industry: Interview with Piotr Wozniak, the Author of SuperMemo," *Bajtek* (Poland), July 1994, translated and corrected April 1997. You can find the full version here: www.supermemo.com/articles/bajtek.htm.

78 **"200 to 250 words per minute . . .":** SuperMemo user survey, data gathered in Fall 1994, www.supermemo.com/articles/survey1994.htm#Speed of learning.

80 **"Music is the silence between the notes":** French composer Claude Debussy actually said, "Music is the space between the notes," but variations on that abound.

83 **"I use only e-mail communication":** From a section called "Apology" on Wozniak's website, www.supermemo.com/english/company/wozniak.htm.

83 **"research done since Ebbinghaus's first experiments . . .":** To find out more about the spaced repetition, we'd recommend you read this paper: Pimsleur, "A Memory Schedule," 73–75.

85 **"a quiet, small tribe of timing seekers":** The authors thank the New York chapter of the Quantified Self movement for welcoming us.

87 **this kind of timing can have a major impact:** John Tierney, "Do You Suffer From Decision Fatigue?" *The New York Times*, August 17, 2011.

88 **"Craig not only won":** Alexandra Carmichael, "Roger Craig Wins *Jeopardy!* Championship with Knowledge Tracking," *Quantified Self*, November 17, 2011, quantifiedself.com/2011/11/roger-craig-on-knowledge-tracking.

90 **"an average of eighteen months . . .":** Jennifer Van Brunt, "Approval Times Increasing," *Signals*, February 12, 2010.

90 **"dubbed 'slumbertech'":** Scott Kirsner, "On the Cutting Edge—In the Arms of Morpheus," *The Boston Globe*, August 21, 2011.

91 **"carries Zeo products in its stores":** Scott Kirsner, "Sleep Measurement

Company Zeo Announces New Mobile Product and Best Buy Distribution Deal," *The Boston Globe*, September 26, 2011.

91 **twelve to twenty "breath cycles every minute":** For a good discussion on rethinking the way we breathe and potential health benefits visit: www.coherence.com.

93 **"studying Buddhist monks in Tibet":** Lisa Takeuchi Cullen, "How to Get Smarter, One Breath at a Time," *Time*, January 10, 2006.

93 **the thickness of their cerebral cortex:** Ibid.

93 **"Smart Person's Bubble Bath":** "Just Say Om," *Time*, August 4, 2003.

94 **"Italian doctor named Luciano Bernardi":** Charnicia E. Huggins, "Mantras, Rosary May Help the Heart, Study Shows," Reuters, December 21, 2001.

97 **Dieticians recommend thirty-day experiments:** There's plenty of debate about how long it takes to "reset" taste buds, which individually only live for about two weeks. It's obviously a combination of biology and psychology, but here's one discussion: Kieve Kavanaugh, "Diet to Reset Taste Buds," *eHow Mom*, undated, www.ehow.com/way_5656351_diet-reset-taste-buds.html.

98 **"the urge to pick variety":** Alain Sampson, "Do You Diversify," *Psychology Today*, March 15, 2012.

5. FLOW MECHANISMS

105 **"If two people can paint a house":** Please excuse the gratuitous length of this note as it touches a subject very near to Hugh and Bob's heart—the math, not the house painting. If two people can paint a house in two hours, that means that 2 people × 6 hours = 12 total man-hours of labor needed to complete the house. Assuming that all painters work at the same rate, you just need to divide 12 total hours by 3 painters, which gives you 4 hours needed by each painter to get the house painted.

109 **"Al Roker—who, coincidentally, is from the Bahamas":** Hugh insisted on writing this note to point out some other interesting Bahamians: "List of Bahamians American," *Wikipedia*, last modified September 8, 2012, en.wikipedia.org/wiki/List_of_Bahamian_Americans. "List of Bahamians," *Wikipedia*, last modified August 18, 2012, en.wikipedia.org/wiki/List_of_Bahamians.

110 **naming continues alphabetically after that:** It's not as easy as you think: "Tropical Cyclone Names," National Weather Service National Hurricane Center, last modified April 16, 2012, www.nhc.noaa.gov/aboutnames.shtml.

110 **"average number of named systems":** Data from the National Hurricane Center: "Tropical Cyclone Climatology," National Weather Service National Hurricane Center, last modified June 18, 2012, www.nhc.noaa .gov/climo.

110 **"Just ask Seth Rubin, owner of Rise & Shine":** We did! The quotes from Seth are based on a phone interview we did with him in 2011. Seth, if you're reading this, keep a biscuit warm for us.

116 **"more than 143 million personal information records":** Verizon RISK Team, *2010 Data Breach Investigations Report*, www.verizonbusiness.com/ resources/reports/rp_2010-DBIR-combined-reports_en_xg.pdf.

116 **"the price of a single stolen credit card number":** This may be even cheaper by the time you read this book. To get some current pricing information just type "CVV2 CC" into your favorite search engine (although, for the record, Bob and Hugh would strongly recommend against actually buying a stolen credit card number).

116 **"the customer service policies of one such, ahem, merchant":** These sites don't tend to stay around that long, so it's long since removed from the Web.

117 **The scheme is called "repackaging":** The Internet is rife with tales of repackaging scams. Here's one retelling: Eve Tahmincioglu, "Don't Fall for Work-at-Home Scams," *NBC News*, last modified April 21, 2008, www .msnbc.msn.com/id/24132244/ns/business-careers/t/dont-fall-work-at-home-scams.

118 **CAPTCHA was the brainchild of Luis von Ahn:** To find out more on the history of CAPTCHAs and reCAPTCHA, start here: "reCAPTCHA: Telling Humans and Computers Apart Automatically," Google, accessed October 8, 2012, www.google.com/recaptcha/captcha. Luis von Ahn also has given a TED talk on the subject and has some other ideas on massive collaboration. Luis von Anh, "Massive-scale Online Collaboration," TED talk, 16:40, filmed April 2011, posted December 2011, www.ted .com/talks/luis_von_ahn_massive_scale_online_collaboration.html.

119 **"special-purpose optical character recognition (OCR)":** While we don't recommend downloading any of these tools, here is a paper

describing some of them: Elie Bursztein, Matthieu Martin, and John C. Mitchell, "Text-based CAPTCHA Strengths and Weaknesses," *Proceedings of the ACM Conference on Computer and Communications Security,* 2011.

119 **"pay people in low-income countries to solve":** There are many sources for this. Here's one: Vikas Bajaj, "Spammers Pay Others to Answer Security Tests," *The New York Times,* April 25, 2010.

119 **"Cybercrime gangs set up porn sites online":** Oh my! Well, ahem, in the name of decency, how about we just give you an article that *describes* the porn sites: Munir Kotadia, "Spammers Use Free Porn to Bypass Hotmail Protection," *ZDNet,* May 6, 2004, www.zdnet.com/spammers-use-free-porn-to-bypass-hotmail-protection-3039153933.

120 **more than "150,000 hours of labor per day wasted":** That's a lot of time. We got the stats from the reCAPTCHA site: "reCAPTCHA: Digitizing Books One Word at a Time," Google, accessed October 8, 2012, www.google.com/recaptcha/learnmore.

124 **"90 percent of the lentils grown":** Donna St. George, "National Origins: Washington-Idaho Border; America's Golden Land of Lentils," *The New York Times,* September 24, 1997.

124 **"personal greeting from Steve and Kevin Mader":** Interview with the authors. Our thanks to Kevin Mader for his insight into farming and crop rotation.

127 **"a Hungarian doctor named Ignaz Semmelweis":** Sherwin B. Nuland, *The Doctors' Plague: Germs, Childbed Fever, and the Strange Story of Ignac Semmelweis* (New York: W. W. Norton, 2003).

127 **The well-known phenomenon of the placebo effect:** Our thanks to Dr. Robert Ang for explaining the nuances of the placebo effect. Here is a paper that looks at its impact: TJ Kaptchuk et al., "Components of Placebo Effect: Randomised Controlled Trial in Patients with Irritable Bowel Syndrome," *BMJ* 336, no. 7651 (May 2008): 999–1003.

6. DISTORTION MECHANISMS

131 **"Other factors contribute to the way airlines handle this . . .":** These include the fact that making multiple planes late could cause disruption for those trying to make connections. It also could cause overflow gate trouble or force airlines to pay overtime to more employees.

133 **"rose 25 percent!":** Joanna Zelman, "Shark Attacks in 2010 Rose by 25%,"

The Huffington Post, February 9, 2011, www.huffingtonpost.com/2011/02/09/shark-attack-numbers-on-t_n_820406.html.

133 **three "billion people on the planet . . .":** The section that follows is a back-of-the-envelope calculation by the authors—a risky proposition, we know.

135 **the "reptilian" portion of our brains:** There are many places to read about the reptilian brain. Our favorite is this primer: Thomas Lewis, Fari Amini, and Richard Lannon, *A General Theory of Love* (New York: Vintage, 2001). For a very simple breakdown visit Buffalo State College's website at www.buffalostate.edu/orgs/bcp/brainbasics/triune.html.

138 **"choose a known mildly uncomfortable outcome":** Plenty of tests confirm this so-called status quo bias. One good explanation is offered by decision consultant Lee Merkhofer: "According to psychologists, when people face the opportunity of changing their status quo, the loss aspects of the change loom larger than the gain aspects. Losses represent the certain elimination of visible, existing benefits. Gains, in contrast, are prospective and speculative." Lee Merkhofer, "Part 1: Errors and Bias in Judgment," Lee Merkhofer Consulting: Priority Systems, accessed June 24, 2012, www.prioritysystem.com/reasons1.html.

142 **"The Amazing Randi":** Based on interviews by the authors.

144 **"Brian [Doyle] was basically a career minor leaguer":** Ron Fimrite, "The Yankee D Boys Did Double Duty," *Sports Illustrated*, October 30, 1978, sports illustrated.cnn.com/vault/article/magazine/MAG1094251/2/index.htm.

150 **"can't do something as simple as calculate a tip":** Bob Sullivan, *Stop Getting Ripped Off* (New York: Ballantine Books, 2009).

150 **people downshift from thoughtful, neocortex decision making:** The reptilian brain model, also called the triune brain model, has its detractors. In fact, as a clinical description of the brain, it's fairly useless to neuroscientists. But even as an oversimplification, it's still a helpful metaphor. It's important to note that those who dislike the triune model also dislike the term *downshifting*—if your brain isn't comprised of three distinct parts, how can you shift from one to the other? For an excellent discussion of this see: Robert Sylwester, "The Downshifting Dilemma: A Commentary and Proposal," *21st Century Learning Initiative*, August 19, 1998, www.21learn.org/site/archive/the-downshifting-dilemma-a-commentary-and-proposal.

154 **"landmark experiment by psychologist Solomon Asch":** For more

information on Asch's experiments, we recommend reading the following: S. E. Asch, "Studies of Independence and Conformity: A Minority of One Against a Unanimous Majority," *Psychological Monographs* 70, no. 416 (1956). S. E. Asch, "Opinions and social pressure," *Scientific American* 193, no. 5 (November 1955), 31–35. The image from Asch's experiment is reprinted under Creative Commons licensing. It can be found here: en.wikipedia.org/wiki/File:Asch_experiment.png.

155 **"medical community calls that phenomenon homeostasis":** Elaine N. Marieb and Katja Hoehn, *Human Anatomy & Physiology*, 7th ed. (San Francisco: Pearson Benjamin Cummings, 2007).

155–156 **pressure called 'groupthink' . . .":** W. H. Whyte Jr., "Groupthink," *Fortune*, March 1952, 114–117, 142, 146.

7. ATTENTION

165 **"eight hours per day watching moving screens":** Steven Reinberg, "U.S. Kids Using Media Almost 8 Hours a Day," *Bloomberg Businessweek*, January 20, 2010.

165 **"introduced the first multitasking personal computer":** As with all "firsts," there is some debate about what should rightly be called the first multitasking computer. For our definition here, we have settled on general availability of IBM's ill-fated OS/2 operating system for personal computers. For more see: "A Short History of OS/2," *DataBook*, accessed October 8, 2012, www.databook.bz/?page_id=223.

165 **"dopamine the interruption releases into the brain":** Matt Kwong, "The Opiate of the Messages," *The National*, May 2, 2010.

166 **"decreases your IQ in the moment ten points":** Erik Qualman, "Social Media Multi-tasking Worse Than Marijuana," *Socialnomics*, November 8, 2010, www.socialnomics.net/2010/11/08/social-media-multi-tasking-worse-than-marijuana.

166 **people like Lord Chesterfield knew this:** Philip Stanhope, fourth Earl of Chesterfield, in a letter to his son dated April 14, 1747, as quoted in: Christine Rosen, "The Myth of Multitasking," *The New Atlantis*, Spring 2008, 105–110. The full letter is available through Project Gutenberg at snowy.arsc.alaska.edu/gutenberg/3/3/6/3361/3361-h/3361-h.htm.

166 **"eleven continuous minutes on a project":** Clive Thompson, "Meet the Life Hackers," *The New York Times*, October 16, 2005, www.nytimes.com/2005/10/16/magazine/16guru.html.

167 **"a series of cognitive tests"**: Adam Gorlick, "Media Multitaskers Pay Mental Price, Stanford Study Shows," *Stanford Report*, August 24, 2009, news.stanford.edu/news/2009/august24/multitask-research-study-082409.html.

167 **"40 percent of the time"**: Erik Qualman, "Is Social Media Multitasking Worse Than Marijuana?" *ClickZ*, November 5, 2010, www.clickz.com/clickz/column/1868147/social-media-multitasking-worse-marijuana. Also, multitasking and the expense of task switching can cost workers up to 40 percent of their productive time. See: Cora Dzubak, "Multitasking: The Good, the Bad, and the Unknown," Association for the Tutoring Profession Conference, 2007, paper accessed from www.myatp.org/wp-content/uploads/2012/06/Synergy-Vol-2-Dzubak.pdf. She puts it this way: "Although switching costs may be relatively small as individuals alternate between tasks, sometimes just a few tenths of a second per switch, they can add up to large amounts of time when people switch repeatedly back and forth between tasks. Thus, multitasking may seem efficient on the surface but may actually take more time in the end and involve more error. Rubinstein et al (2001) found that even brief mental blocks created by shifting between tasks can cost as much as forty percent of someone's productive time. Again, even though one might feel more productive when switching among tasks, research demonstrates that a large percentage of time is spent on the act of switching, requiring rule activation and disablement."

167 **Basex found that its employees lose 2.1 hours per day:** Jonathan B. Spira et al., "The Cost of Not Paying Attention," Basex Inc. report, 2006.

169 **"He studied students' listening skills . . ."**: Ralph G. Nichols and Leonard A. Stevens, *Are You Listening?* (New York: McGraw-Hill Book Company, 1957). For more on Nichols and his "Minnesota Method" for listening see: Ralph Nichols, interview by Rick Bommelje, "Listening Legend Interview," *Listening Post* 84 (Summer 2003), www.listen.org/Legend.

170 **"400 words per minute . . ."**: Other data cited in this section comes from: Dick Lee and Delmar Hatesohl, "Listening: Our Most Used Communication Skill," University of Missouri Extension, October 1993, extension.missouri.edu/p/CM150.

171 **project conducted with researcher Larry Ponemon:** We recorded three approximately five-minute videos. They were shown via Internet delivery to 1,009 volunteers, who answered a series of questions after the

viewing as a test of comprehension. While the sample wasn't as scientific as a random telephone survey would be, the group was representative of US adults—meaning volunteers were screened to match the population on factors such as income, home state, gender, and so on. As we say in the text, it was a fun project, and we're fairly certain we've shown that women are better listeners than men, and that very few people are great listeners. Our gratitude to Larry Ponemon for his work on this project.

172 **we partnered with Carnegie Mellon University:** The authors thank Eyal Peer for his execution and analysis of this research, and Alessandro Acquisti for coming up with the idea.

174 **"1.6 million accidents are caused annually by cell phone use . . .":** "National Safety Council Estimates That at Least 1.6 Million Crashes Each Year Involve Drivers Using Cell Phones and Texting," press release issued by the National Safety Council, January 12, 2010.

174 **"the "Great Speedup":** Monika Bauerlein and Clara Jeffery, "All Work and No Pay: The Great Speedup," *Mother Jones*, July/August 2011, www .motherjones.com/politics/2011/06/speed-up-american-workers-long-hours.

174 **"what *The Wall Street Journal* calls 'superjobs'":** Anne Kadet, "Superjobs: Why You Work More, Enjoy It Less," *The Wall Street Journal*, May 8, 2011.

176 **Stephen Covey's five levels of listening:** Covey's nearly ubiquitous five levels of listening are referenced in many of his works, but most of the world heard about them as habit five in his classic *7 Habits of Highly Effective People* (New York: Free Press, 1989).

177 **Alan Turing was a British mathematician:** Alan Turing's work is available at www.AlanTuring.net. "Intelligent Machinery," published in 1948, with handwritten notes and all, can be seen here: www.alanturing.net/turing_archive/archive/l/l32/L32-001.html. The relevant portions of "Computing Machinery and Intelligence" can be found on the Loebner web site at www.loebner.net/Prizef/TuringArticle.html.

180 **"Lucas says that if the Turing test is passed . . .":** Eric Chinski, "Brian Christian on the Most Human Human," *Paris Review*, March 14, 2011.

180 **"93 percent of all communication is nonverbal":** Albert Mehrabian, a professor at UCLA, first mentioned this formulation after research conducted in 1967. He's subsequently discussed it in several books, including *Silent Messages* (Belmont, California: Wadsworth Publishing Company, 1972). As with all research, it is not as conclusive as journalists would have

you believe. Mehrabian has frequently been forced to clarify his asser-
tion, explaining that it only applies under certain circumstances, such as
when there is significant emotional content in the speaker's comments.
It is still illuminating.

186 **"Typical SC":** Story originally told in Bob Sullivan's *Stop Getting Ripped
Off*. For more visit www.CustomersSuck.com.

188 ***Yoga Journal* soared 300 percent":** Alexis Grant, "Yoga Teaching Increasingly Popular as Second Career," *US News & World Report*, April 26, 2011.

189 **"runaway best seller *The 4-Hour Workweek*":** Tim Ferriss, *The 4-Hour
Workweek* (New York: Crown, 2007).

190 **"Intel instituted 'Quiet Time' ":** Nathan Zeldes, " 'Quiet Time' and 'No
Email Day' Pilot Data Is In!" *Open Port IT Community* (blog), June 14, 2008,
communities.intel.com/community/openportit/blog/2008/06/14/-
quiet-time-and-no-email-day-pilot-data-is-in.

8. AGILITY

193 **the Agile Manifesto:** The manifesto and its signatories can be found
here: agilemanifesto.org.

193 **Beck is the creator of an approach called Extreme Programming:** Kent
Beck helped to transform the field of software development. Our description of Extreme Programming at the beginning of this book is inspired by
Beck's book *Extreme Programming Explained*. The driving story is also a
quote from that book. Kent Beck with Cynthia Andres, *Extreme Programming Explained: Embrace Change*, 2nd ed. (Boston: Addison-Wesley, 2005).

194 **followed a model known as "waterfall":** A good reference for software
development models in general is: Steve McConnell, *Code Complete*, 2nd
ed. (Redmond, WA: Microsoft Press, 2004).

195 **"third of business software projects were canceled":** The Standish
Group, "Chaos," 1995, available from net.educause.edu/ir/library/pdf/
NCP08083B.pdf.

197 **the *just-noticeable difference*:** Its origins go back to the 1800s, but here is
a paper that puts it in perspective: D. A. Booth and R. P. J. Freeman, "Dis-
criminative measurement of feature integration," *Acta Psychologica* 84,
1–16.

199 **"percentage of adults who owned their homes":** Based on US Census
data, Housing Vacancies and Homeownership. See: www.census.gov/
hhes/www/housing/hvs/historic/index.html.

199 **eleven million US households were "underwater":** Les Christie, "Underwater Borrowers Are on the Rise," *CNN Money*, March 1, 2012, money .cnn.com/2012/03/01/real_estate/underwater_borrowers/index.htm.

200 **"slipped below 50 percent":** "Home Debt Greater Than Equity for First Time Since '45," Associated Press, March 24, 2008.

201 **the field of agile software development:** Robert C. Martin, *Agile Software Development: Principles, Patterns, and Practices* (Upper Saddle River, NJ: Prentice Hall, 2002).

201 **Scrum is organized into *sprints*:** Ken Schwaber and Mike Beedle, *Agile Software Development with Scrum* (Upper Saddle River, NJ: Prentice Hall, 2002).

201 **"agile methods as opposed to waterfall":** A CA Technologies survey, October 2010.

202 **"bring the Internet down in thirty minutes":** "Hackers Testifying at the United States Senate," YouTube video, 59:04, testimony given to the United States Senate on May 19, 1998, posted by "kingpinempire," March 14, 2011, www.youtube.com/watch?v=VVJldn_MmMY&feature=player_ embedded.

203 **Mudge gave a DARPA colloquium presentation:** Peiter "Mudge" Zatko, "If you don't like the game, hack the playbook," presentation given to the DARPA Cyber Colloquium, Arlington, Virginia, November 7, 2011. Also see Mudge's talk at the ShmooCon conference in 2011: Peiter "Mudge" Zatko, "ShmooCon 2011: Keynote: Analytic Framework for Cyber Security," YouTube video, 53:17, posted by "Christiaan008," February 5, 2011, www.youtube.com/watch?v=rDP6A5NMeA4.

203 **Alberto Savoia told a class at Stanford:** See Alberto's talk on pretotyping at Stanford in 2012: Alberto Savoia, "The Pretotyping Manifesto: Stanford Graduate School of Business," YouTube video, 52:39, posted by "Pretotyping," February 14, 2012, www.youtube.com/watch?v=t4AqxNekecY. Also take a look at his keynote on testing at the Google Test Automation Conference: Alberto Savoia, "GTAC 2011: Opening Keynote Address—Test Is Dead," YouTube video, 57:52, posted by "GoogleTechTalks," www.youtube .com/watch?v=X1jWe5rOu3g. Our thanks to Alberto for his insights during our interview.

205 **Savoia prefers what he calls the "pretotype":** Alberto Savoia's website on the concept of "pretotyping:" www.pretotyping.org. Savoia also has a book on pretotyping: Alberto Savoia, *Pretotype It*, 2nd ed., October 2011.

207 **"cats that look like Adolf Hitler":** www.catsthatlooklikehitler.com.

207 **"Pets.com, the online shopping destination":** David Goldman, "10 Big Dot.com Flops," *CNN Money*, last updated March 10, 2010, money.cnn .com/galleries/2010/technology/1003/gallery.dot_com_busts.

207 **"Webvan went all in":** Ibid.

207 **just ask Jeff Hawkins:** Shawn Barnett, "Jeff Hawkins: The Man Who Almost Single-handedly Revived the Handheld Computer Industry," *Pen Computing*, 2000, www.pencomputing.com/palm/Pen33/hawkins1.html. Also see: Savoia, *Pretotype It*.

210 **"You never see an unmotivated baby":** This and other quotes from Carol Dweck taken from her talk at Stanford University on mind-sets: Carol Dweck, "Brain Research at Stanford: Mindsets," YouTube video, 8:42, posted by "StanfordUniversity," November 7, 2011, www.youtube .com/watch?v=WvIBG98wj0Q&feature=player_embedded.

210 **Dweck believes that this is a *growth mind-set*:** Carol S. Dweck and Ellen L. Leggett, "A Social-Cognitive Approach to Motivation and Personality," *Psychological Review* 95, no. 2 (April 1988), 256–273. Carol Dweck, *Mindset: The New Psychology of Success* (New York: Random House, 2006).

9. APPLICATION

220 **"their groundbreaking book on learning":** We are among the long list of authors who owe a debt of gratitude to psychologists Paul Fitts and Michael Posner for their tome *Human Performance*.

223 **"rounded up 100 creative, career-oriented women":** Gordon L. Flett, a psychology professor at York University in Toronto, in an interview with the authors.

225 **"Flett's 10 signs your a perfectionist":** Gordon Flett's test has been published in multiple places. Here's one: Melissa Jackson, "Why Perfect Is Not Always Best," *BBC News*, June 19, 2004, news.bbc.co.uk/2/hi/ health/3815479.stm.

225 **children were given a computer test:** "Perfectionism Can Lead to Imperfect Health: High Achievers More Prone to Emotional, Physical and Relationship Problems," *Science Daily*, June 14, 2004, www.sciencedaily .com/releases/2004/06/040614074620.htm.

226 **"the ragingly popular FlyLady":** FlyLady's advice, and the data provided in this section, can be found at FlyLady.net.

227 **"Harrison set about solving perhaps: . . ."** For a good discussion of

Harrison's technological (and perfectionist) pursuits, see: Shahan Cheong, "Time in Motion: The Story of the Sea-Clock, or Harrison's Chronometers," *Not Yet Published* (blog), March 25, 2010, scheong.wordpress.com/2010/03/25/time-in-motion-the-story-of-the-sea-clock-or-harrisons-chronometers. There's also a good discussion here: "John Harrison and the Longitude Problem," Royal Museums Greenwich, accessed October 8, 2012, www.rmg.co.uk/Harrison.

230 **Izsak uses a simple card track:** Eric Abrahamson and David H. Freedman, *A Perfect Mess: The Hidden Benefits of Disorder* (New York: Little, Brown and Co., 2007).

234 **"mathematical computations can actually be more exhausting":** Allison Bond, "Do You Burn More Calories When You Think Hard?" *Science Line*, October 27, 2008, scienceline.org/2008/10/ask-bond-obesity-thinking-calories. It's also interesting to note that studies show mental work can actually leave people drained of energy for physical exercise. See: Rick Nauert, "Mental and Physical Fatigue Linked," *PsychCentral*, February 26, 2009, psychcentral.com/news/2009/02/25/mental-and-physical-fatigue-linked/4343.html.

234 **"John Perry is a confessed procrastinator":** When you get around to finding the time, Perry's work can be found at www.Structured Procrastination.com.

237 **groundbreaking study on this uniquely modern malady:** Aner Sela and Jonah Berger, "Decision Quicksand: How Trivial Choices Suck Us In," *Journal of Consumer Research* 39, no. 2 (August 2012), 360–370.

240 **Sheena Iyengar of Columbia University:** Matthew Boyle, "How to Fix your 401(k)," *CNN Money*, December 23, 2005, money.cnn.com/2005/12/23/pf/401k_fortune_122605.

242 **Angelika Dimoka, director of the Center:** Sharon Begley, "I Can't Think," *Newsweek*, February 27, 2011, www.thedailybeast.com/newsweek/2011/02/27/i-can-t-think.html.

246 **"it's worth doing badly":** Chesterton actually said, in his book *Orthodoxy* (1908): "It is, on the contrary, a thing analogous to writing one's own love-letters or blowing one's own nose. These things we want a man to do for himself, even if he does them badly." It appears Chesterton wasn't actually writing about perfectionism but rather the rights of men and women to do things for themselves, even if they often failed. The phrase still provides great meaning, however. Meanwhile, if you are interested in the

great inaccuracy fraud perpetuated on self-help gurus everywhere through this phrase, read: Hollis Robbins, "Familiar (Mis)Quotations," *Inside Higher Ed*, April 8, 2011, www.insidehighered.com/views/2011/04/08/robbins.

249 **"translation of the very English word *perfect*":** For lively discussion of misuse of the word *perfect* see: Dennis Bratcher, "The English Term *Perfect*: Biblical and Philosophical Tensions," *The Voice*, November 8, 2011, www.crivoice.org/terms/t-perfect.html.

THE ENDING

253 **Elderly folks who learn a new language:** Clara Moskowitz, "Second Language Protects Against Alzheimer's," *CBS News*, February 18, 2011, www.cbsnews.com/2100-205_162-20033422.html.

254 **"famous Christian writer of the twentieth century":** See Lewis's *The Screwtape Letters* New York: Time Inc., 1961), which was initially published as a series of columns in *The Guardian* newspaper during 1941.

ACKNOWLEDGMENTS

It's folly to try to thank everyone who helped you write a book, so we won't try here. There are endless large and small moments of love, friendship, honest criticism, and inspiration that go into an effort like this. We remember them all, and the people we shared them with. Large and small, every one is important.

At Dutton, our editor Stephen Morrow has guided us through every step of the process, with a light touch here and major suggestion there, and every one on the mark. We connected with him on the Plateau concept immediately, which was essential in a project like this. Plenty of other Dutton folk deserve our gratitude: editor Stephanie Hitchcock, production editor Andrea Santoro, copy editor Mary Beth Constant, along with director of publicity and marketing Christine Ball and her amazing team, including Katie Burns, Liza Cassity, and Cassie Mandel. Editor Jill Schwartzman also deserves our thanks for her early support. We would also like to thank Drs. Alessandro Acquisti and Eyal Peer from Carnegie Mellon University and Larry Ponemon of the Ponemon Institute for the original research studies they conducted for this book, and Dr. Robert Ang for his contributions and insights on plateaus in medicine. And our agent, Dan Lazar, was a constant voice of support.

Hugh would like to thank his wife, Megan, for her love, encouragement, patience . . . and for her incredible chocolate chip cookies. Hugh would also like to thank his Creator for his two beautiful children, Ava and Hunter, who were born while writing this book. They have provided an endless supply of brief plateaus, spectacular breakthroughs, and infectious giggles. Hugh loves them all more than words could say. The list of people who gave him their support during this process would perhaps fill three pages, but Hugh would like to single out his mom (Frankie Mae), dad (Herbert), sister (Maria), Jeanne Friedman, David Murphy, Sandra LaPedis, Robert Ang, David Ascioti, and Jason O'Briant for their constant encouragement. He'd also like to thank his former students at Columbia University for putting up with his classroom hijinks and his colleagues in the technology industry for their inspiration.

Bob would like to thank a long list of colleagues at NBC News and MSNBC who have supported the project and supported Bob through the process. Editor Michael Brunker offered endless encouragement, and Jennifer Sizemore created an environment where writers could thrive. There's an even longer list of friends and family he'd like to thank: Dad, Mom, Donnie, Jimmie, Margaret, Sue, Shannon, Catie Lou, and Karen. Also Rusty and Lucky, his pooches who provided enough comic relief to keep him sane, and Helen, who provided enough dog walks that he could get some work done. And finally, a special thanks to the millions of people who have read Bob's columns and the countless readers and viewers who were angry enough at something to take the time to contact Bob and let him know how they felt. They mean everything to him.

INDEX